Praise for Gamboa's World

"*Gamboa's World* offers a powerful new vision of governance in New Spain, detailing the ways of a regime that was primarily judicial by focusing on the career of one of its most engaged judges. We see anew how 'Bourbon reforms' were contested and contained by jurists committed to working with—and at times against—powerful economic interests and diverse popular communities to preserve the kingdom that sustained Spain's empire and fueled its trades through the eighteenth century."

—JOHN TUTINO, author of *Mexico City, 1808:
Power, Sovereignty, and Silver in an Age of War and Revolution*

"This book is both very smart and highly entertaining, even funny at times. It is a treasure trove of material on law and legal culture, the silver economy, and late-colonial Spanish rule overall. Yet because the author smuggles all this in with a skillful narration of the life and times of a scrappy, brilliant Mexican jurist named Gamboa, readers hardly need to work for it at all."

—BIANCA PREMO, author of *The Enlightenment on Trial:
Ordinary Litigants and Colonialism in the Spanish Empire*

"In exploring the private life, educational trajectory, and distinguished legal career of Francisco Xavier de Gamboa, Christopher Albi challenges various long-held assumptions regarding eighteenth-century New Spain. This is required reading for all those interested in Spanish America's tumultuous eighteenth century."

—FRANCES L. RAMOS, author of *Identity, Ritual, and
Power in Colonial Puebla*

Gamboa's World

Diálogos Series

KRIS LANE, SERIES EDITOR

Understanding Latin America demands dialogue, deep exploration, and frank discussion of key topics. Founded by Lyman L. Johnson in 1992 and edited since 2013 by Kris Lane, the Diálogos Series focuses on innovative scholarship in Latin American history and related fields. The series, the most successful of its type, includes specialist works accessible to a wide readership and a variety of thematic titles, all ideally suited for classroom adoption by university and college teachers.

Also available in the Diálogos Series:

The Conquest of the Desert: Argentina's Indigenous Peoples and the Battle for History edited by Carolyne R. Larson
From the Galleons to the Highlands: Slave Trade Routes in the Spanish Americas edited by Alex Borucki, David Eltis, and David Wheat
A Troubled Marriage: Indigenous Elites of the Colonial Americas by Sean F. McEnroe
Staging Frontiers: The Making of Modern Popular Culture in Argentina and Uruguay by William Garrett Acree Jr.
A Woman, a Man, a Nation: Mariquita Sánchez, Juan Manuel de Rosas, and the Beginnings of Argentina by Jeffrey M. Shumway
The Origins of Macho: Men and Masculinity in Colonial Mexico by Sonya Lipsett-Rivera
Mexico in the Time of Cholera by Donald Fithian Stevens
Tides of Revolution: Information, Insurgencies, and the Crisis of Colonial Rule in Venezuela by Cristina Soriano
Mexico City, 1808: Power, Sovereignty, and Silver in an Age of War and Revolution by John Tutino
Murder in Mérida, 1792 by Mark W. Lentz

For additional titles in the Diálogos Series, please visit unmpress.com.

Gamboa's World

Justice, Silver Mining, and
Imperial Reform in New Spain

~✘

CHRISTOPHER ALBI

University of New Mexico Press • Albuquerque

ISBN 978-0-8263-6294-0 (cloth)
ISBN 978-0-8263-6295-7 (paper)
ISBN 978-0-8263-6296-4 (electronic)

Library of Congress Control Number: 2021942867

Founded in 1889, the University of New Mexico sits on the traditional homelands of the Pueblo of Sandia. The original peoples of New Mexico—Pueblo, Navajo, and Apache—since time immemorial have deep connections to the land and have made significant contributions to the broader community statewide. We honor the land itself and those who remain stewards of this land throughout the generations and also acknowledge our committed relationship to Indigenous peoples. We gratefully recognize our history.

Cover illustration: Gamboa, Francisco Javier. Anonymous, 18th century. Reproduction authorized by the Instituto Nacional de Antropología e Historia.
Composed in Minion Pro 10.25/13.5

In memory of my parents, Dr. Wilfred and Marjorie Albi

Contents

~⅊

Acknowledgments

I am indebted to many people for their help over the long gestation of this book. First of all, I am grateful to my family. My parents, Dr. Wilfred and Marjorie Albi, are no longer around to see the completion of this project, but without their love and support it could not have started in the first place. I thank my sister Andrea, my brother-in-law Brent, and my nephews Max and Liam for their encouragement and the use of the man cave in Bellingham as an occasional writing retreat.

I owe an enormous debt to the University of Texas at Austin, where this book began its life as my doctoral dissertation. Susan Deans-Smith and Jorge Cañizares-Esguerra, in their distinct but complementary ways, were both superb mentors. I appreciate the help I received from Alan Tully, Ann Twinam, Jonathan Brown, Virginia Garrard, Seth Garfield, and Julie Hardwick. I also want to thank my fellow graduate students at the University of Texas at Austin, many of whom have already made their marks in the profession. Special thanks to Kenny Aslakson, Adrian Howkins, Pablo Mijangos, Heather Peterson, Michael Anderson, José Adrián Barragán, Andrew Paxman, Jackie Zahn, Matt Gildner, Emily Berquist, Evan Ross, Jennifer Hoyt, and Renata Keller.

John Tutino, Kris Lane, Pablo Mijangos, and José Adrián Barragán all read the manuscript carefully and provided expert comments. They have made this book much better than it would have been otherwise. Thanks as well to the people at the University of New Mexico Press, especially Michael Millman for his patient guidance and Bridget Manzella for her expert copyediting.

I am grateful to Brian Owensby for serving on my dissertation committee, Gabriel Paquette for getting my work in print at an early stage, and Linda and Richard Salvucci for their friendship during my two years at Trinity University in San Antonio. Conversations with colleagues at conferences, as well as in bars in Spain, cantinas in Mexico, and baseball stadiums in Chicago, have sharpened my arguments over the years. Particular thanks to Jeremy Adelman, Matthew Restall, Bianca Premo, Esther González, Mara Wade, and Paul Ramírez. I feel especially privileged that John Elliott and Bernard Bailyn took the time to read and comment on early drafts of my work. I also want to thank Peter Bailey for his mentorship during my undergraduate days at the University of Manitoba.

The writing of this book was supported by a number of fellowships. I am grateful to have received a three-year dissertation fellowship from the Social Sciences and Humanities Research Council of Canada. The Spanish government, through its Program for International Cooperation, provided funds for travel to Spanish archives. I received a lot of support from the University of Texas, including an affiliation with its Institute for Historical Studies that bridged a year between graduation and success on the job market. I have been fortunate to have been awarded fellowships from the Lilly Library at Indiana University in Bloomington, the John Carter Brown Library in Providence, and the Newberry Library in Chicago. I especially want to thank Neil Safier at the JCB and D. Bradford Hunt at the Newberry for fostering such diverse and supportive scholarly communities at their institutions.

I would not be an historian if I didn't love archives. I thank the librarians and archivists at the Nettie Lee Benson Library in Austin; the British Library in London; the Hispanic Society of America in New York; the Archivo General de la Nación, the Archivo Histórico del Colegio de las Vizcaínas, and the Augustinian archive at the parish of Nuestra Señora del Socorro in Mexico City; and the Archivo General de Indias, the Archivo Histórico Nacional, the Biblioteca Nacional, the Real Academia de Historia, and the Real Biblioteca in Spain.

Living in Oaxaca and Mexico City in the 1990s, I discovered Mexico in the company of great friends like Xóchitl Carrasco García, Greg Dechant (who reached up one day in a used bookstore on Doncelas and pulled down a copy of Gamboa's *Comentarios*), Gerardo Copca, Ann Ginsburg, Bond Snodgrass, Elisabeth Malkin, Eduardo García, Andrew Downie, Laura Martínez, and the late Peter Gutrich. Similarly, without my friends Javier Mata and Juan Vicente Bachiller, my understanding of Spain would be much poorer.

Since 2012 I have been a faculty member of the State University of New York at New Paltz. I am grateful to the administration for giving me the time to finish this project and especially the support of my colleagues in the History Department, above all Andrew Evans, Heather Morrison, and Lou Roper. Finally, I want to thank all the students I have taught at New Paltz, San Antonio, and Austin over the years; teaching history remains an enviable way to make a living.

Introduction

≈≫

> If one day the literary and social history of Mexico is written, this person
> [Gamboa], born at the beginning of the eighteenth century and dying at its
> end, will play a major role, since his epoch was great and he was great in it.
>
> —MARIANO OTERO, 1843

✦ MARIANO OTERO CERTAINLY THOUGHT HIGHLY OF FRANCISCO
Xavier de Gamboa. Otero, a Mexican writer and statesman of the early
republican period, depicted Gamboa, in a short biographical sketch, as one
of the great figures of eighteenth-century New Spain. Gamboa, born in
Guadalajara in 1717, enjoyed a long and illustrious legal career. In the 1740s
he became one of top *letrados* in Mexico City, advising merchants, miners,
and religious organizations. In 1755 he traveled to Madrid to represent the
Consulado of Mexico, the merchants' guild, at the royal court. In the decade
he lived in Spain, he wrote *Comentarios a las Ordenanzas de Minas*, immediately recognized as the authoritative guide to mining law.[1] From 1764 to
1794 Gamboa served as an *audiencia* (or high court) magistrate in New Spain
and Santo Domingo. In 1788 the crown named him the regent of the Real
Audiencia of Mexico, the first locally born judge to hold the position equivalent to chief justice.[2] Upon his death in 1794, his contemporaries recognized
him as the most impressive jurist of his era.

But despite Otero's prediction, Gamboa has not played an especially
prominent role in any of the hundreds of histories of Mexico written since
the 1840s. This is not surprising if you consider how history has generally
been written. Gamboa was not a major political or military leader. He did
not amass a great fortune or otherwise gain popular fame during his lifetime.
He led the studious, mostly uneventful life of a jurist, surrounded by books
and paper. He has thus been easy to ignore by those writing conventional
top-down history, which focuses on the dramatic actions of the movers and
shakers of society. Nor was Gamboa in any way a subaltern, someone who

challenges societal norms from the margins. He was a well-educated white man of Basque descent who enjoyed notable social, racial, and gender privileges in New Spain. He thus makes a poor subject for those writing history from below. Rather, Gamboa, as both a Spanish American and a lawyer, can be situated in the pivotal middle of *novohispano* society, a mediator between the power of the Spanish monarchy above and the intractable reality of Spanish America below. To really understand New Spain and the Spanish Empire in the eighteenth century, the career of Gamboa offers invaluable insight.

Reappraising Spanish American Law

In 2012 Jorge Castañeda, political scientist and former Mexican foreign minister, declared in a book intended for readers in the United States that "from the start, Mexican society was imbued with the quite logical notion that the law was meaningless, and that this was a forgivable sin."[3] This has long been a popular view of the legal order of the Spanish Empire, held even by many historians. Law was weak, merely an elaborate facade that masked the brutal exercise of colonial power. Scholars routinely cite the legal formula, *obedezco pero no cumplo*, "I obey but do not comply," as proof of the cynical attitude American subjects supposedly felt towards the law. Law could be safely ignored, they suggest, as long as you first remembered to pledge your allegiance to the king.[4] But in the words of historian Lewis Hanke, one of the first North American scholars to take Spanish law seriously, "If Spaniards in America were so ready to disregard the law, why did so many dread it?"[5] And if law didn't matter, why did so many American subjects, including poor indigenous villagers and plebeian women, flock to Spanish courts throughout the colonial period seeking justice?[6]

Rather than point out its weakness, other critics of Spanish law in America dwell on its oppressiveness. In this version, Spanish law propped up an absolutist colonial state that secured the dominance of a small elite of white men. It shaped exclusionary institutions that impeded natural economic development.[7] In the words of John Coatsworth, people in Spanish America "tolerated royal monopolies (*estancos*), conformed to endless regulations for fiscal and other purposes, and had no choice but to accept a legal system that failed to define property rights clearly or to provide an efficient court system to enforce them."[8] But if this is true, that oppressive law stunted economic growth, how do you explain the dynamic silver-mining industry in New Spain, which by 1800 was producing almost two-thirds of the world's refined silver?[9] And if the law did little to protect property rights, why did so many individuals invest their capital in an industry as inherently risky as mining?

Historians are now studying with renewed enthusiasm the legal regime of colonial Spanish America, what Spanish-language scholars call *Derecho Indiano*. Their main task has been to historicize it properly, that is to frame it within its own particular historical context.[10] This new legal history of Spanish America draws upon two larger historiographical trends of recent years: the reconsideration of political power under the ancien régime in Europe and the renewed interest in the governance of colonial empires.[11] One fundamental point made by scholars engaged in this work is that the state, as we know it today, with its monopoly on force and legislation, simply did not exist before the nineteenth century. Law should thus be studied more in its broader social and cultural context than as an ordering tool by the state.[12]

The new scholarship has brought into relief four fundamental attributes of the juridical order of colonial Spanish America. First, its foundation was profoundly religious. Human law fit into a larger, explicitly Christian normative framework. In the Spanish world, where only Catholicism was tolerated, a form of religious totalitarianism prevailed, although obviously without much of a state to enforce it.[13] People simply accepted, with few exceptions, the existence of a divine order in the universe superior to human society. This did not mean that Spanish America was governed theocratically, but it did mean that even the king was subject to a higher constitution, the principles of justice, fairness, and mercy inscribed in nature by God. Positive laws, those enacted by human authorities, were thus always subject to challenge on the basis they were not in accord with the universal norms dictated by God. In the words of Isidore of Seville, a renowned seventh-century scholar and bishop, to be enforceable, the laws of society had to be "honest, just, possible, appropriate to the time and place, necessary, useful and clear."[14]

Understanding this Christian foundation and the weakness of the state makes the legal pluralism of Spanish America easier to understand. State legislation was just part of a diverse mixture of normative instruments that included the unwritten natural law emanating from God, the canon law of the Catholic Church, Roman jurisprudence, and local customs. Lawyers learned to read Latin to penetrate the *Corpus Juris Civilis*, the compendium of Roman law and jurisprudence assembled under Emperor Justinian in the sixth century. Along with canon law, Roman law constituted the foundation of the *ius commune*, the common law of Europe.[15] What we now think of as law—legislation issued constitutionally by the state—was still too narrow and inconsistent to monopolize the legal field. The *Recopilación de las leyes de Indias*, the collection of royal legislation for Spanish America published in 1680, served more as a handy reference than an unassailable code of law.[16] Custom, the unwritten rules of a community that arise from repeated practice and gain force through majority consent, played an especially big role in the Spanish American legal order.[17] Custom shaped the rules of everything from how mine workers got paid to the prerogatives of audiencia magistrates. Perhaps because Spanish America lacked local legislatures, custom was particularly useful as a way for ordinary subjects to "make law" for themselves. What remained custom in New Spain in the eighteenth century might have been codified into written law by the assemblies of colonial British North America.

A third key feature of the juridical order was the importance of jurisdiction, the power to make law and adjudicate disputes over a specific area, activity, or group of people. Jurisdiction ordered society. The Catholic Church, for instance, controlled jurisdiction over moral and religious matters, with its own laws and court system. It enjoyed an exemption from the civil jurisdiction controlled by the king. In addition, the military enjoyed a degree of jurisdictional independence from the ordinary civil courts. In Spanish America, the viceroys exercised jurisdiction over matters of government, with residual adjudicative powers although only through streamlined administrative processes.[18] The audiencias exercised superior jurisdiction, independent from the viceroys, over all matters of civil and criminal justice, although with little power over the exempt clergy and soldiers. The consulados of Mexico and Lima, the merchants' guilds, handled all commercial law matters. These multiple jurisdictional lines were always subject to dispute. The audiencias and viceroys fought incessantly over what constituted a matter of *justicia* or *gobernación*. Could a civil official arrest a suspected criminal on church grounds? Did the military *fuero* protect a drunk militiaman who caused a ruckus in a pulqueria? Could the viceroy protect Spanish merchants facing sanctions before the consulado? These turf battles consumed time, energy, and masses of paper, but they had their beneficial effect. They acted to increase institutional accountability and check and balance power;

jurisdictional rivals denounced the abuses of each other. Absolutist government, however much the crown might have yearned for it at times, could never be established with such a fluid system of mixed and unsettled jurisdictions.

Finally, the preeminent concern of the legal regime of Spanish America was justice, not administrative efficiency or economic growth. This flowed from the understanding that the king was, first and foremost, a judge, obligated by God to dispense justice to the people in his realms. He was responsible for assuring that everyone got what was justly theirs and that the weak were protected from the strong. In the words of the *Digest*, one of the principal books of the *Corpus Juris Civilis*, justice was "the constant and perpetual desire to give to each his own." [19] This philosophy of government required that everyone had access to the law and its instrumentalities, such as the right to petition higher authorities or bring suit in court.[20] The preoccupation with justice, however much you can criticize the results in practice, led naturally to a casuistic approach to both lawmaking and adjudication. What was important was justice as defined in the particular case, not the application of abstract or general rules.[21]

The audiencias, the high courts of royal justice exercising jurisdiction over ordinary civil and criminal matters, were the principal institutions of the Spanish American justice system. The first ones were established in Santo Domingo in 1511 and Mexico City in 1527, even before the creation of the viceroyalty of New Spain in 1535.[22] Audiencia magistrates, the king's foremost representatives in matters of justice, never forgot the fact that they came before the viceroys.[23] The high courts in the viceregal capitals of Mexico City and Lima could overrule decisions by the viceroy if they violated rules of justice, but the viceroy exercised no corresponding power to quash the courts' judicial decisions. Juan Solórzano Pereyra, the most authoritative jurist of Spanish America, formerly an audiencia magistrate himself in Peru, described the audiencias, a bit hyperbolically to be sure, as "the stone fortresses of the Indies, where justice is safeguarded, the poor find protection from the aggravations and oppressions of the powerful, and everyone gets what is justly theirs." [24] To serve on an audiencia required university training, a higher requirement than for any other civil position. Candidates were screened by the Council of the Indies in Madrid, the chief administrative and judicial body for Spanish America. Magistrates received decent salaries, which allowed them to live decorously and protected them from the temptation of bribes. They also enjoyed life tenure. Viceroys, treasury officers, and military commanders came and went but audiencia judges could remain on the bench for decades, accumulating deep local knowledge and valuable connections to local elites.[25] The relative independence of the audiencias is one of the most overlooked aspects of Spanish rule.

This juridical order, imported from Castile, worked well in the difficult social and geographic conditions of America.[26] Its inherent flexibility suited the kaleidoscopic diversity of the New World. Spanish law provided the language, procedures, and institutions for the negotiations and accommodations, especially between royal officials and American subjects, that made Spanish sovereignty possible.[27] This is not to deny at all the obvious shortcomings of this legal system. The rich and powerful enjoyed stark advantages over the poor and weak. Even if a court ruled in your favor, there was no reliable mechanism to ensure the decision was enforced. People still frequently resorted to extra-legal and sometimes violent means to secure what they thought they deserved and the law promised. But such problems were hardly unique to early modern Spanish America; even in the most advanced societies today legal equality and consistent enforcement remain problematic. If it did not redeem Spanish colonialism, the law at least made life more tolerable for most people. They found the tools it provided, especially petitions and lawsuits, useful in resolving problems in their daily lives. It thus fostered the legitimacy of Spanish rule and made the empire more durable.

Where does Gamboa fit into all of this? His life, I argue, allows us to examine the full panorama of law and legal culture in eighteenth-century New Spain. I chart his career chronologically. The first chapters examine his life and career before he became an audiencia magistrate in 1764. Chapter 1 starts with his upbringing in Guadalajara, his Jesuit education, and his legal studies at the University of Mexico. Erudition was an important tool for lawyers, and Gamboa came superbly equipped. Chapter 2 analyzes some of his most notable cases as a private lawyer in Mexico City in the 1740s and 1750s. He gained more practical experience at the bar than any other audiencia magistrate of his time. Chapter 3 investigates his social network, the transatlantic Basque community. This world of merchants, clerics, and officials of Basque descent, whether born in Spain or America, was instrumental in both advancing his career and shaping his thinking about such crucial matters as the relationship between local autonomy and imperial loyalty. As the lawyer of the Basque confraternity Nuestra Señora de Aránzazu, Gamboa helped to establish the Vizcaínas, a residential school for girls in Mexico City. As the deputy appointed by Basque merchants to represent the Consulado of Mexico in Madrid, he composed submissions on trade and fiscal matters, including on the future of the fleet system for colonial commerce. Chapter 4 analyzes the *Comentarios a las Ordenanzas de Minas*, the ambitious book he wrote while in Spain, published in Madrid in 1761. The *Comentarios* accomplished several things: it clarified the confusing legal treatment of silver mining in New Spain, based on the Royal Mining Ordinances of 1584; it described technical processes, such as the patio method of mercury amalgamation; it proposed concrete reforms to make the industry more productive, such as a consulado-led mining bank; and it burnished Gamboa's juridical credentials before the ministers of the Council of the Indies, responsible for audiencia appointments. In the *Comentarios* Gamboa articulated his thinking about the legal regime of Spanish America. It thus helps to explain what happened after 1764, when the Spanish crown appointed the novohispano lawyer to the bench of his local high court, the Real Audiencia of Mexico.

The Bourbon or Galvesian Reforms?

An examination of the legal regime in eighteenth-century New Spain naturally prompts a reappraisal of what historians have called the Bourbon Reforms. This phenomenon encompassed a diverse range of administrative, fiscal, economic, military and cultural measures. Their underlying purpose—if one can be discerned—was to strengthen Spain both economically and militarily by taking better advantage of its overseas territories. Major reforms included enhanced state control over tax collection; the establishment of new crown monopolies; the creation of the viceroyalty of Rio de la Plata; the abolition of the Cadiz monopoly on trade with America; and the implementation of the intendancy system of local government.[28] In this book I focus on the reforms attempted in New Spain during the reign of Charles III (1759–1788) and under the direction of José de Gálvez, first as visitor general of New Spain from 1765 to 1771 and then as minister of the Indies from 1776 to 1787. This period coincides almost exactly with Gamboa's years as an audiencia magistrate from 1764 to 1794.

Rather than the Bourbon Reforms, I suggest a more apt term for this process, at least in the case of New Spain, might be the Galvesian reforms. Gálvez was both a true believer in the cause of reform and the principal agent of implementation in New Spain. He acted under the assumption, as did the government of Charles III as a whole, that the old juridical and governmental systems of Spanish America were broken and no longer served the economic interests of Spain or the financial needs of the crown. To Gálvez, a lawyer from Málaga in southern Spain, American subjects flouted royal laws with impunity, defending themselves with spurious invocations of immemorial custom. The judiciary was a willing partner in this game, always ready to soften the rigor of royal law to please local constituencies. The first remedy for such ills, in Gálvez's eyes, was the strict application of existing legislation, which could best be effected if Spaniards from Spain supplanted locals in American government. In addition, the audiencias, the guardians of the old system, exercised, in Gálvez's opinion, a dangerously broad jurisdiction. Conservative magistrates could thus jam up desirable fiscal and administrative changes. To curtail their power, Gálvez supported the expansion of exemptions for favored groups, including policemen, militiamen, bureaucrats and miners. He also advocated for the implementation of the intendancy system throughout Spanish America, which would turn regional government over to executive-style officials reporting directly to Madrid. This reform would also deprive the audiencias of power, since they oversaw in matters of justice the *alcaldes mayores* and *corregidores* whom intendants would replace.[29]

In his groundbreaking first book, *Miners and Merchants in Bourbon Mexico, 1763–1810*, David Brading identified Gamboa as a fierce opponent of Gálvez and the crown's reform program.[30] To explain Gamboa's stance, Brading emphasized his close ties to the merchants of the Consulado of Mexico, whose plan for a mining bank he had folded into the *Comentarios a las Ordenanzas de Minas*. According to Brading:

> Despite the legal and technical brilliance of his commentaries, Gamboa emerged as the political advocate of the great import houses and silver banks of Mexico City. Precisely at the time when the statesmen of the Bourbon dynasty were moving to undercut the position of the colonial merchant-monopolists, Gamboa wished to subject the entire Mexican silver mining industry to the control of the Consulado and the mercantile oligarchy.[31]

This research project began years ago as an attempt to challenge Brading's assessment of Gamboa as basically the mouthpiece of self-serving, monopolistic merchants. Yes, Gamboa was close to the merchants, especially those who shared his Basque ancestry, like Manuel Aldaco, who sent Gamboa to

Spain in 1755 to pitch the idea of a consulado mining bank. But after 1764, when the crown named Gamboa to the Real Audiencia of Mexico, he no longer acted as the consulado's representative; his primary concern was the administration of justice and especially the integrity of the audiencias. Justice and not the economic concerns of the merchants of the consulado better explains Gamboa's opposition to Bourbon or Galvesian reform. He saw no reason to tamper with a system of law that had proven its effectiveness in maintaining public order and respect for the monarchy.

Gamboa did not stand alone. By examining the eighteenth-century reform process through the lens of law, we can better understand the stiff opposition it aroused among veteran crown officials. Tomás Ortiz de Landázuri, a fellow Basque and the accountant-general on the Council of the Indies in the late 1760s and 1770s, was a case in point. He had spent two decades as a royal servant in New Spain. He came to know the country well, better perhaps than any other top official in Madrid at the time. He understood, for instance, that local customs that deviated from royal law and thus looked suspect to reformers in Madrid often served valuable purposes in America. He would have agreed with Solórzano, who wrote in *Política Indiana* that "the ancient customs of a province should not be changed easily, for each province has many, and it is better to adjust the law to suit local reality than to try to change reality to suit the law." [32] Landázuri, in his opinions for the Council of the Indies, urged a cautious approach to reform, with respect for local custom and the tradition of consultation with local experts. Along with Gamboa and many others, including Antonio María de Bucareli, the viceroy of New Spain in the 1770s, Landázuri saw no reason to upset the complex matrix of customs, practices, and institutions that had long kept New Spain both loyal and profitable to the Spanish crown.

This book analyzes two particular episodes of conflict between Gamboa the audiencia magistrate and Gálvez the imperial reformer. First, in chapter 5, I examine how Gamboa, as an *alcalde del crimen*, or criminal court magistrate, in the Real Audiencia of Mexico's Sala de Crimen, opposed reforms to the administration of criminal justice. In November 1766, prompted by a police corruption scandal in Puebla, the viceroy, Carlos Francisco de Croix, backed by Gálvez, stripped the *sala* of jurisdiction over police captains outside of Mexico City. The viceroy's decree granted the Tribunal of the Acordada, an independent force created in the early eighteenth century to combat rural banditry, the right to operate in all the cities of New Spain besides the countryside. Unlike the sala, the Acordada ignored formal rules of procedure. A few months later, in early 1767, Gálvez endorsed another viceregal decree. It required the courts of New Spain to send all prisoners to military *presidios*. Intended to bolster the workforce needed to rebuild Spanish defenses, the measure deprived the sala of the funds it had long raised through the sale of convict labor to private businesses, such as *obrajes*, or textile mills. Coupled with the loss of jurisdiction over policing in 1766, the presidio decree of 1767 crippled the Sala de Crimen. It could no longer function as a high court for criminal matters. This episode, largely overlooked by historians, epitomized the danger that Galvesian reform posed to the larger administration of justice in New Spain. The crown turned to fast and cheap solutions that sacrificed due process while shifting power from judicial to executive officials. Gamboa paid a high price for his defiance; in 1768 the Spanish government, desiring to reimpose order after the tumultuous expulsion of the Jesuits the previous year, ordered Gamboa out of New Spain. He spent three years in exile, separated from his wife and children, in Valladolid in northern Spain.

The second dispute I explore between Gálvez and Gamboa, the subject of chapter 6, concerns the creation of the Mining Tribunal. This organization, patterned on the consulados, gave silver miners control over their own bank, adjudicative system, and technical college. Gamboa, back in New Spain in 1773, thought the whole scheme preposterous. Miners, in his opinion, had no capacity to manage their own bank or adjudicative tribunal. They were by nature solitary risk takers. It was better if they stuck to what they knew best, digging ore from the ground, and leave financial and judicial matters to more responsible men. He particularly attacked the plan of relieving the audiencias of jurisdiction over mining disputes. Gamboa's arguments against the tribunal convinced all of the members of the Real Audiencia of Mexico, Viceroy Bucareli, Landázuri, and the Council of the Indies of the impracticalities of the plan. But in 1776, Gálvez, after becoming minister of the Indies under Charles III, secured royal approval for the Mining Tribunal anyways. He then got rid of Gamboa again by transferring him against his will to the Audiencia of Santo Domingo in 1783. The Mining Tribunal, so often lauded as an example of enlightened Bourbon reform, proved to be a failure on almost all counts, just as Gamboa predicted. It could not even improve the technical level of mining in New Spain since local methods turned out to be better than what imported European experts tried to implement. Yet the tribunal did succeed in one very important matter, perhaps what Gálvez sought all along: it served as an effective financial intermediary to arrange loans and donations for the crown supported by silver revenue.[33]

Gamboa's own perseverance, I would argue, symbolized the larger resilience of the juridical order, the subject of chapter 7. He survived five lonely years in Santo Domingo, again separated from his family. He participated in an attempt to remake the Spanish colony in the image of its French neighbor, Saint-Domingue, which, fortunately, failed. In 1788, after the death of Gálvez and the dissipation of the reform impulse, the crown approved his return to New Spain as the first American-born regent of the Real Audiencia of Mexico. Since the 1760s, he and his allies had managed to block or deflect many measures that would have transformed the legal regime of Spanish America. Because of this resistance, Bourbon reformers had little choice but to compromise. For example, it took twenty years for the crown to implement the intendancy system in New Spain and then only with major modifications that diluted the authority of the new officials. In fact, Gamboa as regent exercised significant power to frustrate the ambitious intendants Gálvez had appointed. But he refused to let down his guard, dueling with the second Conde de Revillagigedo, viceroy during his time as regent, on the most picayune matters, even the amount of barley consumed by horses in Mexico City, in order to safeguard the prerogatives, jurisdiction, and independence of the high court he led. He died in 1794.

CHAPTER ONE

The Education of a Novohispano Lawyer

~ↄℓ

It is attested that he is a native of the city of Guadalajara in the kingdom
of New Galicia, the legitimate son of the marriage between Don Antonio
de Gamboa and Doña Maria de la Puente y Aramburu, Old Christians of
recognized nobility and clean of all bad blood.

—GAMBOA, *RELACIÓN DE MÉRITOS*, 1757

⊹ FRANCISCO XAVIER DE GAMBOA WAS BORN ON DECEMBER 17, 1717, IN
Guadalajara, the capital of the kingdom of New Galicia in the viceroyalty of
New Spain. He came from an honorable family of Basque descent. Gamboa's
father, Antonio de Gamboa, was a merchant. He and his wife, Maria de la
Puente y Aramburu, had eight children, of which Francisco Xavier was the
eldest son. The small city of Guadalajara was prospering in Gamboa's childhood. It was founded in 1531 by Nuño Beltrán de Gúzman, the brutal conquistador of New Galicia, and reestablished in the fertile Atemajac Valley in
1542. At the time of Gamboa's birth, the region around the city produced a
cornucopia of agricultural products, from old-world livestock, wheat, and
pomegranates to new-world corn, beans, squash, and medicinal plants. They
were cultivated by indigenous villagers, mestizo ranchers, and Spanish estate
owners. In the nearby town of Tequila, people were already distilling a potent
spirit from the juice of the agave cactus. Guadalajara, with about six thousand inhabitants in the early eighteenth century, served as the commercial
entrepôt for northwestern New Spain. Its merchants, including presumably
Gamboa's father, ferried agricultural products and merchandise north to
mining camps like Zacatecas and shipped silver back to the capital.[1]

Guadalajara's economic importance was enhanced by its administrative
functions. It was the home of an audiencia, a high court of royal justice,

founded in 1548.[2] Spain, or more accurately, Castile, established its sovereignty in the New World by extending jurisdiction. This required high courts to deliver the services of royal justice to the new American vassals of the king. In the words of historian J. H. Parry in his study of the Audiencia of Guadalajara:

> Spain carried over from the age of feudalism into the age of sovereignty the notion of jurisdiction as the essential function of authority. Though he legislated continually, the king was still regarded primarily as a judge, the chief of judges. His authority was most directly and characteristically represented by the high courts of justice and in the government of his dominions the school-trained lawyer was his most useful servant.[3]

The establishment of an audiencia in the frontier area of Nueva Galicia in the 1540s was intended to bring order after the ravages of Beltrán de Guzmán and the subsequent Mixtón Rebellion of 1541, when Native warriors attacked and drove out Spanish settlers. The Spanish crown also wanted to crack down on the encomenderos, those privileged colonists who had received encomiendas, or grants allowing them to extract tribute in the form of labor and goods from Native villages. An audiencia was the means for the crown to assert its authority in the turbulent region.

By the eighteenth century, the high court in Guadalajara administered civil and criminal justice over a vast territory, from New Mexico in the north to the present-day state of Jalisco in the south. Within its district lay Zacatecas, the first great silver-mining center in New Spain. The four magistrates of the audiencia were kept busy hearing and reviewing cases, administering various crown offices, and advising the governor of New Galicia, the titular president of the audiencia. The presence of this high court attracted commerce to Guadalajara, as people with business before the court hired notaries and lawyers, sought lodging, bought food and drink, and frequented places of entertainment. The presence of an episcopal court handling canon law matters brought in more people. Although still small in population, Guadalajara was thriving in Gamboa's childhood, the most important agricultural, commercial, and administrative hub in western New Spain.

Antonio de Gamboa's trading business was prospering in the early eighteenth century. He might have profited from connections with Basque

Map 1. New Spain in the eighteenth century: its main cities, mining districts, and roads. Map by Joshua Korenblat.

wholesalers in Mexico City who needed the silver from Zacatecas to purchase imported manufactured goods. He apparently built up a moderate fortune. But then in the mid-1720s tragedy struck. Gamboa's father died suddenly, of unknown causes. The family was left nearly destitute after careless or dishonest executors mismanaged the estate.[4] Gamboa recalled later that "at the age of eight, when I began my education, I studied in the streets while going door-to-door to collect charity for my family."[5] The ordeal marked him for life. From a very early age, Gamboa felt a strong sense of responsibility "to relieve my household, mother, and siblings" of the suffering caused by the premature death of his father.[6] Rebuilding his family's modest fortune became an enduring preoccupation.

A Jesuit Education in New Spain

Like most young boys of Spanish descent, Gamboa received his first lessons from a parish priest. But one day, perhaps while reading a book in the shade of the arcades around Guadalajara's main square, Gamboa attracted the attention of a young Spanish *oidor* on the audiencia, José Mesía de la Cerda y Vargas.[7] Learning of his family's struggles, Mesía de la Cerda offered to pay for Gamboa's education at the local Jesuit college of San Juan Bautista. The Jesuits, the richest and most influential order of the Catholic Church, founded the Colegio de San Juan Bautista in 1696. It was supported by a number of Jesuit-owned agricultural estates around Guadalajara, most notably the hacienda of Toluquilla, which supplied the city with flour.[8] Like all Jesuit schools, its curriculum was based on the Ratio Studiorum, the pedagogical plan adopted by the order in the 1590s. Young boys first concentrated on language and literature, with the goal of mastering Latin grammar and rhetoric. They read excerpts of Roman writers such as Livy, Seneca, Virgil, and Cicero. They learned to speak fluently and think on their feet.[9] After this primary stage, called humanities, students moved on to philosophy, which included more advanced subjects like logic, metaphysics, theology, history, and mathematics. After graduating from philosophy, students would be ready to enter university to study theology, law, or medicine.

One subject that left a deep imprint on Gamboa was mathematics, which had always been an important part of Jesuit education. In Madrid, the Colegio Imperial, the most prestigious Jesuit college in the Spanish world, was particularly renowned for its mathematicians. In the seventeenth century, Hugh Sempill (ca. 1590–1654) and José de Zaragoza (1627–1679) both taught there and wrote textbooks used in Jesuit schools throughout the Catholic world.[10] By tradition, the chair of mathematics at the Colegio Imperial served as the official cosmographer of the Indies, essentially the chief scientific advisor to the Council of the Indies.[11] Zaragoza held the position in the mid-seventeenth century. This Jesuit priest began his career in Valencia, where he taught the future scholar Tomás Vicente Tosca (1651–1723), who in turn mentored Gregorio Mayans i Síscar, one of the leading intellectuals in mid-eighteenth-century Spain.[12] Gamboa's teachers at San Juan might have used Tosca's nine-volume *Compendio mathematico*, published between 1707 and 1715, which covered the full range of applied mathematics, from trigonometry to architecture. Otero suggested that the study of mathematics, in particular geometry, was fundamental in the development of Gamboa's rigorous approach to legal analysis and argumentation.[13]

Gamboa also gained from the Jesuits a grounding in what was called at the time natural philosophy, encompassing the life and physical sciences. Jesuit priests had always been active in scientific work, assisted by their global network of colleges and missions. They had educated many scientific revolutionaries, like Galileo Galilei and René Descartes, and carried out their own scientific research. For instance, Athanasius Kircher (1602–1680), who taught for decades at the Jesuit college in Rome, peered into his microscope, collected fossils, and pondered the cause of volcanoes. Eusebio Kino (1644–1711) brought with him to northern New Spain a telescope to observe the stars at night while he preached to the nomadic peoples of the region during the day. Wherever they went, Jesuits observed nature closely, not just out of curiosity but for potential profit. In Peru they noticed that Natives used the bark of the cinchona tree to treat fevers. In the early seventeenth century the samples the Jesuits sent back to Rome, which contained quinine, proved effective against malaria. The Jesuits controlled the trade in this medicine, widely known as Jesuit's bark.[14]

The Jesuits, as the most educated and worldly of the regular orders, had to protect themselves from conservative churchmen quick to pounce on any challenge to theological, philosophical, or cosmological orthodoxies.[15] Jesuits learned to take indirect approaches when discussing potentially radical ideas. One "nudge-nudge-wink-wink" method was to present something like Newtonian physics to their students as an unproven theory that they should learn to rebut with scholastic reasoning. In the case of Descartes, in 1706 the general congregation of the order decided their schools could teach his science but not his philosophy, even though this unlikely kept Cartesian rationalism under wraps.[16] It is easy now to mock such methods, but they worked to spread challenging ideas in an intensely Catholic society. Just because it was difficult to publish radical books in the Spanish world did not mean that radical ideas were not thoroughly discussed and debated, even in Catholic schools.[17]

In 1733, at the age of fifteen, Gamboa completed his studies in philosophy. He later boasted in his official résumé—which was hardly the place to be modest—that he was the best student of his class. From the Jesuits, he gained a deep knowledge of classical history and literature as well as an understanding of mathematics and science. His ability to memorize vast passages of texts and think on his feet allowed him to excel in the academic acts popular at the time, in which students demonstrated their knowledge by parrying questions in public from their masters. Gamboa mentioned that he was tested in two comprehensive examinations in his final semester at San Juan Bautista, covering all of the subjects of philosophy. This qualified him for a bachelor of arts degree, which only the University of Mexico could confer in New Spain. He was granted this degree on January 8, 1734, at the age of sixteen. He was now ready for the study of law.

The Royal College of San Ildefonso

In the early 1730s Mesía de la Cerda, Gamboa's patron, ran into trouble in Guadalajara. In 1731 the crown rebuked him and his friend Fernando de Urrutia, a supernumerary magistrate on the audiencia, for excessive gambling. While games of chance were ubiquitous in New Spain, they were considered dangerous for audiencia magistrates. If they fell into debt, their impartiality, the highest virtue of a royal judge, could easily be compromised. A host of legal provisions tried to keep audiencia judges isolated from the temptations of local society. Even their children needed royal approval before marrying someone from a local family. In practice, however, the crown recognized the difficulties in enforcing such rules, especially on young single men from Spain in remote corners of the empire. In the case of Mesía de la Cerda, he not only gambled with Fernando de Urrutía but also courted Fernando's sister, Maria. The crown allowed him to marry María but, at the same time, perhaps to prevent further scandal in the city's gambling dens, moved him out of Guadalajara. In November 1733 he joined the Sala de Crimen, the criminal law chamber of the Real Audiencia of Mexico, as an alcalde del crimen. He brought with him to Mexico City his young protégé, Gamboa.[18]

Gamboa entered the Real Colegio de San Ildefonso, the most prestigious Jesuit school in New Spain.[19] San Ildefonso was the American equivalent of a *colegio mayor*, one of the richly endowed colleges of old Spanish universities where the aristocracy sent their sons. These students, known as *colegiales*, used the connections they made in the colegios mayores to dominate the top positions in Spanish government and the church. Students without noble pedigrees attended less prestigious universities and typically rented rooms in private homes rather than resided in colegios mayores. They were known as *manteístas*, for the long cloaks, or *manteos*, they traditionally wore. In the eighteenth century, thanks to the Bourbon desire to reinvigorate the government, the crown promoted manteístas over colegiales. Many of the top ministers of Charles III, notably Pedro Rodríguez de Campomanes, José Moñino, and José de Gálvez, came from this middle segment of society, prosperous enough to attend university but without the aristocratic ties to enter a colegio mayor in Salamanca or Alcalá de Henares. Gamboa shared with the Spanish manteístas a relatively humble origin but his membership in the Jesuit college of San Ildefonso gave him a bit of the elite sheen of Spanish colegiales. In New Spain, graduates of San Ildefonso felt entitled to occupy high offices of government and church.[20]

Gamboa arrived at the college at an auspicious moment. Flush with cash from the growing novohispano economy, the Jesuits had embarked on an ambitious rebuilding program.[21] Cristóbal Escobar y Llamas, the rector from 1727 to 1742, headed the effort. College chronicler Felix Osores described Escobar as "the most notable protector and promoter of the letters in the cited Seminary, whose grandiose and magnificent building he raised from the foundations, adorning Mexico with it, and providing an example of the magnificence corresponding to the dignity of an empire of knowledge."[22] Construction on the massive three-story building—with exterior walls of red tezontle stone trimmed by carved limestone, three interior patios, an ornate chapel, assembly halls, classrooms, dormitories, refectories, and one of the most extensive libraries in Mexico—continued throughout Gamboa's years in the college. At a cost of over 400,000 pesos, the expansion of San Ildefonso was one of the largest construction projects in Mexico City of the early eighteenth century.[23] Escobar also expanded the college's academic program. He endowed new prizes in theology and law as well as securing for San Ildefonso chairs for the study of the *Four Books of Sentences* by Peter Lombard, a medieval classic of theology, and the works of Francisco Suárez, the great sixteenth-century Spanish Jesuit, theologian, and jurist.[24]

Life for the students at San Ildefonso, known as *alonsíacos*, can be gleaned from the pages of a little handbook, *El discreto estudiante: Reglas de buena crianza, para la educación de los colegiales del Colegio Real de San Ildefonso*, printed in Mexico City in 1722.[25] The typical day began with mass at dawn. In chapel, boys were admonished to "keep your body composed, the eyes modest and serious, walking slowly, remembering to show courtesy to the persons you pass."[26] They should not gawk at the chapel's adornments and decorations "because that is silliness, and you will be judged as a man who has never seen such a thing before."[27] After mass and a light breakfast,

Figure 1. The ornate principal entrance of the Real Colegio de San Ildefonso, constructed during Gamboa's residence in the 1730s. Photograph by Sandra Guerrero.

students filed out to their morning classes. At the noonday meals, they were expected to keep their elbows off the table and use only their right hand to cut meat, so as not to be mistaken for gluttons. During meals, students took turns giving academic talks, presenting arguments drawn from their reading and facing tricky questions from their teachers. Classes resumed in the afternoon. After a light supper, students would pray the rosary between 7:30 and 8:00 p.m., before turning in for the night. *El discreto estudiante* cautioned students never to brag or gossip or use silly nicknames. They were to keep their hair short and nails clipped. Once a year they practiced the *Spiritual Exercises of Ignatius de Loyola*, a rigorous program of prayer and meditation devised by the founder of the Jesuit order. The whole regimen at San Ildefonso was designed to produce disciplined and devout students. For Gamboa, however, a university student in residence at the college, life was not quite as regimented as for the younger boys studying humanities and philosophy.

Gamboa was residing in San Ildefonso when the worst epidemic of the eighteenth century hit Mexico City. Natives called the plague *matlazahuatl*; today we believe it was likely an outbreak of typhus. The Valley of Mexico had suffered drought since 1734, leading to shortages of corn, wheat, and beef, which prepared the ground for the high death toll.[28] The epidemic struck in the late summer of 1736. By January 1737 matlazahuatl had spread to the whole city but was especially virulent in the poorer indigenous neighborhoods. The Real Colegio de San Ildefonso was largely spared. The Jesuits, who operated four hospitals in Mexico City, spent 3,500 pesos to set up additional facilities to care for the sick.[29] The death toll reportedly reached an extraordinary thirty thousand, meaning that a third of the population of the city could have perished.[30] Bodies were buried with little ceremony in churches or burned in mounds at the paupers' cemetery of San Lázaro. Priests swung censers in the streets to mask the stench of rotting flesh.

To contain the epidemic, the authorities took extraordinary measures. First, they banned the sale of pulque, the fermented juice of the agave plant, under the belief that its consumption weakened Native bodies and made them more prone to infection. Second, they sought the intercession of the most holy religious figures of Mexico City. Processions were organized in honor of Our Lady of Loreto, Our Lady of Remedios, and the Christ of Ixmiquilpan, praying for their help to end the crisis.[31] Finally, city authorities appealed to the most holy of local saints, the Virgin of Guadalupe. The cloak of Juan Diego imprinted miraculously with her image was brought from her shrine in Tepeyac. Sure enough, a few days later, rain began to fall, the drought abated, and the plague subsided. In May 1737, in thanksgiving, the archbishop of Mexico, Juan Antonio de Vizarrón y Eguiarreta, declared Guadalupe the patroness of the city.[32] In 1746, the bishops and cathedral chapters of New Spain united to proclaim the Virgin of Guadalupe the universal patroness of the viceroyalty. And in 1754, the pope confirmed her as the patroness of New Spain. She remains the most popular icon of religious devotion in Mexico today.[33]

The apotheosis of Guadalupe coincided with an upsurge in local patriotism. It began as a reaction to an insult thrown America's way in 1735 by the Spanish humanist, Manuel Martí, known as the dean of Alicante. He claimed the Indies had never produced a writer of merit. This comment outraged Spanish American intellectuals, among them Juan José Eguiara y Eguren, a faculty member of San Ildefonso and a professor and later rector of the university.[34] Eguiara began work immediately on an ambitious project, the

Bibliotheca Mexicana, meant to profile the most noteworthy Spanish American authors. He only managed to finish the first volume, which covered authors up to the letter C, but he did leave manuscripts of later volumes. The fact that he wrote it in showy Latin instead of Spanish surely limited his audience. But the *Biblioteca Mexicana* did help shape the ideas that later flourished with Mexican nationalism. For instance, Eguiara claimed, as did Carlos de Sigüenza y Góngora fifty years earlier, that creoles, Americans of Spanish descent, could look back with pride to the glorious Aztec past. He presented creoles as the rightful heirs of Mesoamerican civilization. They did not need Europe to validate their work. This potent myth obscured the rather inconvenient truth that it was the ancestors of the creoles who had destroyed the Aztec Empire in the first place.

Within the community of San Ildefonso, Gamboa, a poor boy from Guadalajara, met the sons of the elite and the future leaders of New Spain. He befriended José Miguel Calixto de Berrio y Zaldívar, the scion of one of the wealthiest landowning families in New Spain, who later assumed the showy titles of Marqués de Jaral de Berrio and Conde de San Mateo Valparaiso.[35] They became life-long friends and compadres, with Gamboa later acting as the executor of Berrio's huge and complicated estate. Gamboa also met many of his future legal colleagues within the walls of the Real Colegio de San Ildefonso. He studied under Agustín Bechi y Monterde, a Veracruz-born priest, canon law professor, and audiencia advocate.[36] Manuel Ignacio Beye de Cisneros, another canon law professor and rector of the university in the late 1750s and early 1760s, was a classmate in the 1730s.[37] With these men, along with his future audiencia colleague Baltasar Ladrón de Guevara, who studied at San Ildefonso in the 1740s, Gamboa helped to establish in the early 1760s Mexico City's Colegio de Abogados, a mutual aid society for the legal profession.[38] Two of New Spain's most noted men of science in the eighteenth century, José Antonio de Alzate, a polymath secular priest, and Antonio de León y Gama, an astronomer and mathematician, also attended San Ildefonso. Gamboa knew them both.

Another notable alonsíaco of Gamboa's generation was José Rafael Campoy, praised by Osores as "the wisest of the wise in the eighteenth century."[39] Born in 1723, he entered San Ildefonso in 1735 as a philosophy student. But he had difficulty coping with the school's strict regime, especially the discipline meted out by his primary master, Father Miguel Quijano. In 1737 Campoy ran away and found work with a widow outside of the city. Her harsh treatment, however, was even worse than Quijano's. Fortunately,

Escobar, the rector, learned of the boy's whereabouts and brought him back to San Ildefonso. Later ordained a Jesuit priest himself, Campoy taught the next generation of young scholars at San Ildefonso, which included the poet Diego José Abad, the theologian Francisco Xavier Alegre, and the historian Francisco Xavier Clavijero.[40] Clavijero, from exile in Italy after the suppression of the Jesuit order in 1767, wrote a history of Mexico that picked up the patriotic message from Eguiara, linking New Spain to the glories of the pre-Columbian past. This was the social and intellectual milieu Gamboa enjoyed in his years as a law student.

Studying Law at the University of Mexico

From San Ildefonso it was a short walk through the teeming Plaza Mayor to the Royal and Pontifical University of Mexico. Students passed by the massive viceregal palace, rebuilt after the damage sustained during the popular riot of 1692.[41] It housed, besides the office and residence of the viceroy, the two chambers of the Real Audiencia of Mexico, a jail, the Mexico City mint, apartments, and even a popular tavern. The university, founded in 1553 on the model of the University of Salamanca, had five faculties: arts, theology, civil law, canon law, and medicine. It was run as a joint venture, as its name implied, between the crown and the church, but had jurisdictional independence.[42] Its permanent faculty members were all clergymen. Theology and the two laws were the most popular fields of study.[43]

The study of law in eighteenth-century Mexico was still based on the sixth-century Roman legal texts discovered in an Italian library in the eleventh century. These writings made up the *Corpus Juris Civilis*, an immense compendium of Roman law and jurisprudence assembled under Justinian, the last native Latin-speaking emperor of Rome. Justinian hoped his legal collection would help to revitalize imperial control in the West; instead, the *Corpus Juris Civilis*, after its medieval recovery, established the foundation for the legal order of Europe.[44] It provided a transnational common law of unimpeachable pedigree. The *Corpus Juris Civilis* consisted of four parts: the *Digest*, itself divided into fifty volumes and containing the writings of the principal Roman jurists; the *Code*, divided into twelve books and containing historic legislation; the *Novels*, a compendium of legislation passed during the reign of Justinian; and the *Institutes*, a summary of the other books and used primarily as a teaching text.[45] The Spanish world also had its own

Figure 2. The National Palace, once the home of the viceroy, the audiencia, the mint, a jail, and even a raucous tavern. Photograph by Sandra Guerrero.

unique legal code derived from Roman law, *Las Siete Partidas*, written in the thirteenth century under the auspices of Alfonso X of Castile.[46] Even in the late eighteenth century, few lawyers in New Spain would not have had access to *Las Siete Partidas*, usually the 1555 edition by the humanist jurist Gregorio López.[47]

Why would future lawyers in eighteenth-century Mexico City need to study Roman law? It was not as if the legislation of Justinian or the opinions of Roman jurists like Ulpian still applied as valid law. But what Roman law supplied, in the words of legal historian Peter Stein, was "a conceptual framework, a set of principles of interpretation that constituted a kind of universal grammar of law, to which recourse could be made whenever it was needed."[48] Students applied this grammar of law to concrete legal problems discussed in the classrooms and assembly halls.[49] In time, with the vocabulary and principles derived from Roman law and elaborated by generations of European jurists, students would learn how to think like lawyers, with the discernment to see differences where others just saw similarities and similarities where others saw differences and the skill to craft persuasive verbal and written arguments.[50] In addition, Roman legal categories, namely the laws of family, inheritance, property, torts, unjust enrichment, contracts, and remedies, still defined much of civil law in the eighteenth century.[51]

The *Corpus Juris Civilis* was considered almost a sacred text, akin to the Bible, which reflected the transcendent norms of divine and natural law. And just as Catholics relied on theologians to make sense of Holy Scripture, lawyers in the Spanish world needed jurists to guide them on how to use the timeless principles of Roman law to resolve everyday legal problems. The most esteemed of the early glossators and commentators was Bartolus of Saxoferrato (1313–1357).[52] According to a common refrain at the time, *Nemo bonus iurista nisi bartolista*—you could not be a good jurist without being a follower of Bartolus. Over the centuries, following the examples of Bartolus and his student Baldus of Ubaldis, European jurists produced a massive literature, covering all areas of law, to explain how Roman principles could be applied to everyday cases. The most skilled of these juridical authors acquired *auctoritas*: their opinions gained authoritative status in legal disputes.[53] This was the *ius commune*, the common body of norms derived from Roman law that filled in the gaps of state legislation, whether municipal, national, or imperial. Lawyers cited juridical opinions in their briefs just as lawyers in the English common law system would cite the binding decisions of high courts. In the civil law world, judicial decisions themselves never became an important source of law. Since adjudication remained casuistic, the resolution of one dispute did not necessarily bear on the outcome of others. In addition, unlike in the English world, courts did not issue the reasons for their decisions; it was believed that transparency was dangerous for judicial authority as it would reveal the inner politics of decision-making.

The canon law of the Catholic Church also evolved from Roman antecedents.[54] After the fall of the empire in the West, the church continued to pass legislation and adjudicate disputes according to Roman procedures. Medieval jurists organized the church's laws in a series of compilations, beginning with Gratian's *Decretum* in the twelfth century. Italian jurists of the Middle Ages, like Giovanni D'Andrea (Joannes Andreas) and Nicolò de Tudeschi, known as Panormitanus, wrote on canon law in the same manner as Bartolus did on civil law. The Council of Trent in the late sixteenth century endorsed an omnibus of canon law known as the *Corpus Juris Canonici*, the canon law equivalent of the *Corpus Juris Civilis*. It included Gratian's *Decretum*, the *Decretals* of Pope Gregory IX, and the *Clementines* of Pope Clementine V. Students at the University of Mexico in the 1730s continued to pore over the *Decretals* and *Clementines*. Even law students planning careers in private practice or the civil administration studied canon law, another reflection of the Christian foundation of the juridical order.

Increasingly in the eighteenth century, critics in Spain asked why students had to spend so much time studying ancient legal texts at the apparent expense of the legislation of their own king. After all, in Spain, there was no question that domestic laws, whether royal or municipal, took priority over the ius commune; both the *Ordenamiento de Alcalá* in 1348 and the *Leyes de Toro* in 1505 spelled that out clearly. This was reaffirmed again in 1713 by the first Bourbon king Philip V.[55] In 1738, José Berní Catalá, a young reformist jurist from Valencia, wrote in his guidebook for novice lawyers, *El abogado instruido en la practica civil de España*, that "lawyers in Spain who are only guided by the Authors and who fill their bookshelves with their works proceed in error, for they do not pay sufficient attention to the Royal Laws."[56] In 1741, the Council of Castile reminded "the endowed chairs and professors in both laws to take care in reading with the Roman law the laws of the Kingdom that correspond to the subjects under consideration."[57] The Bourbon crown worried that universities produced lawyers with scant knowledge of the actual laws that governed the kingdom and with undue reverence for a foreign body of law. Roman law should be studied by historians, not lawyers.[58]

This reformist criticism of the ius commune, however, exaggerated the problem. Just because the curriculum was structured around the ancient texts of civil and canon law did not mean that professors, many practicing lawyers themselves, would not teach their students Spanish legislation, such as the laws contained in the *Recopilación de las leyes de Indias*.[59] The casuistic orientation meant that students studied concrete cases in classes, drawn from local experience, which they would attempt to resolve by employing the full repertoire of legal sources. This inevitably introduced them to royal and municipal laws, local customs, and the writings of jurists who focused on Spanish legislation rather than the ius commune. Law students like Gamboa residing at San Ildefonso also participated in weekly seminars specifically dedicated to the discussion of practical jurisprudence hosted by the college.[60]

For instance, there is little doubt that Gamboa and his classmates would have read closely Solórzano's *Política Indiana*, considered since its publication in the mid-seventeenth century the outstanding guide to the Spanish American juridical order. Solórzano, born in 1575, spent over a decade as an audiencia magistrate in Lima before returning to Spain in 1627.[61] He wrote the *Política Indiana* after he retired in 1644, attempting to sum up all his experience and knowledge about the legal order of the Spanish Indies. Its six books cover Spain's title to its New World empire; Native labor; the encomienda; the *real patronato*, the crown's powers over the church in America; the powers and duties of secular government, from municipal officials to the viceroy; and financial and economic matters, including mining and commerce. *Política Indiana* was probably intended as a companion to the *Recopilación de las leyes de Indias*, which Solórzano edited in the 1630s.[62]

Política Indiana not only analyzed government in Spanish America but also exemplified its juridical culture. Solórzano made it clear that the king's primary duty, an obligation from God, was the deliverance of justice to his subjects. In discussing the big questions of law and justice, Solórzano demonstrated both the casuistic approach to legal analysis and the pluralism of law. He canvassed a dizzying variety of material, the whole literature of the ius commune, royal laws (of which he likely had the best knowledge in Spain, thanks to his editing of the *Recopilación de las leyes de Indias*), and local customs. Solórzano stressed throughout *Política Indiana* the necessity of respecting the social and geographic diversity of America. Only people with practical experience in America could fully grasp how to govern it while preserving justice. Although a firm Spanish imperialist, in the sense that he did not question the validity of Spain's title to the New World, he believed people born in America had a natural right to occupy high offices of civil and ecclesiastical government.[63] Solórzano's *Política Indiana* remained an unassailable authority into the eighteenth century. In 1733, just before Gamboa entered law school, the Spanish jurist Alonso Varela de Ureta commented, "it was easier to ignore the disposition of the law than the authority of that work."[64]

In his official résumé, Gamboa boasted that his professors recognized him as "the best student of his time" at San Ildefonso and the University of Mexico. He won scholarships after his third and fourth years, which might have helped relieve Mesía de la Cerda of some of the financial cost of supporting Gamboa. He performed admirably in the major academic acts, as he had as a schoolboy in Guadalajara. Gamboa ended his formal education participating in two prestigious ceremonies. In the December 1739 celebration of the Immaculate Conception, the rector of the university chose Gamboa to give the traditional Latin prayer in honor of the Blessed Mother. This was one of the most solemn religious feasts in New Spain and would have brought together the religious and civil elite of Mexico City.[65] Around the same time, he and the top theology student of San Ildefonso, Cayetano Torres Tuñón, were chosen by Escobar to perform *actos mayores* to inaugurate the college's new chapel and general assembly hall. Ironically, Gamboa, the law student, performed at the opening for the chapel, and Torres, the theology student, opened the assembly hall.[66] Gamboa graduated with degrees in both civil and canon law and then completed the required bar admission course in procedure and practical jurisprudence organized by San Ildefonso. On November 28, 1740, he took his oath before the Real Audiencia of Mexico, qualified to represent clients in the high court of the viceroyalty. It was time to make good on his pledge to rebuild his family's lost fortune.

The Legacy of Mesía de la Cerda

José Mesía de la Cerda, Gamboa's first mentor, did not do much to distinguish himself on the bench. After his promotion to the Real Audiencia of Mexico in 1734, he remained stuck in the Sala de Crimen for the next three decades. He never received promotion to the more senior Sala de lo Civil. Perhaps the reprimand for excessive gambling tarnished him for the rest of his career. The viceroy of New Spain from 1746 to 1755, Juan Francisco de Güemes y Horcasitas, the first Conde de Revillagigedo, thought him arrogant and suspected he profited illicitly from his post.[67] The Jesuits of San Ildefonso, however, did honor Mesía de la Cerda. In a 1748 poetry contest hosted by the college to commemorate the ascension to the throne of Ferdinand VI, he was praised for the "extraordinary love with which he favored and protected this college."[68] But his most memorable accomplishment might simply have been rescuing the precocious Gamboa from poverty in Guadalajara and making sure he received an education. Thanks to the Spanish judge, Gamboa studied with the Jesuits, received a solid grounding in the Latin classics of literature, history, and philosophy, acquired a sound knowledge of geometry and mathematics, and a gained familiarity with some of the new ideas about the natural world emerging from the Scientific Revolution. Gamboa then followed his mentor's footsteps by studying law. Thanks to the unheralded Mesía de la Cerda, Gamboa, an orphan from Guadalajara, got the start he needed to become one of Mexico City's top lawyers in the 1740s and 1750s.

CHAPTER TWO

Courtroom Combat

Gamboa, courtrooms and Parnassus
For you the same I judge;
Here you resemble Papinius;
There a cultured Papinian.
Of the buckles that you wear
To cinch your buskin,
Do not fear the spur,
For that is your sharpest talent.

—SAN ILDEFONSO POETRY CONTEST, 1748

✦ NO JUDGE ON THE REAL AUDIENCIA OF MEXICO IN THE LATE eighteenth century had more practical experience at the bar before rising to the bench than Francisco Xavier de Gamboa. From the time he entered legal practice in 1740 to when he departed for Madrid in 1755, he did everything a lawyer could do in New Spain. In his 1757 résumé, he boasted that he "gained such credit as an astute, eloquent, and wise jurisconsult that in recent times hardly could there be an important matter in which one party did not benefit from my prudent advice."[1] He represented religious orders, notably the Discalced Carmelites, on all matters of property and estates. His work on behalf of silver miners made him an expert in this lucrative field for lawyers, not only on the intricacies of the Royal Mining Ordinances of 1584 but also on the technical and economic problems of the industry. Just when the Spanish crown was pushing to strengthen its leverage over the church in America, he handled a case for the new college of canons at the Basilica of Nuestra Señora de Guadalupe, Mexico City's holiest shrine, which plunged him deep into the fraught jurisdictional politics of throne and altar. His most famous case, his representation of the merchant Manuel de Rivas Cacho, touched not only the law of wills and estates but also the delicate matters of honor and reputation in novohispano society. He also served the Inquisition as an official defender of those accused of religious offenses. His work therefore touched on many of the most vital social, economic, and religious issues in eighteenth-century New Spain.

Although the arguments a professional lawyer makes for clients obviously do not necessarily conform with his personal beliefs, we can detect in Gamboa's briefs in the 1740s and 1750s certain themes that recur again and again in his thinking as a jurist. Most conspicuously, even before he was appointed to the bench, Gamboa believed in the vital importance of protecting the broad jurisdiction of the audiencias over ordinary civil and criminal matters. This was the key to the health of the administration of justice in his eyes. His arguments also reveal his mastery of the prodigious pluralism of Spanish American law. He studded his briefs with erudite references to a vast array of juridical, historical and even theological material. He epitomized what the late seventeenth-century Spanish jurist Melchor Cabrera Núñez de Guzmán had written about legal practice in his *Idea de un abogado perfecto*: "the main part of the craft and skill consists in looking at and handling many and diverse books." [2] But even with the flurry of citations, something expected then in legal writings, Gamboa crafted tight and logical arguments, which brought clarity to difficult areas of the law while also highlighting the equitable considerations in his clients' favor. In this sense, he would also have agreed with his contemporary, the Spanish jurist Juan Francisco de Castro, who wrote in 1765 that ultimately "the operations of law are always guided by the light of reason." [3]

In the eighteenth century, university-trained lawyers like Gamboa did not dirty their hands in routine legal matters. Notaries handled transactions like property transfers, wills, loans, and contracts. Unlicensed legal agents did the paperwork for lawsuits and advised on litigation strategy. Scribes and crown attorneys handled courtroom proceedings. A letrado like Gamboa might provide an initial opinion about the merits of a case but typically only became involved near the end, either to write the formal brief for a litigant or to instruct the judge, who might not have legal training himself, on underlying questions of law. [4] In addition, in the Spanish inquisitorial system, there were no public trials featuring cross-examinations and emotional addresses to a jury. Rather, lawsuits generated reams of paper, starting with the initial plea for justice and continuing on with notarized witness statements, copies of interlocutory writs, summaries of previous proceedings, the opinions of the letrados, and finally the decisions of the court. As Bianca Premo aptly put it in her study of eighteenth-century litigation, "law was conceived as a circulation of texts."[5] Ironically, one of the only things not reduced to writing was the reasoning behind judicial decisions, what formed the foundation of English common law.

The Discalced Carmelites

In 1740, as an aspiring lawyer, Gamboa started off on the right foot by landing a clerkship in the law office of José Méndez Meléndez, one of the top letrados in Mexico City. Born in the early 1680s, Méndez enjoyed the reputation as "a truly learned subject, respected as the master of lawyers."[6] The highlight of his career was acting as the official legal counsel to Juan de Acuña, the Marqués de Casafuerte, the much-respected Peruvian-born viceroy of New Spain from 1722 to 1734. This would have made him, in effect, the most influential lawyer in New Spain during the years of Gamboa's early education. Méndez had a busy practice when Gamboa joined the office, representing clients from every branch of novohispano society.

Yet shortly after he took Gamboa on as associate, Méndez dropped dead, reportedly in court while arguing a case.[7] If the death of his father in the 1720s had been an unmitigated tragedy, at least until Mesía de la Cerda came to the rescue, the sudden death of Méndez proved to be something of a lucky break. As Gamboa explained it, the day after the death of Méndez, he had to appear in court in his principal's place and proceeded to make such "an effective argument that I won justice for the party and the applause of the court."[8] This early success convinced the existing clients of Méndez to stick with the young Gamboa, who immediately had a thriving practice. As he later put it, "I began my career where other lawyers ended theirs."[9]

One of the mainstays of his legal practice from the start was the Discalced Carmelites. This austere order, founded in Spain in the 1560s, lived a cloistered life devoted to prayer. They nevertheless needed a lawyer to handle their worldly affairs, such as the management of income-producing properties. Gamboa likely inherited the Carmelite file from Méndez and the early triumph of 1742 might have been the case of a bequest gone wrong in San Luis Potosí.

The facts were the following: In 1732 Nicolás Fernando de Torres, a prosperous Spanish immigrant, died and left two large agricultural estates or
haciendas, the Pozo and Peotillos, to the Carmelites with the proviso that
they use the income from them to fund a new convent and a *beaterio*, a home
for single women. If the Carmelites were unable to start work on these projects within six years, the haciendas would go to the Jesuits. In the meantime,
his widow would continue to occupy the two properties. The Carmelites
immediately applied for the requisite royal approval for their new convent
building. The beaterio, which only required local approval, went ahead without complication. Three years after Fernando de Torres's death, while still
waiting for an answer from Madrid, his widow passed away and the two
haciendas went to her brother, Francisco Zapata, a secular priest. Zapata
evidently had no desire to see the properties go to the Carmelites. He dragged
his heels in providing Madrid with the documentation requested to approve
the convent. In 1738, after the six-year limit stipulated by the will had expired
but before the crown had given its approval for the convent, the Carmelites
took legal action against Zapata. They asked the Real Audiencia of Mexico to
order the sequestration of the two haciendas on the grounds that Zapata had
deliberately sabotaged their efforts to build the convent. The court took this
action and then appointed an independent appraiser who found that Zapata
had grossly mismanaged the two properties, with their value declining from
650,000 pesos at the time of Torres's death in 1732 to just 200,000 in 1738.
Zapata next exercised his right to request a *revista*, or review, of the decision.
He argued that since the six years had expired without any progress on the
new convent, the haciendas of Pozo and Peotillos should go to the Jesuits.
They had incidentally promised Zapata a generous annual payment in the
event they got their hands on the haciendas. This was in many ways a classic
novohispano case. It featured competitive religious orders, the frustrated last
will of a pious Spanish immigrant, an unscrupulous secular priest, and the
standard delays in transatlantic decision-making.

Gamboa handled the revista at the audiencia on behalf of the Carmelites.
He had a number of tricky legal questions to address. Did the Real Audiencia
of Mexico have jurisdiction since the dispute concerned an ecclesiastical body?
If so, had the court acted properly in the first place in ordering the sequestration of the properties? Were the Carmelites at fault because the six-year limit
had expired without the start of construction on the convent? Spanish legislation furnished no answers to these questions. Gamboa had to turn to the ius
commune, beginning with Roman jurists digested in the *Corpus Juris Civilis.*

He cited the Italian jurists Giacomo Menochio on procedural matters and Antonio Peregrino on trusts. He drew upon the authority of the Spanish jurist Francisco Salgado de Somoza, whose 1646 *Labyrinthus creditorum concurrentiae* remained the leading text on debtor-creditor law throughout Europe and America. And he referenced the work of Antonio Gómez, the sixteenth-century Spanish juridical expert on marriage and inheritance. Yet what counted at the end of the day was finding a logical path to a just outcome. According to Gamboa's analysis, the Carmelite friars had done everything in their power to fulfill the wishes of Torres. They had set up the beaterio without delay and applied immediately for crown approval of the new convent. They were just the victims of the dilatory Spanish bureaucracy and especially the duplicity of Zapata. Justice would therefore be best served by ignoring the expired six-year limit and recognizing Carmelite title on the properties.

The audiencia accepted Gamboa's reasoning in full and turned the haciendas over to the Carmelites, pending final approval for their convent. This came soon enough, and construction of the new convent complex finally commenced in the late 1740s. In 1764, more than thirty years after the death of Torres, the convent finally opened, with its magnificent baroque Templo de Nuestra Señora del Carmen, which remains one of the architectural splendors of San Luis Potosí.[10]

With victory in the Torres case, the Carmelites entrusted Gamboa with a lot of legal work in subsequent years. A significant number involved bad estate managers, a problem that religious orders, especially those confined to monasteries and convents, continually faced. Perhaps the most intriguing case concerned the internal government of the Carmelites. According to the order's sixteenth-century rules, the members of each province elected from among themselves a *definidor*, or provincial administrator. When the Carmelites first came to New Spain in the late sixteenth century to form the new province of San Alberto, they lacked local candidates to serve as definidor. So the pope approved an exception to this rule allowing the Carmelite friars of San Alberto to elect an outside candidate. Over time, this exception hardened into a custom; a Spanish monk always served as head of the order in New Spain. Gamboa was asked to determine, presumably at the behest of American-born Carmelites, whether it was time to return to the original rule favoring local candidates.

As a Spanish American himself, Gamboa would have likely sympathized with the local Carmelites. He also knew well the patriotic apologetics of Juan José Eguiara y Eguren, the author of *Bibliotheca Mexicana*, as well as the long history of American complaints against *peninsulares* for taking jobs and opportunities from worthy locals. In his opinion, however, Gamboa did not refer to these arguments. Instead, he stuck to a neutral natural law argument, citing Francisco Suárez, the influential Spanish Jesuit theologian and jurist. In *De Legibus* (1612), Suárez had explained that any positive law or rule could become unjust over time if circumstances changed. This was obviously the case here: the exception might have made sense in the sixteenth century, but now there were many local candidates who could serve as definidor. Justice thus demanded that the Carmelites revert to their original rule. We know little more about the case, including the outcome.[11] It might just have been an internal legal opinion Gamboa wrote for the Carmelites. But it is noteworthy for Gamboa's deployment of a natural law argument to defend the right of people born in America to occupy leadership positions. Personally, he was one of the few novohispanos of his era to rise above this discrimination, although he obviously understood the frustration of his less fortunate paisanos.

Gamboa also represented a rather famous Franciscan friar, José Torrubia, considered one of Spain's first paleontologists. In 1749 Torrubia found himself imprisoned in the Morro Castle in Havana, accused of embezzlement and neglecting his duties while serving as a missionary in the Philippines in the 1720s and early 1730. Torrubia, like many churchmen of the eighteenth century, found a stronger vocation in science than preaching the Gospel. With a microscope at hand, he scoured the countries where he was sent by his order to look for fossils. On his behalf, Gamboa wrote a letter to the viceroy of New Spain, Juan Francisco de Güemes y Horcasitas, Conde de Revillagigedo, arguing that the charges against Torrubia were spurious.[12] It was a straightforward plea that Torrubia had indeed fulfilled his evangelical duties, not a defense of his paleontological endeavors. We don't know if it was Gamboa's defense that sprung Torrubia from jail in Cuba, but the friar did manage to return to Spain. In 1754 his groundbreaking *Aparato para la historia natural española* was published. He explained that the fossils of sea creatures found in high mountains far from oceans must have been carried there by the Great Flood of Noah.[13] Even in the mid-eighteenth century, the biblical chronology for the history of the earth remained rock solid. Natural scientists may have been collecting the necessary data to shatter the old paradigm, but it held firm until the late eighteenth century.[14]

A Gold Mine for Litigators

The search for silver drove Spanish conquest and settlement, and silver mining powered the novohispano economy, stimulating ranching, farming, and manufacturing. It encouraged the migration of indigenous groups from the settled farming villages of the center to the irrigated haciendas of the Bajío to the rangeland of the northern plateau. It juiced commerce, both domestic and overseas. Demand for silver came not just from Europe but also from China, whose government demanded tax payments in silver.[15] After a slowdown in the seventeenth century, part of a global phenomenon tied to the Little Ice Age, mining bounced back beginning in the late seventeenth century. The first great mining center of Zacatecas revived, Guanajuato took off, and the new camp of Bolaños experienced a bonanza. New Spain produced around half of the world's silver in the eighteenth century. As the viceroyalty's chief export, silver linked New Spain to the global economy, paid for imports, and generated the tax revenue necessary to uphold Spanish sovereignty in the Indies. For a young lawyer looking to make his mark and restore his family's economic standing, mining offered Gamboa opportunity.

Like his work for the Discalced Carmelites, Gamboa inherited from his deceased mentor his first big mining case, the representation of Antonio de Arrieta, a miner from Chihuahua.[16] The basic facts of the case might have been straightforward, but the path of its litigation was tortuous. In Santa Eulalia, a new mining district in Chihuahua, Arieta and his neighbor Manuel de San Juan both claimed title to a vein of silver that lay between their mines. In 1735, in accordance with ordinance twenty-eight of the 1584 statute governing the industry in New Spain, Arrieta received permission from the local alcalde mayor to restake his claim. He enjoyed this right as first registrant. Naturally, Arrieta's new stakes incorporated the dispute vein. San Juan appealed to the Audiencia of Guadalajara, the high court for the district. To clarify any doubts as to property lines, the court ordered a new survey of the entire area. On the basis of this, on December 4, 1736, the audiencia confirmed the local judge's decision in favor of Arrieta. To ensure enforcement of its decision, the court asked the viceroy of New Spain, Juan Antonio de Vizarrón, to send an army officer to Santa Eulalia. By April 30, 1737, Arrieta was back at work on his mine, beginning the excavation of the promising vein of silver ore.

San Juan however did accept defeat easily. He managed to convince Viceroy Vizarrón to intervene on his behalf. Viceroys often grabbed jurisdiction over mining cases, with the argument that mining was more a matter of government, for its importance to royal revenue, than of justice. Mining cases also offered viceregal officials opportunities to plunge their beaks into rich waters, although that did not seem to be the case here. It is not clear why, but the viceroy evidently helped San Juan obtain from Madrid a *real cédula*, a royal order confirmed by the Council of the Indies, dated November 12, 1737, which recognized San Juan's title to the disputed property. For two years, however, San Juan did not try to enforce this order. He knew that the local judge favored Arrieta. But when a new royal official arrived in June 1740, San Juan moved quickly to present the cédula and managed to get Arrieta evicted from the mine. San Juan then sent workers to chase Arrieta and his local legal representative out of town. Such was justice in a northern novohispano mining town in the eighteenth century. San Juan took over the mine with access to the rich silver vein and soon hit pay dirt.

Arrieta came south in the summer of 1740. Local justice had failed him, so he looked to the authorities in Mexico City for relief. He sought the advice of Méndez, who evidently recommended a direct appeal to the new viceroy of New Spain, the Duque de la Conquista. With little experience in America, Conquista refused to reverse the decision of his predecessor Vizarrón in assuming jurisdiction over the matter. Arrieta then sought justice at the Real Audiencia of Mexico, which had the authority to contest viceregal decisions that violated law. On May 12, 1742, the high court in Mexico City ruled in Arrieta's favor. It declared that Vizarrón had had no legal right to intervene in a judicial matter before its sister court in Guadalajara and the original 1736 decision in favor of Arrieta should be enforced.

Meanwhile, San Juan, whose pockets must have now clanged with silver, somehow managed to secure a second cédula from Madrid that reaffirmed his title to the mine. The only way to stop him, therefore, was to convince another new viceroy, Pedro Cebrián y Agustín, Conde de Fuenclara, to recognize the jurisdiction of the high courts.[17] With the death of Méndez, Gamboa, just twenty-five years old, took over the representation. On January 14, 1743, he submitted an extensive brief to the legal advisor of Fuenclara. The *alegato* summarized the complicated proceedings so far and laid out the reasons to support Arrieta's claim. First and foremost, the Audiencia of Guadalajara retained jurisdiction and thus its ruling on December 4, 1736, in favor of Arrieta still stood as determinative. On this point Gamboa cited both royal law and the revered Solórzano: "This is the principal spirit of the Jurisdiction of the Royal Audiencias, of which our *Recopilación* is clear, especially in laws XXXVI and XXXVII of Title III, Book III, that in matters of civil or criminal justice the Viceroys leave it to the Audiencias, without being able to intervene in any way (as Sr. Solórzano teaches as well in Book V, Chapter III of his *Política Indiana*)."[18] Here was a bedrock principle of the Spanish American justice system that Gamboa never forgot: viceroys had no power to interfere in judicial matters before the courts. Gamboa argued Arrieta was right to seek justice in the Real Audiencia of Mexico since, as Solórzano also taught, only the senior court could overturn a viceregal decision.[19] As for the two cédulas of 1737 and 1742 in favor of San Juan, Gamboa argued they must have been obtained fraudulently and thus lacked legal force. He wrote that San Juan had tried "to win by malice, what he could not win by law."[20] Finally, Gamboa ended his defense of his client with an emotional invocation of equity. Poor Arrieta, he wrote, "after imponderable expenses and difficulties, won judgments in Chihuahua and Guadalajara, obtained possession of his old measurements for three years, only to see them suddenly stripped from him again at a time of bonanza."[21] In the period that San Juan occupied the mine illegally, he had extracted the huge sum of 150,000 pesos in silver. Gamboa's arguments persuaded Viceroy Fuenclara to give up the claim for jurisdiction assumed by his predecessor Vizarrón and recognize that of the Audiencia of Guadalajara. At the end, Arrieta won back his mine but whether there was any silver left after San Juan's unlawful occupation is unknown.

Gamboa represented miners in all the major mining districts of New Spain. Perhaps no case had higher stakes and a more intriguing connection to his later work as an audiencia magistrate than his early 1750s representation of Agustin Moreno y Castro, the Marqués de Valle Ameno, in his fight with Pedro Romero Terreros over title to a mine in Real del Monte. This district close to Mexico City and adjacent to the town of Pachuca was the site of the most ambitious rehabilitation project in the eighteenth century. In 1739 José Alejandro de Bustamante negotiated an agreement with the viceregal government that guaranteed him a number of valuable concessions, including tax relief, discounted mercury, and government-supplied draft labor. In return, he promised to dig a tunnel that would drain the flooded Vizcaína vein, well known as one of the richest in New Spain. He brought in Pedro Romero Terreros, a young Spanish merchant based in Querétaro, as his principal financial backer.[22] The first tunnel they dug, however, came in at the wrong angle to fully drain the water-filled mines. In 1747 Bustamante sought additional investors, including his brother-in-law Valle Ameno, a fellow Andalusian who already owned the Todos Santos mine in Real del Monte, to fund a second tunnel. In exchange for his investment, Valle Ameno received the title to the already registered San Vicente mine along the vein. In 1750 Bustamante died after he fell from his horse and contracted gangrene from his injury. Terreros, the merchant-financier, assumed control over the project. His first move was to get rid of Valle Ameno. In proceedings that commenced in 1753, Terreros claimed that Valle Ameno's title to San Vicente was revocable upon his decision. In the alternative, Terreros argued that Valle Ameno had forfeited his title to the mine by failing to keep at least four men at work continuously as the 1584 mining statute stipulated.[23]

Gamboa handled Valle Ameno's case before the Real Audiencia of Mexico. He made short work of Terreros' arguments. First, why would Valle Ameno invest his hard-earned money in a risky venture without secure title to the mine? It was ridiculous for Terreros to argue that Valle Ameno's title over San Vicente was revocable. Terreros' second argument was equally specious. According to the terms of the 1739 agreement with the viceregal government, ordinance thirty-seven of the 1584 statute, which stipulated that four men had to work a mine for the title to remain good, had been suspended for as long as work continued on the drainage tunnel. Terreros himself benefited from this concession; it was the height of hypocrisy for him to deny the same privilege to his fellow investor Valle Ameno. The Real Audiencia of Mexico accepted Gamboa's arguments and validated Valle Ameno's title to the San Vicente mine.[24]

Like San Juan in Chihuahua, Terreros would not let an adverse judicial decision stand in his way. Rather than seek the intervention of the viceroy, however, Terreros went directly to the Council of the Indies, the supreme judicial authority for America. Only an extremely deep-pocketed litigant could consider this option. By this time, Valle Ameno had died, and Gamboa had moved to Madrid to represent the merchants of the Consulado of Mexico. But he kept an eye on the litigation, maintained by the widow and children of Valle Ameno. The Council of the Indies rejected Terreros's plea, since "if the appeal were admitted, the greatest inconvenience would ensue, as everyone would abandon the courts of first instance, and the ordinary remedies of law, and would have recourse to new and extraordinary remedies, tending to bring the superior courts into disrepute, to detract from the authority of decisions, which ought to be regarded as definitive, to prejudice the interests of the public, and to bring irreparable injury upon the parties concerned."[25] Terreros still had the right to request the Real Audiencia of Mexico to review its decision.

The story did not end there. Terreros had not become one of New Spain's most successful capitalists by accepting no for an answer. In 1759 after the audiencia refused his application to reopen the case, he sent a crew of armed men to occupy the San Vicente mine by force. The Valle Ameno family responded by sending their own men to defend it. Fighting broke out in the streets of the neighboring town of Pachuca. The audiencia fined Terreros 5,000 pesos for his illegal seizure of the mine, a pittance considering the wealth then flowing from his other mines in Real del Monte. In January 1766, the Valle Ameno family, worn down by almost fifteen years of litigation, surrendered the title of the San Vicente mine to Terreros.[26] Then at the peak of his powers in 1766, Terreros was about to push his luck again, this time trying to squeeze the wages of his workers. As we shall see, Gamboa once again was required to provide his legal expertise to forestall violence.

By representing silver miners in the 1740s and 1750s, Gamboa gained a comprehensive knowledge of New Spain's anchor industry. He learned the intricacies of its laws and the troubles that ensued when litigants and other authorities did not respect the jurisdiction of the audiencias. Along the way he learned about how mines were financed and how operators contracted labor. Not least, he came to understand the technical questions, such as how mines were drained and ventilated and how raw ore was turned into shining bars of silver. And by representing miners in court, he gained a feel for their psychology. These were men willing to put everything at risk for the slim chance of great fortune. They were unlike his father and other Basque merchants, who understood caution and diversification.

The Colegiata de Guadalupe

By the early 1750s Gamboa had reached the top of the legal community in Mexico City. He was the lawyer that took on the highest profile cases, such as the representation of the *colegiata* at the Basilica of Nuestra Señora de Guadalupe against the archbishop of Mexico, Manuel José Rubio y Salinas. The colegiata was the college of canons, a residential community of secular clergy, first proposed for the basilica in 1709. After decades of fundraising and organizing by Father Juan de Alarcón, the colegiata was ready to open in the late 1740s. Alarcón had raised an impressive endowment of 500,000 pesos, enough to support himself as abbot, ten canons, six prebendaries, and six chaplains.[27] It would be the most important canonical chapter in New Spain after that of the cathedral itself. On May 27, 1749, the crown approved its creation, issuing a cédula that put the new ecclesiastical institution under royal patronage. This would exempt it from the jurisdiction of the archdiocese of Mexico controlled by Rubio.

It seemed the perfect time to seek royal protection for a church body. The Spanish crown in the mid-eighteenth century was determined to strengthen its power over the church. In Europe it was negotiating a new concordat with the Papacy that would reinforce the real patronato, the crown's historic rights over church appointments and financial matters in Spain and America. And in New Spain and Peru the crown had already launched the secularization of the *doctrinas*, which would strip the regular orders of control over Native parishes, putting secular priests under episcopal authority in charge. Such a move, it was hoped, would help assimilate Natives into Spanish culture while enhancing the crown's control over crucial matters of religion.[28] While a contentious time in church-state relations, it seemed that the crown definitely had the upper hand. Thus the prospect of the Colegiata de Guadalupe opening under royal patronage and thus exempt from episcopal control looked like a sure bet.

Rubio y Salinas, the archbishop of Mexico, a canon lawyer before his appointment in 1748, refused to relinquish his authority over the college of canons of Guadalupe. He simply ignored the royal cédula granting the colegiata independence and refused to carry out the investiture ceremony to allow the college to open. He demanded that Alarcón, as the new abbot, inform him regularly on the "status of the sanctuary; its rents, collected and what should be collected; its expenditures, for what ends and with what powers."[29] He must have considered it absurd that a college of canons attached to the sanctuary of Guadalupe, so closely associated with the archdiocese since the apparition of the Virgin to Juan Diego in December 1531, would not come under his full control.

Alarcón came to Gamboa for advice. The lawyer recommended enlisting the support of the viceroy of New Spain, the Conde de Revillagigedo. Gamboa wrote a long alegato addressed to Revillagigedo, which put forth a full-throttled defense of the real patronato. "The high powers of kings," Gamboa wrote, "do not need defenses among the vassals, as they rest on the throne of His Majesty as attributes of his sovereignty, and do not only oblige veneration and respect but demand all of the vassals' attentions."[30] Here Gamboa sounded more like a Spanish regalist than a novohispano jurist steeped in the pluralism of American law. This was an argument, however, designed to appeal to a viceroy with a heightened sense of his own authority. Revillagigedo, an assertive military commander, had few qualms about trespassing on established jurisdictions, as the audiencia and consulado of Mexico knew well. Gamboa prudently avoided accusing Rubio of any misconduct or disloyalty but did go after the archbishop's legal advisor, Antonio Medina, who had questioned the legitimacy of the royal cédula. This charge was extremely dangerous, according to Gamboa, since it impugned royal authority itself. All officials in America had the responsibility, he asserted, to "conduct themselves with honor as well as to validate the royal rights and authority in the kingdom, where there are no arms but the yoke of obedience."[31] Again, to win the support of Revillagigedo, he argued that royal power was at risk in America if the cédula was not enforced in favor of the colegiata.

Revillagigedo refused to bite. He did not want any trouble with Rubio at the time as they both grappled with the contentious implementation of the secularization decree. Removing Native parishes from the control of the Franciscans, Dominicans, and Augustinians was a higher priority than giving a new college of canons at the Basilica of Nuestra Señora de Guadalupe royal protection from episcopal control. Without viceregal support, Alarcón had no choice but to accept defeat. On October 25, 1752, Rubio carried out the investiture ceremony under his own terms, and the colegiata opened under his jurisdiction. The archbishop's victory in the case made it clear to Gamboa and his friends in the Basque community of Mexico City that they faced a formidable defender of episcopal jurisdiction. If Rubio would not accept an independent college of canons, would he accept an independent school for girls?

The Case of Manuel de Rivas Cacho

By the early 1750s Gamboa was the lawyer of choice for wealthy merchants in Mexico City, and not only those of Basque descent. Manuel de Rivas Cacho, the leading *montañés* merchant on the Consulado of Mexico, hired Gamboa to represent him in a case not only with significant financial consequences but also social and reputational. It involved the estate of Rivas Cacho's deceased wife, Josepha María Franco Soto.

Don Manuel de Rivas Cacho married Doña Josepha in the early 1730s, a second marriage for both. Don Manuel had at least one child from his first marriage, a daughter Ana. Doña Josepha, childless but rich, brought significant assets to their union. After almost twenty years of marriage, Doña Josepha died following a lengthy illness on March 2, 1751. On the night of her death, Juan José de la Roca, her confessor and spiritual advisor, stunned the family by presenting a will, dated February 4, 1749, and notarized on April 22, 1750, that declared him her sole heir and executor. On March 24, 1751, three weeks after Doña Josepha's death, Roca launched proceedings in the Real Audiencia of Mexico to have this will recognized and enforced. Don Manuel responded by submitting to the court another will, dated February 24, 1751, dictated by his wife on her sick bed a week before her death. Although an oral or nuncupative will, seven people had witnessed its making, and a notary, Juan Antonio de Arroyo, had recorded its contents. This document recognized her husband as her sole heir and executor and expressly revoked all previous testamentary instruments.

Gamboa's old mentor, José Mesía de la Cerda, heard the case in first instance, as one of the responsibilities of alcaldes del crimen on the Real Audiencia of Mexico was to hear local civil cases of consequence. Mesía de la Cerda ruled in favor of Roca, the priest. Don Manuel then appealed this decision to the full panel of the Sala de lo Civil of the audiencia, the civil law chamber of the high court. At this stage, Roca came up with two more testamentary instruments, one dated May 15, 1750, which divided Doña Josepha's estate into three equal parts: one for Don Manuel, another for Roca, and the third for the construction of a church; and another, a letter purportedly signed by Doña Josepha just before her death, that repudiated the will of February 24, 1751, in favor of her husband. It said her true intention was to leave everything to Roca. The basic question facing the court in this confusing mess was whether the will of February 4, 1749, in favor of Roca should be preferred over the will of February 24, 1751, in favor of her husband, Don Manuel de Rivas Cacho.

Gamboa's alegato in defense of Rivas Cacho was a tour de force of juridical erudition.[32] In order to work out which testamentary instrument should prevail, he cited ius commune authorities on such questions as the freedom to dispose of one's assets, the requirements for the validation of oral or nuncupative instruments, and the scope of revocatory clauses in testamentary documents. He referenced the medieval commentators Bartolus and Baldus; leading Spanish juridical authorities of the sixteenth century, such as Diego de Covarrubias, Antonio Gómez, Gregorio López, and Martín de

Azpilcueta; and the canonist Cardinal Luca, who commented on the decisions of the Roman Rota, the church's highest court of appeal. On the question of the priest's duty to avoid influencing women and other inherently weak persons in the making of wills, Gamboa referred to the *Codex Theodosianus*, a fifth-century Roman law collection that predated the *Corpus Juris Civilis*. He also referred to the Gospel of Matthew and the writings of church Fathers Jerome and Ambrose. Gamboa did not ignore Spanish legislation either, citing *Las Siete Partidas*, the 1505 Leyes de Toro, the 1569 *Recopilación de leyes de Castilla*, and a recent judicial decision of the Council of the Indies.

The core question was whose reputation would survive, that of merchant or of the priest? Both sides held back nothing in trying to destroy the honor of the other. Roca produced witness statements that described Rivas Cacho as an abusive and miserly husband. Angel Franco, Doña Josepha's cousin, testified that Rivas Cacho was "a subject full of hate, unaccustomed to work, who dissipated his fortune because he hadn't made it himself."[33] Agustín de Jauregui, a Jesuit friend of Roca, swore that "the public fame of the Colonel, as he was commonly called, was of a miserly spirit."[34] He allegedly tried to prevent his wife from spending on such good causes as dowries for poor girls and feast days at local parishes. Other witnesses swore that she had to sell off her jewelry in secret to fund her beneficiaries. Roca's lawyer also brought up an earlier lawsuit in which Rivas Cacho apparently tried to gain control of Doña Josepha's assets even before she died. Finally, in what Gamboa called "the most ignominious calumny" of them all, several witnesses testified that Rivas Cacho and his wife occupied separate bedrooms, thus demonstrating allegedly a lack of spousal love and affection.[35]

To defend Rivas Cacho, Gamboa amassed twenty-three witness statements. One declared that there was always "an abundance of clothes and food in the house, not only for the masters but for all the relatives and servants."[36] Whenever Doña Josepha needed money, she just sent a leather pouch to her husband's bookkeeper who filled it immediately, no questions asked, with up to 400 pesos. According to this testimony, in the course of the marriage, Doña Josepha had paid for nine thousand masses, an annual expenditure of around 500 pesos. As for sleeping in separate bedrooms, there was nothing suspicious about that. Doña Josepha was often sick, she liked to pray in private, and wanted extra space to play with her step-grandchildren, the children of Ana and her husband Francisco de la Cotera, who lived next door.

In his presentation of the evidence, Gamboa portrayed Roca as a greedy scoundrel in cahoots with an unscrupulous legal agent, Nicolás de Rivera Ortuño, whom he described as "not a lawyer, not a notary, not versed in procedure . . . just a poor man, without money, trade, or any known occupation."[37] It was hardly credible, Gamboa argued, that a woman of such high social standing as Doña Josepha would go against nature and leave her entire estate to an outsider rather than her own husband. He pointed out the suspicious circumstances of the will of February 4, 1749. It appeared on the night of her death and was printed on ordinary paper, which was enough to cast doubt on its provenance. Gamboa even adduced the evidence of two handwriting experts, who testified that the signature of Doña Josepha on the deathbed will of February 28, 1751, in favor of Roca, had been forged. As for Roca, his self-interest in profiting from the estate was obvious. As a capper, Gamboa reminded the court, as a matter of both civil and canon law, a woman's confessor could not play any role in the making of a will. He could certainly not be its beneficiary.

Gamboa won the case for Rivas Cacho. The definitive ruling came down on February 6, 1754, less than three years after Doña Josepha's death. Considering the complexities of the legal issues, the speed of the proceedings was remarkable. This was no Jarndyce v. Jarndyce, the interminable English estate case lampooned by Charles Dickens a century later in his novel *Bleak House*. Litigation, almost always slower than at least one of the parties would like, was not delayed unreasonably, it would seem, in eighteenth-century New Spain. Gamboa wrote a book about the case. More specifically, to restore the reputation of his client Rivas Cacho and, perhaps more importantly, to burnish his own standing as a jurist of note, Gamboa arranged for the publication of his thick alegato in the Rivas Cacho case.

The Courtroom Experience

No other audiencia magistrate of the late eighteenth century knew New Spain as well, both practically and legally, as Gamboa. His experience as a private lawyer for almost fifteen years, from his graduation at the University of Mexico to his departure to Madrid in 1755, gave him first-hand knowledge of the jurisdictional frontiers of New Spain, the ins and outs of mining law, and the place of the ius commune, local custom, and royal legislation in defining the rules of everyday life in America. He realized quickly the importance of respecting the jurisdiction of the audiencias to assure the expeditious and authoritative administration of justice. Viceroys could fulfill their own responsibilities to the king by allowing the courts to do their work without interference. To be sure, like any lawyer, Gamboa made arguments at times solely to serve a client. His strong regalist argument for the Colegiata de Guadalupe went against his position later in his career that royal authority had clear limits, especially if opposed by local custom. He pulled out all stops for Rivas Cacho, even if the merchant only won because the priest was even less trustworthy than Gamboa's client.[38]

This survey of Gamboa's years as a private lawyer suggests that the administration of justice in mid-eighteenth-century New Spain, at least at the audiencia level, was not nearly as bad as often assumed. People went to court to resolve their difficulties and used other legal processes available to them, like writing letters to royal officials. The high courts moved quickly once proceedings commenced, with the complicated Rivas Cacho litigation completed within three years. On the other hand, a judicial decision, like a royal cédula, did not guarantee compliance. Losing parties, at least those with sufficient wealth, could ignore contrary rulings, as San Juan did in Santa Eulalia and Terreros in Real del Monte. Violence could still erupt. This was, however, hardly unique to New Spain at the time and remains common today, even in the most outwardly law-abiding societies.

CHAPTER THREE

The Basque Atlantic

~⊱

Even though a vizcaíno finds himself absent from his patria, he always
finds himself in it when he meets a fellow countryman. They have among
themselves such unity, that the best recommendation one can have for
another is the simple fact of being vizcaíno.

—JOSÉ CADALSO, CA. 1774

✦ TO UNDERSTAND POWER YOU HAVE TO STUDY SOCIAL NETWORKS.
This was especially true in the eighteenth century, before the rise of institutions like state bureaucracies and business corporations. The safest way to
undertake any risky, long-distance, or long-term enterprise—whether trading merchandise across oceans or administering distant corners of empire—
was to rely on trusted friends and kinfolk.[1] And to forge a career, one looked
first to one's own community. For Francisco Xavier de Gamboa, that meant
members of the Basque diaspora in New Spain. The Basques, originating in
northeastern Iberia, had laid out an extensive network that spanned the
Atlantic and covered the entire Spanish Empire. Its anchor in New Spain was
the religious confraternity of Nuestra Señora de Aránzazu, where merchants,
clerics, and officials of Basque descent came together to worship, solidify
ethnic ties, and talk business.[2] Gamboa joined Aránzazu as a young lawyer
and met the men who would propel his career, none more important than
Manuel Aldaco, a consulado merchant, silver banker, and acknowledged
leader of the Basque community in Mexico City. Gamboa acted as the lawyer
of Aránzazu in their project to open an independent residential school for
girls, known then and now as the Vizcaínas. This pitted Gamboa for a second
time against the formidable archbishop of Mexico City, Manuel Rubio y
Salinas, whose approval was necessary to exempt the school from episcopal

control. Then in 1755 the Basques on the consulado chose Gamboa as one of two deputies to send to Madrid to represent the body before the royal court. Gamboa would spend nine years in Spain, before returning to Mexico City as an audiencia judge.

In this chapter I examine Gamboa's connection with the Basque community, in particular the powerful Basque merchants, like Aldaco, who largely controlled overseas commerce in the mid-eighteenth century. Gamboa embraced the classic Basque understanding that local autonomy was a right earned by proven loyalty to the larger entity. For instance, eighteenth-century Basques revered their ancient *fueros*, which guaranteed a large degree of self-government for the Basque country; they believed they earned these rights by virtue of their long loyalty and service to the Castilian monarchy.[3] This worked in religious matters as well. As Old Christians of impeccable racial purity, Basques had played prominent roles in the Catholic Church, perhaps most notably as founders of the Jesuits. They thus expected to be trusted to manage their own religious affairs without interference from the Church hierarchy. This notion of the complementarity of local autonomy and imperial loyalty informed Gamboa's work for the Basques of New Spain and surely influenced his own thinking about the relationship between New Spain and the Spanish Empire.

Gamboa's work for the consulado deserves attention. He has been maligned as the spokesman of monopolistic Spanish-born merchants, who were supposedly more interested in extracting profit from New Spain than helping their adopted country develop on its own. Yet in the submissions he made to the crown on behalf of the consulado, including his proposal for a consulado-led mining bank, Gamboa advanced a vision of the novohispano economy consistent with Basque thinking: the autonomous development of New Spain would benefit rather than hurt the larger Spanish Empire. For instance, he advocated the resumption of the fleet system for overseas trade since he argued it retained capital in New Spain, which stimulated mining, agriculture, and commerce. The consulado mining bank he proposed would be a powerful engine of autonomous development. At least in the 1750s and 1760s, the Basque merchants who controlled the Consulado of Mexico saw their economic interests in keeping their money at work in New Spain. They wanted to loosen not tighten colonial controls. There was thus nothing contradictory about a patriotic novohispano like Gamboa acting as the lobbyist of Spanish-born consulado merchants. One could be a local patriot, a transatlantic Basque, and a loyal subject of the Spanish monarchy all at the same time.

The Imperial Basques

Basques have long thought of themselves as exceptional among the people of the Iberian Peninsula. The Basque language, Euskera, is unique, with no relationship to the Indo-European linguistic family. In the seventeenth century, Baltasar de Echave, a Basque priest living in New Spain, proposed that Euskera must have been one of the languages that originated from the Tower of Babel.[4] Basques were presumed to be the first Spaniards, descendants even of the first humans to make the peninsula home. From their rocky enclave in northeastern Spain (and southwestern France) they had resisted all invaders, from the Celts and Romans to the Visigoths and Moors. They had maintained their racial purity, making them the oldest of the Old Christians of Spain. In 1590 the Castilian crown recognized this supposed *limpieza de sangre* by declaring the universal nobility of the Basque people.[5]

The privilege of universal nobility opened doors for the Basques. They could aspire to the highest offices of Castilian government and the Catholic Church without having to worry about proving their racial bona fides. Basques from Navarre, for instance, dominated the administration of Castilian royal finances in the late seventeenth and early eighteenth centuries.[6] Basques played pivotal roles in the church. Juan de Zumárraga, a native of Durango from Biscay, was the first bishop of Mexico in 1527. Ignatius de Loyola, a former soldier from Gipuzkoa, founded the Jesuit order in 1539 with his fellow Basque Francisco Xavier. The ties between Basques and Jesuits remained intimate in the eighteenth century. Universal nobility also inoculated Basques from the stigma of having to use their hands to make a living. Basques hunted whales and fished cod, shepherded and sheared sheep, navigated ships, mined iron and silver ore, and handled cargos of merchandise and bills of lading across the empire. In the eighteenth century, when the crown sought to put to rest old prejudices attached to ignoble manual trades, the industrious Basques were held up as models for the rest of the monarchy.[7]

No matter how much Basques cherished their mountainous homeland, many had to emigrate to make a living. The Basque country lacked much arable land, and the non-partible inheritance system, in which only one son took over the family homestead, or *beserri*, meant that there were always young people looking for opportunities far from home.[8] This was one reason Basques put a premium on education, including the teaching of Castilian, or Spanish, in Basque schools.[9] An anonymous member of the Real Sociedad

Bascongada de Amigos del País (RSBAP), the Basque economic society, joked in 1775 that "in the limited, mountainous and sterile territory of the Basque country, from no other branch of business could one extract such profits than the distribution of young men to Andalusia and America, preparing them first with a careful instruction in the use of the pen and arithmetic."[10]

Emigrant Basques especially gravitated to commerce as a profession.[11] Basque family enterprises shipped wool and iron to England out of Bilbao and imported English cloth and North Atlantic codfish. Bilbao itself was barred from direct trade with America due to its status as a duty-free port under the terms of the fueros.[12] But capitalizing on the old trade of Basque iron for Andalusian farm products, Basque merchants established themselves in Seville and then Cadiz to take advantage of imperial trade. These mercantile Basques laid out extended family networks throughout the Spanish Empire, from Cadiz, Havana, and Mexico City to Caracas, Lima, and Manila.[13] In the eighteenth-century Basques formed the dominant party in the consulados of Mexico City and Lima.[14]

Nuestra Señora de Aránzazu

In 1469, the Virgin Mary appeared to a shepherd boy in the mountains near the village of Aránzazu, close to where the three Basque provinces of Álava, Biscay, and Gipuzkoa adjoined. Speaking Euskera, the Virgin pledged her special love for the Basque people. The cult of Our Lady of Aránzazu spread to America in the seventeenth century, with the first confraternity founded in Lima in 1635.[15] In Mexico City the Basques founded a brotherhood in honor of Aránzazu in 1681. A few years later, in 1686, Juan de Luzuriaga, a Basque Franciscan friar, published in Mexico City a panegyric that explained that the Virgin had appeared in Aránzazu to sanctify the universal nobility of the Basques and to promote national unity.[16] In 1696 the archbishop of Mexico recognized the legal status of the confraternity of Nuestra Señora de Aránzazu and conceded the right to choose its own chaplain and maintain its own financial accounts without ecclesiastical interference.[17] By the mid-eighteenth century, Aránzazu had 120 members, including women and a few non-Basques.[18] All of the established Basque families in Mexico City belonged. Its leadership in the eighteenth century was dominated by consulado merchants.[19]

Aránzazu combined religion with banking. On August 16 its members celebrated the feast of Nuestra Señora de Aránzazu with a solemn mass and fireworks. Throughout the year they honored the Basque saints Ignacio de Loyola, Francisco Xavier, and Fermín, the patron of the Basques of the kingdom of Navarra. On December 12 the Basques of Aránzazu, many of them Spanish-born, celebrated the patroness of New Spain, the Virgin of Guadalupe. On the financial side, the confraternity covered dowries and funeral expenses for poorer members. It owned property in its own name and received testamentary bequests. Its directors lent out this accumulated capital at interest to members.[20] Business was typically done before mass, held at the sprawling San Francisco monastery complex across the street from what is now the Casa de los Azulejos in downtown Mexico City. A notary would be on hand to record transactions. The financial clout of Aránzazu explains why even non-Basques, such as José González Calderón, a montañés merchant from Santander, sought membership.[21]

As an ambitious young lawyer without family in Mexico City, Gamboa naturally joined Nuestra Señora de Aránzazu as soon as he could. Perhaps his close friend from San Ildefonso, Miguel de Berrio, a scion of an immensely rich Basque American family, sponsored him. By 1745, at the age of twenty-seven, Gamboa was already putting his name forward as a candidate for its board of directors.[22] He was not successful the first time but did win election the following year. He represented the American Basques on the board from 1746 to 1750.[23]

Gamboa was also starting a family of his own. On October 14, 1747, two months before his thirtieth birthday, Gamboa married seventeen-year-old María Manuela de Urrutia. Like her husband, María Manuela was an American-born Basque, born in Chihuahua in 1730. She was probably related to the Urrutia family of Guadalajara, perhaps a younger relative of Maria de Urrutia, who had married Gamboa's old mentor, José Mesía de la Cerda, in 1734. There was nothing unusual about the large age difference between Gamboa and his wife. White men in Spanish America who did not come from rich families typically had to establish themselves financially before they could compete in the tough marriage market for respectable young women. The couple had five children in their first decade together, three girls and two boys. Gamboa also supported in his household his sisters and widowed mother from Guadalajara.

The most important person Gamboa met through Aránzazu was Manuel Aldaco. Born in 1696 in Oiartzun, a Basque village with a strong link to the

New World, Aldaco arrived in Mexico City in 1715.[24] He came from humble
stock, allegedly the illegitimate son of a father studying for the priesthood
and a mother who ran a tavern.[25] Aldaco joined the business empire of his
relative Francisco de Fagoaga, who imported merchandise from Spain, ran a
silver bank, and managed the Mexico City mint, at least until the government took back control in 1727. Aldaco married Fagoaga's daughter, a typical
way to maintain wealth within extended families. Upon his father-in-law's
death in 1736, Aldaco assumed control of the mining bank while Ambrosio
de Meave, a younger kinsman from Durango in Biscay, took over the trading
company. As a well-connected and trusted businessman, Aldaco served as
the executor of many Basque estates, particularly those that required the
transfer of large sums of money across the Atlantic. And he never forgot his
hometown, leaving funds in his will to establish an altar dedicated to the
Virgin of Guadalupe in the parish church of Oiartzun. Aldaco was the epit-
ome of the transatlantic Basques, with one foot in his ancestral village and
another in his adopted home of New Spain. Thanks to his support, Gamboa's
career took off.

The Controversy over the Vizcaínas

In the early 1750s Aldaco was both rector of Aránzazu and prior, the elected
chief executive, of the consulado. It was his task to see through the completion of the great project of the confraternity, a residential school for girls,
known officially as the Colegio de San Ignacio de Loyola but colloquially,
from the start, as the Vizcaínas. Construction of the school, a massive
Baroque-style structure of red tezontle and limestone covering an entire city
block and containing a lavish Churrigueresque chapel, began in 1734, in a
ceremony presided over by Juan Antonio de Vizarrón, the Basque-born archbishop of Mexico and the viceroy of New Spain from 1734 to 1740.[26] Aldaco,
Meave, and fellow merchant Francisco de Echeveste oversaw the fundraising
campaign.[27] The main purpose of the Vizcaínas was to shelter and educate
poor girls and unmarried women of Spanish descent, to protect their honor
from the evils that abounded in the streets of Mexico City.

As construction neared completion in 1750, Aldaco tasked Gamboa,
Aránzazu's lawyer, with writing a charter for the new college to set out its
rules and procedures.[28] Since the main objective was to instill Christian virtue in the girls and women it sheltered, residents followed a strict regime

Figure 3. Colegio de San Ignacio de Loyola, Las Vizcaínas. The school remains in operation today, educating boys and girls of modest means and still managed by a board of Basque businesspeople. Photograph by Sandra Guerrero.

patterned on convent life. Every morning they would rise before dawn to attend 6:00 a.m. mass. Once or twice a year they would undertake the spiritual exercises of San Ignatius. The girls would learn how to read, write, and count but would not get the humanistic education offered in Jesuit schools for boys. They did not study, for example, Latin, rhetoric, or philosophy. Instead, they concentrated on the skills expected of honorable ladies in society, such as sewing, embroidery, and singing. The older residents, mainly widows and spinsters, were expected to look after the young girls, creating a family atmosphere within the imposing walls of the college.[29]

The second article of Gamboa's constitution declared that the Vizcaínas would operate with "total exemption and absolute independence" from the jurisdiction of the church. The Basques on the board of Nuestra Señora de Aránzazu wanted to manage the school themselves, without the obligation to pay fees or report to the archdiocese of Mexico City. This was essentially the same demand made by the abbot and canons of the Colegiata de Guadalupe, also represented by Gamboa. This was a bold provision to include in the charter of a school. Education was unquestionably under the jurisdiction of the church, even though there were exceptions, such as the Colegio de la Caridad, a school for orphan girls founded in the sixteenth century by another confraternity, Santísimo Sacramento. The call for autonomy was consistent with the Basque devotion to self-rule. Just as Basques claimed their service to the Castilian crown earned them the right to self-government in their homeland, protected by their fueros, they also believed their exemplary devotion to Catholicism should excuse them from strict ecclesiastical supervision.[30]

The problem in the early 1750s, as we have seen in the previous chapter, was that the episcopal palace in Mexico City was occupied by Manuel Rubio y Salinas, a canon lawyer determined to defend ecclesiastical authority against all comers. He had already defeated Gamboa in the fight over the Colegiata de Guadalupe. Was there any hope for the Vizcaínas?

The board of Aránzazu, led by Aldaco and advised by Gamboa, first tried a conciliatory approach. They invited the archbishop to visit the almost-completed school in September 1751. But right after this cordial encounter, Rubio informed Aldaco that he would never surrender his rights over the school. He demanded the power to inspect it whenever he wanted and oversee all religious services through the nearby parish of Veracruz.[31] The board of Aránzazu offered to compromise. In exchange for accepting the school's exemption, the brotherhood would compensate the archdiocese for the fees it would forego as well as allow the archbishop an annual inspection. This was still not enough for Rubio. He told Aldaco that only a papal bull, a direct order from the pope, could make him surrender his jurisdictional rights. After one more fruitless exchange of letters with the archbishop, Aldaco asked Meave to relay to Gamboa that "insofar as it is in my power, not another word will be spoken, only to the royal court and to Rome." Aldaco then added ominously, "if we come out of this badly we will set fire to what has cost us our fortune."[32]

Aldaco and the board of Aránzazu appealed for help in Madrid. They could count on powerful friends in the Congregation of San Ignacio, the Basque religious brotherhood in the imperial capital. Since 1729 the two organizations were formally linked, with the Madrid Basques handling transatlantic financial matters for their cousins in Mexico City and helping them with business in the royal court.[33] Members of San Ignacio included some of the most important men in government, including Sebastián de la Cuadra, the Marqués de Villarias, a key minister under Philip V. Villarias had been the patron of Zenón de Somodevilla, the Marqués de la Ensenada, the chief minister of Ferdinand VI from 1746 to 1754.[34] In the 1750s, Ensenada's most loyal collaborator, Agustín Pablo de Ordeñena, the secretary of the Council of State, served as rector of San Ignacio.[35] Many crown officials of Basque descent, after service in America, joined San Ignacio on their return to Madrid. At least three, all members of the Council of the Indies, served as rectors of the congregation in later years, Tomás Ortiz de Landázuri in 1766, Francisco Antonio de Echavarri in 1772, and Francisco Leandro de Viana in 1782.[36]

Aldaco wrote to San Ignacio to explain their predicament.[37] Ordeñena, the confidante of Ensenada and rector of the congregation, promised his help.[38] He quickly got Ensenada to issue a royal cédula dated March 31, 1753, that authorized the opening of the Vizcaínas according to the original terms of Gamboa's charter. The crown would grant the school royal patronage in order to protect it from the jurisdiction of the archbishop.[39] Ensenada also wrote directly to Rubio in September 1753 in the name of the king to "request and order you very particularly that in respect to the exemptions and prerogatives that the cited board and congregation [Aránzazu] desire and request for the named college . . . that you ratify and enforce in this case the orders that are sent to you through prudent and pious conduct, whose particular service will be very much to my royal pleasure."[40] But the bishop simply ignored this royal order, just as he had in similar circumstances in the case of the Colegiata de Guadalupe. Only a command from the pope, he repeated, would force him to relax his jurisdictional claim. With the board of Aránzazu equally stubborn, the huge, recently finished building remained empty as the Basques of Mexico City and Madrid began the arduous process of securing the papal bull demanded by Rubio.

Basques on the Consulado

The stalemate over the Vizcaínas was just one headache for the Basque merchants at the time. Business, they complained, was also bad. The core problem was the change in the organization of Atlantic trade since hostilities began with Britain in 1739, in the confrontation now known as the War of Jenkins' Ear. This had forced Spain to suspend the dispatch of fleets from Cadiz. Instead, licensed ships (*registros sueltos*) left Cadiz alone or in small groups throughout the year. The end of the so-called fleet system fundamentally transformed Atlantic commerce, as Xabier Lamikiz has demonstrated in his insightful study of Basque merchants in the eighteenth century.[41] It greatly increased market risk for all participants and put a higher premium on accurate commercial intelligence. The Consulado of Mexico complained frequently to Madrid about the disruptions caused by the unexpected arrival of registros, bringing merchandise for which there was no demand.[42] Merchants in Cadiz did not like the situation either. Both sides yearned for a return to the more predictable fleet system. Historians have focused on the official abolition of the Cadiz monopoly in 1778 as the turning point for Spanish imperial trade; far more consequential, it would seem, was the move decades earlier to replace the *flotas* with registros sueltos.[43]

Making a bad situation worse, in the eyes of the Consulado of Mexico, were the actions of the viceroy of New Spain from 1746 to 1755, the Conde de Revillagigedo. He systematically favored Cadiz-based merchants at their expense. He allowed the sales agents from Cadiz to set up shop in Mexico City in violation of the established rules of the Jalapa trade fair. According to the 1729 regulations, merchants from Spain were supposed to transact business exclusively in Jalapa and then return promptly home, in respect of the Consulado of Mexico's legal monopoly over wholesaling in New Spain.[44] Revillagigedo also violated the consulado's jurisdiction over the adjudication of commercial cases to help Spanish parties involved in disputes. He refused to enforce the consulado's established exemption from paying sales taxes on goods brought into Mexico City for resale; in their view, this amounted to double taxation.[45] The most damaging measure came in 1753 when the viceroy revoked the consulado's old contract to collect the *alcabala* sales tax in Mexico City.[46] This lucrative concession had funded many of the consulado's activities, including public works, like construction of Mexico City's drainage system. It also channeled capital to the silver banks run by Aldaco and other consulado merchants. With the loss of alcabala income, the consulado had no choice but to draw upon funds from a smaller tax concession, the *avería* import duty, which was supposed only to be used to fund the consulado's operating expenses, like the salaries of its executives.

In early 1755 the consulado received some good news and some bad news. The good news was that the crown had finally decided to resume the dispatch of fleets.[47] The bad news was that the first fleet in decades would set sail the following year, even though inventories in Mexico City remained high. The consulado, led by Aldaco, decided in a general meeting on March

Figure 4. The first Conde de Revillagigedo, viceroy of New Spain from 1746 to 1755, an assertive reformer willing to breach established jurisdictional boundaries. Photograph by Leonardo Hernández; reproduced by permission of the Instituto Nacional de Antropología e Historia.

18, 1755, to send representatives to Madrid at once to plead for a delay in the fleet for at least one year. At the same time, these deputies could bring to Madrid's attention all the problems caused by Revillagigedo's constant interference. They might even be able to rescind his order taking away the alcabala contract. On May 16 the consulado met again to choose the deputies. The Basque party nominated Gamboa while the *montañeses* chose Francisco de la Cotera, the son-in-law of Gamboa's former client Manuel de Rivas Cacho. Gamboa and Cotera received a general power of attorney to pursue all of the consulado's business in Spain.[48] As the trusted lawyer of both factions on the consulado, Gamboa would take the lead. For travel and living expenses, as well as for any gifts or gratifications that might be necessary, the consulado authorized Gamboa and Cotera to draw as they saw fit from the 400,000 pesos remaining in alcabala funds.[49]

Gamboa of course was also the lawyer of Nuestra Señora de Aránzazu. He could thus keep Aldaco, Meave, and the other Basque merchants apprised of ongoing negotiations in Madrid and Rome to secure the papal bull necessary to open the Vizcaínas. Aldaco wrote a particularly warm letter of recommendation for Gamboa to the Congregation of San Ignacio:

I hope that you will extend to him all the influence in his favor, as our
business demands, and for being the son and grandson of countrymen.
He knows how to handle himself with the highest honor; and his
accomplishments, long personal experience and most honorable conduct have earned the confidence of this mercantile community, especially my own. He will know how to instruct and inform you up to the
latest particulars of our negotiation over San Ignacio [Vizcaínas].[50]

There was a third reason for Gamboa to go to Madrid. It was the only
realistic way to win a seat on the audiencia. After the crown stopped the sale
of judicial seats in 1750, candidates had little choice but to present themselves
in Madrid before the ministers of the Council of the Indies who made the
selections. This, as intended, gave the advantage to Spanish-born candidates.
The Basque merchants in Mexico City expected their friends at San Ignacio
in Madrid to do what they could to help Gamboa beat the odds. Having a
friend like him on the bench, one who understood their business concerns,
would be of immense value.

Enlightenment Madrid

Gamboa was thirty-seven when he set off for Madrid in the fall of 1755. He
left behind his wife, Maria Manuela, then twenty-five, their eldest son Juan
José, not quite six, and four younger children, including an infant son.
Perhaps he expected that his wife and children would join him at a later date.
On the other hand, it was hardly uncommon in this era for men to endure
long absences from their families. Typically, they left Europe for the economic opportunities available in America. Gamboa went in the opposite
direction. He brought with him from New Spain a black domestic slave,
Nicolás Márques, which would have marked him out conspicuously as a
prosperous *indiano*.[51]

In the fall of 1755 Gamboa landed in the bustling port of Cadiz. The merchants there built towers above their homes to spot ships approaching from
the west, still a charming architectural feature of the city. We don't know
how long Gamboa remained in Cadiz. Presumably he set off as soon as he
could for Madrid. He thus likely missed the horrific events of November 1,
1755. First, a massive earthquake, felt in much of the Iberian Peninsula, shook
the city for nine terrifying minutes. Then came a tsunami, which battered

the exposed Atlantic coast of Portugal and Spain. Compared to Lisbon, where ninety thousand people died, and most of the buildings were destroyed by the combination of earthquake, fire, and tsunami, Cadiz fared relatively well. Its stout seawalls managed to break the force of the tsunami, and then— at least according to pious *gaditanos*—the Virgen de la Palma stopped the seawater from inundating the city. Only about twenty people died in Cadiz.

We know little about Gamboa's life in Madrid; any letters he wrote to his wife and children have disappeared. He had friends in the city, such as Santiago Saenz, the long-time agent of the Consulado of Mexico. In addition, the Basque members of San Ignacio would have welcomed him, as would the members of the confraternity of the Virgin of Guadalupe, established in 1741 for Americans in the capital. In fact, this brotherhood had been founded by acquaintances of Gamboa, Francisco de Berrio, the older brother of Miguel, and Juan de Alarcón, the abbot of the Colegiata de Guadalupe.[52] Gamboa likely rented rooms in Madrid's crowded center, perhaps with his fellow deputy Cotera. He would then have been within walking distance of the Plaza Mayor, with its shops and taverns; the Church of San Felipe el Real, whose front atrium was a popular gathering spot to catch the latest news and gossip; and the new royal palace, whose construction was just nearing completion. Madrid was larger than Mexico City, with approximately 150,000 residents. Like Mexico City, it was dirty and dangerous, with poor sanitation and haphazard security. Although there is no indication that Gamboa ever strayed from the straight and narrow, he would have had no difficulty finding occasional sexual companionship. Prostitutes abounded, with numerous brothels concentrated along the Calle Mayor.[53]

Gamboa would have found the cultural and intellectual life of Madrid in the 1750s invigorating.[54] It was the heyday of the Spanish Enlightenment.[55] In Spain, one of the most important advocates of intellectual renewal, the Benedictine monk Benito Jerónimo Feijóo y Montenegro, was at the height of his influence. Since the 1720s he had been writing short essays, collected in *Theatro crítico universal* (1726–1739) and *Cartas eruditas y curiosas* (1742–1760), both bestsellers of their day. Feijóo skewered scholasticism, superstition, and archaic customs. Influenced by the English empiricism of Francis Bacon and Robert Boyle, both instrumental in laying out the scientific method, Feijóo promoted a more rational, skeptical approach to knowledge.[56] As an ordained priest, he was obviously not against religion or Catholicism but, like other Spanish *ilustrados*, did oppose the more exuberant and emotional forms of religious practice. Ferdinand VI, king from 1746 to 1759, so appreciated Feijóo's writings that in 1750 he tried to ban criticism of them, a rather ironic tribute to an advocate of rational inquiry.[57] In the *Comentarios a las Ordenanzas de Minas* Gamboa called Feijóo "our Spanish sage."[58]

The Catholic Church played an ambivalent role in this intellectual ferment. Clerics in Spanish universities continued to defend scholasticism, which regarded Aristotle, for example, as the highest authority in questions of cosmology. The entrenched conservatism of Spanish universities led many ilustrados to support the establishment of independent academies to educate young men in useful sciences, whether medicine, navigation, or even metallurgy. On the other hand, many priests, especially among the Jesuits, advocated for Enlightenment thinking, especially in the physical sciences. The Inquisition, renowned for its harsh enforcement of religious orthodoxy, in fact did little to staunch the flow of new ideas into Spain. While maintaining its list of prohibited books, it also issued licenses for people to read them. Gamboa got his permit while in Spain. In Cadiz, booksellers openly displayed prohibited titles published in Paris, Geneva, and Amsterdam.[59] The Republic of Letters was thriving in mid-eighteenth-century Spain, with religious authorities apparently no more effective there in limiting free discussion than in Britain or France.[60]

Spain saw a particular upsurge in economic writing in mid-century, another hallmark of a wider Enlightenment phenomenon. The most important Spanish book of political economy in the first half of the eighteenth century, Gerónimo de Uztáriz's *Theórica y práctica de comercio y la marina* of 1724, gained readers across Europe after its translation into English in 1751 and French in 1753.[61] It was the only book by a Spanish author cited by Adam Smith in *The Wealth of Nations*.[62] Uztáriz offered a well-informed program to boost Spanish manufacturing. He urged tariff reform and government concessions to protect domestic factories. He did not think that an overhaul of the colonial trading system was necessary; he endorsed the existing fleet system and the Cadiz monopoly, albeit with changes to the tariff regime. The Spanish republication of Uztáriz's book in 1757, the edition Gamboa cited in the *Comentarios*, reflected the growing fascination with political economy. Everyone aspiring to a high government position felt obliged to put pen to paper to offer the crown their invaluable insights on the big economic problems of the day. José de Gálvez, a lawyer from Málaga, wrote *Discurso y reflexiones de un vasallo sobre la decadencia de Nuestras Indias* in 1759 and Pedro Rodríguez de Campomanes, a lawyer from Asturias, wrote *Reflexiones sobre el comercio español a Indias* in 1762. Both tracts advocated reform of the imperial trading system as the starting point for Spain's own revival. Newspapers in Madrid at this time, like *Discursos mercuriales económicos-políticos*, edited by Juan Enrique de Graff, and *El Pensador*, edited by José Clavijo y Fajardo, also beat the drum of social and economic reform. They carried news from abroad, with the implicit message that Spain should emulate its European rivals to overcome its presumed backwardness.[63] In the Basque country, the first economic society in Spain, founded officially in 1765 as the *Real Sociedad Bascongada de los Amigos del País*, had been meeting informally since the early 1750s under the leadership of Xavier María de Munibe e Idiáquez, Conde de Peñaflorida. Gamboa would become a charter member of its novohispano branch in the early 1770s.[64] As the representative of the Consulado of Mexico in Madrid, responsible for articulating its position on a host of economic issues, Gamboa naturally listened to this lively conversation about economics.[65] His *Comentarios a las Ordenanzas de Minas* of 1761, although ostensibly about mining law, dealt extensively with economic questions, such as the role of silver mining in the novohispano economy and the best ways to encourage investment.

Gamboa enjoyed the lively Enlightenment culture of Madrid at the highest levels. Perhaps through Jesuit friends, he met Juan de Iriarte, the royal librarian and a renowned scholar of Latin and Greek. Iriarte had studied in Paris at the Jesuit college Louis-le-Grand in the 1710s, where he met Voltaire. He then lived in London before returning to Madrid in the 1720s. Decades later, in a letter to Iriarte's nephew, Bernardo de Iriarte, Gamboa recalled his halcyon days in Madrid and "your dignified uncle, whose respect and friendship was constant and reciprocated during my long stay at the court. I will never forget that exemplary scholar who knew how to combine profound erudition with profound humility, and with the graciousness and wit that I remember so well."[66] In Madrid Gamboa met the teenaged Bernardo de Iriarte, who would later serve as a Spanish diplomat and member of the Council of the Indies, as well as his younger brother Tomás de Iriarte, who became one of the most popular Spanish literary figures in the late eighteenth century.

In contrast to the bright intellectual and cultural scene, the domestic political situation in Spain in the mid-1750s was murky. In July 1754, a palace coup backed by the British ambassador, Benjamin Keene, ousted the reformist chief minister of Ferdinand, Zenón de Somodevilla, Marqués de la Ensenada. Ricardo Wall, a conservative French-born Irishman who had risen up the ranks of the Spanish military, took over as the king's chief minister. Wall and Keene had managed to convince Ferdinand and his formidable Portuguese wife, Barbara de Braganza, that Ensenada wanted to end Spain's policy of neutrality, which had kept it out of war and restored the health of state finances.[67] They bundled Ensenada off to internal exile in Granada and sent his closest collaborator, Agustín Pablo de Ordeñena, who had helped Aránzazu secure the royal cédula in favor of the Vizcaínas, to Valladolid. The fall of the government of Ensenada marked the end of a fruitful period of domestic reform in Spain. Ensenada had tried to restructure the tax system, increase trade, and rebuild the navy. The new government drew support from more conservative sectors of society, including the merchants of the Cadiz consulado. It was not surprising therefore, with the veteran Julián de Arriaga at the helm of the ministry of the Indies, that the crown announced in late 1754 the resumption of fleet sailings from Cadiz to New Spain, a policy opposed by reformers.

Gamboa and Cotera, once established in Spain, did manage to delay the departure of the first fleet in decades for at least one year.[68] They then prepared a long submission, Gamboa presumably the lead author, explaining the benefits of maintaining the fleet system and detailing the damage done to commerce in New Spain by *registro sueltos* and the interference of viceroy Revillagigedo. This was Gamboa's most explicit economic writing. Employing the standard rhetoric of doom and gloom used for centuries by advocates of reform, Gamboa characterized the powerful Consulado of Mexico as "that stricken body," which sees itself "at the brink of ruin due to the repeated dispatch of registros sueltos and the great confusion with which they have transacted business."[69] Merchant ships from Cadiz arrived without notice laden with goods that buyers did not want. Revillagigedo's decision to allow Spanish sales agents to set up shop in the interior of the country to offload unsold inventory exacerbated the problem. This competition, contrary to the rules of the Jalapa trade fair, had driven a number of Mexico City wholesalers into bankruptcy. This in turn hurt religious institutions, which invested capital with Mexico City merchant houses.

Gamboa set forth an ingenious defense of the fleet system. It started with the recognition of the peculiar nature of New Spain's economy. Because silver was its principal export commodity, New Spain literally exported money. The continual coming and going of registros meant that merchants in Mexico City had to keep silver bars and pesos on hand at all times. This limited their ability to put their capital to work in other sectors of the economy, such as mining, agriculture, and manufacturing. The fleet system, on the other hand, with ships arriving predictably every two or three years, with a well-organized trade fair in Jalapa, ensured that New Spain's silver pesos circulated widely and for a longer duration. Merchants could make bigger, longer-term investments, and consumers and small shopkeepers benefited from the larger supply of legal tender in circulation. The fleet system thus worked to slow the outflow of capital, which allowed the novohispano economy to develop at its own pace. On behalf of the merchants of the consulado, who obviously stood to gain the most, Gamboa defended the fleet system on the grounds that it fostered the autonomous economic development of New Spain.[70]

Were Gamboa's arguments against the registros and for the flotas just self-serving justifications for consulado power? Not if we take the word of Revillagigedo, the nemesis of the consulado. Even before Gamboa and Cotera tabled their submission to the crown on the fleet system, the viceroy had made substantially the same points in his 1755 instructions to his successor. He agreed that the constant arrival of registros had caused severe disruptions in the domestic novohispano market. Supply of merchandise exceeded demand, causing prices to fall to unprofitable levels for all. This limited what merchants could invest in mining, "the primary spring that waters all of commerce."[71] This hurt the crown, which collected less tax revenue than it would have with more managed trade. Revillagigedo did not mention the actions he had taken that had outraged the consulado, such as granting licenses to Spanish-based sales agents to set up shop in Mexico City. But he did refer to the rescinded alcabala contract. He declared it had been managed by the merchants of the consulado with "purity, good faith, and legality."[72] The outgoing viceroy endorsed the consulado's desire for greater economic autonomy for New Spain within the Spanish Empire. For example, New Spain should be allowed to trade directly with Peru. This would support textile manufacturing in Mexico City and Puebla, which would create much needed jobs and displace foreign imports.[73] Here was a major official of the crown, on the cusp of returning to Spain to advise the crown on colonial affairs, who agreed with Gamboa and the consulado that the Spanish monarchy would be best served if New Spain had greater freedom to develop its economy on its own, rather than subordinate it to the needs of the mother country.

The Consulado's Mining Bank

As the argument in favor of the fleet system showed, a major preoccupation of consulado merchants was the future health of the silver-mining industry. Merchants had always been the principal financiers of the mines, whether as local *aviadores*, supplying working capital in exchange for discounted silver bars, or as Mexico City-based silver bankers, who invested in large-scale works like drainage tunnels. Merchants needed a secure supply of silver to buy imported merchandise to wholesale in New Spain. But this was threatened, it would seem, first by the commercial disarray caused by the registros and then by the cancellation of the consulado's alcabala concession. The silver banks of Aldaco and Francisco de Valdivieso, Conde de San Pedro del Álamo, had used the profits from the consulado tax contract to fund mining loans.[74] In the 1756 submission on the fleet, Gamboa admitted that both silver banks were on the brink of ruin, owed more than one million pesos by delinquent borrowers. Meanwhile, mining projects in New Spain were scaling up. The Valenciana mine in Guanajuato, for example, boasted the deepest shaft in the world and employed thousands of workers. It was clear to the business-minded Aldaco, who had invested and lost a fortune in the drainage of Real del Monte, that a new type of mechanism was required to finance such gargantuan projects.

In his 1761 *Comentarios a las Ordenanzas de Minas*, Gamboa included a plan for a chartered, joint stock company under the management of the consulado to invest in mining projects. The consulado, he wrote, was the ideal institution to oversee such an enterprise, since it was made up of "subjects with intelligence, judgment, maturity, and capital, the last of which they have known how to earn through prudent and well-governed economy, without a note of indecency, as well as from the experience of a century and a half administering the alcabala sales tax."[75] Various schemes for mining banks had been proposed over the decades. In the early 1740s, an Italian immigrant miner, Domingo Reboreto, pitched a plan received favorably by the viceroy. The problem with Reboreto's plan, according to Gamboa, was not the concept but the promoter, a foreigner with no capital or track record. In 1743 Aldaco opposed Reboreto's proposal, but he nevertheless embraced the idea of a chartered mining bank.[76] He surely instructed Gamboa to propose it in Madrid. Under the plan as set out in the *Comentarios*, the consulado would raise four million pesos in share capital, including from outside investors like religious communities and landowners. This capital would then be put to work on the rehabilitation of established mines, those with proven reserves but operational difficulties, like flooded or burned-out galleries. To give the fledgling bank credibility from the start, Gamboa requested from the crown three privileges: a fee of one real for every mark of silver the bank delivered to the mint, the right to import mining supplies duty-free, and the provision of mercury at cost.[77] These were essentially the same demands made by Reboreto two decades earlier.

Historians have not looked favorably on Gamboa's plan. According to David Brading, Gamboa, as the advocate of Mexico's monopolistic merchants, wanted to subject the entire mining industry to their control.[78] Stanley and Barbara Stein agreed, seeing the consulado bank as a naked power grab over mining by the privileged merchants, advised by their crafty creole lawyer.[79] Yet these condemnations fundamentally misrepresent Gamboa's proposal. First, the bank would not have extended the consulado's legal monopoly over wholesale commerce to mining. The bank had the limited purpose of rehabilitating old mines, not developing new ones. Second, consulado merchants were already the principal lenders to miners, as Revillagigedo had acknowledged in his 1755 instructions.[80] Gamboa's plan would just have institutionalized an existing relationship. It would have given New Spain its first banking corporation, with the capacity to pool capital from a wide variety of investors to undertake the expensive rehabilitation of mines.

Madrid rejected Gamboa's banking plan not because they thought it would fail but because they feared the consequences of success. Pedro Rodríguez de Campomanes, the influential crown attorney for the Council of Castile, read Gamboa's *Comentarios* as soon as it was published. He praised the book as "truly very useful and the study employed in its composition immense."[81] He particularly appreciated the detailed information it contained on the economics of silver mining in New Spain. But Campomanes vigorously opposed the mining bank. First, like Feijóo and other eighteenth-century Spaniards, Campomanes thought that American precious metal mines had fundamentally stunted the Spanish economy. They had contributed to inflation and the decline of manufacturing and craft production. He compared Spain's situation to that of England: "Gold and silver are not necessary for human life, like manufactured goods, and therefore a country can live without these metals, as happens in England and its colonies, where bank paper replaces them and is legal tender, even if of no intrinsic value."[82] While Campomanes knew the Spanish treasury still relied on New Spain's silver mines, he saw no reason for additional state assistance. "When a branch of industry produces with liberty, it is a fundamental maxim of government," Campomanes wrote, "not to interfere, especially if it is destructive of liberty." [83] Finally, Campomanes believed Gamboa's proposed bank was dangerous since it would make the Consulado of Mexico "the strongest in all of the Monarchy and would impose the law on the metropole itself." [84] For all his talk of economic liberalism, Campomanes ultimately still saw New Spain and the other American dominions in colonial terms. Spain could not allow them to outshine the metropole.

The Doors Open at the Vizcaínas

The members of Nuestra Señora de Aránzazu had to wait over a decade before they could open the doors of their school for girls. Unlike the canons of the Colegiata de Guadalupe, the Basques of Mexico City refused to bend to the will of archbishop Rubio y Salinas. Negotiations in Rome over the papal bull dragged on for years. By the time the pope's order finally arrived in Mexico City in 1767, which accepted the exemption of the Vizcaínas from episcopal jurisdiction, Rubio was dead. The new prelate, Francisco Antonio de Lorenzana, an avowed regalist, would likely have approved the school on the basis of the original royal cédula of 1753. There was an even greater irony about the opening of the Vizcaínas: Lorenzana presided over the inauguration of a school officially named after San Ignacio de Loyola, the founder of the Jesuit order, just a few weeks after he had cooperated with civil authorities to expel the Jesuits from New Spain. Until the Jesuits returned to Mexico in 1816, welcomed back incidentally by Gamboa's son Juan José, a canon at the cathedral, the Vizcaínas remained a covert center of Jesuit devotions. The school remains in operation today, in the same building constructed by Nuestra Señora de Aránzazu. It now educates boys and girls of low-income families, making money on weekends by hosting society weddings in its magnificent chapel and spacious patios. It houses the archive for the Basque community in Mexico, and an independent board of Basque businesspeople still oversee its operations, independent of course from the jurisdiction of the archbishop of Mexico.

CHAPTER FOUR

The Mining Laws of New Spain

～℮

For the law to be in essence law, it has to be honest, just, possible,
appropriate to the time and place, necessary, useful, and clear,
so as not to induce error for its obscurity, and made not for private
convenience but for the common good of all.

—ISIDORE OF SEVILLE, EARLY SEVENTH CENTURY

⁂ FRANCISCO XAVIER DE GAMBOA ARRIVED IN SPAIN IN 1755 AS AN
unknown novohispano lawyer entrusted with the task of representing the
Consulado of Mexico before the royal court; he returned to Mexico City in
1764 a royal magistrate on the Real Audiencia of Mexico. This advance in his
career was largely due to the book he published while in Madrid, *Comentarios
a las Ordenanzas de Minas.* It was recognized immediately, by such influential crown officials as Pedro Rodríguez de Campomanes, the rising star of the
government of Charles III, as the best available guide to the silver-mining
industry of New Spain. As Gamboa put it, his intention in writing the
Comentarios was "to uncover the roots of the problems that afflict the working of the mines, as well as to set out the practical remedies and new methods
for its advancement, which my long experience handling such matters has
allowed me to acquire."[1] Gamboa presented an exaggeratedly bleak picture
of the industry in New Spain, drawing attention to its flooded mines, financial difficulties, and technical shortcomings. He proposed a number of
reforms, such as a more scientific approach to surveying and the establishment of a merchant-run mining bank. The primary purpose of the book,
however, was to slice through the thickets of the complicated mass of legislation and custom that governed silver mining. Most problems, he assured his
readers, could be solved simply by a better understanding of the law. Gamboa

rejected the need for legal reform; he defended the existing framework based on the Royal Mining Ordinances of 1584 and supplemented by subsequent laws and local customs. He also strongly supported the jurisdiction the ordinary courts, headed by the audiencias, exercised over mining lawsuits. The *Comentarios* captured Gamboa's distinctive blend of Enlightenment rationalism and legal conservatism. As a statement of his legal philosophy, the book helps to explain the stands he would take later as an audiencia magistrate.

An Eighteenth-Century Legal Commentary

After he had completed his main tasks for the consulado, such as presenting the body's position on trade and tax issues, Gamboa devoted himself to a more personal endeavor, a commentary on the laws governing silver mining in New Spain. He settled down to work in the library of the Colegio Imperial, the most important Jesuit college in Spain.[2] He discovered there valuable manuscripts, including a report on mercury mining in New Spain by José de Zaragoza, the college's professor of mathematics in the mid-seventeenth century and cosmographer of the Indies, the crown's chief scientific advisor.[3] Gamboa received help from Christian Rieger, the professor of mathematics at the college and also cosmographer of the Indies. The Austrian Jesuit brought to Gamboa's attention a number of German works on mining and metallurgy. These included Abraham von Schönberg's 1693 report on Saxon mining; Nicolaus Voigtel's 1714 work on subterranean geometry; Christopher Andre Schluter's 1738 treatise on metallurgy (translated into French by Jean Hellot in 1750); Johann Gottfried Jugel's 1744 overview of mining and smelting; a 1749 book by Friedrich Wilhelm Von Oppel, one of the founders of the celebrated Freiberg academy of mines; and the 1753 treatise on mineralogy and metallurgy by Johann Gottlieb Lehman (translated into French in 1759).[4] No one else in the Spanish world at the time had access to this German literature on mining and metallurgy. He wanted to share it with miners back in New Spain who were not even familiar, he claimed, with such classic texts as Georgius Agricola's *De re metallica* of 1556 or Alvaro Alonso Barba's *Arte de los metales* of 1640. Gamboa did not just want to explain the laws; he also wanted to publicize the latest technical innovations. This was a classic Enlightenment move, especially in Spain, with its gnawing sense of backwardness compared to northern Europe.

A commentary on the laws was one of the oldest genres of juridical literature, fundamental in the formation of the ius commune. Commentaries were typically showcases of erudition, packed with references to legal, theological, and historical authorities. Gamboa lived up to this tradition.[5] In just one paragraph, in which he described the ancient silver mines of Spain, Gamboa cited the Book of Maccabees of the Old Testament; the Greek writers Aristotle, Herodotus, Posidonius, Polybius, Diodorus Siculus and Strabo; and the Roman writers Gaius Julius Solinus, Lucio Anneo Floro, and Pliny the Elder.[6] Throughout the book, he especially demonstrated his knowledge of European juridical literature of the previous two or three centuries. He referenced the English lord chancellor Francis Bacon's *De Justitia Universali* and the Italian canon lawyer Giovanni Battista de Luca, who collected the judicial decisions of the Roman Rota, the chief appellate court of the Catholic Church. He relied heavily on Spanish jurists, such respected authors as Diego de Covarrubias, Francisco Salgado de Somoza, Juan Larrea Batista, Antonio Gómez, Jerónimo Castillo de Bobadilla and Juan Hevía de Bolaño, to help him untangle the knots of Spanish legislation. Particularly valuable to him were texts that tackled legal issues in America, such as Solórzano's *Política Indiana*, Juan de Matienzo's *Gobierno de Peru*, and Gaspar de Escalona y Aguero's *Gazophilacio Regium Perubicum*, which included the mining legislation the Viceroy Francisco de Toledo approved for Peru in 1574.[7]

Gamboa needed to draw upon all of these authorities to make sense of the perplexing field of mining law. The main statue was the Royal Mining Ordinances of 1584, also known as the Nuevo cuadro. Its enactment, however, did not automatically abrogate the previous mining statute, the Viejo cuadro of 1569. Both remained in the books, and the new law only prevailed where there was direct conflict with the old; in situations in which the Nuevo cuadro was silent, the Viejo cuadro still applied. Gamboa also had to take into account the hundreds of orders, decrees, decisions, and other specific legislative acts issued since 1584. The 1680 *Recopilación de las leyes de Indias* contained just a portion of this material. Gamboa had to comb through *cedularios*, compilations of royal orders, like the one rescued from the fire that almost destroyed the viceregal palace in Mexico City in 1692.[8] Gamboa referred frequently to the separate Peruvian mining code of 1574. As legislation of a sister viceroyalty, Toledo's code, he said, was particularly useful in interpreting the mining law of New Spain. The challenge of Gamboa's analytical task epitomized why state law in the eighteenth century could not monopolize legality: it was still too messy and unsystematic. An external set of principles, like those elaborated by the authors of the ius commune, was needed just to make state legislation coherent.

A basic problem was that lawmakers in Spain never had all the information necessary about conditions in America to legislate comprehensively. The crown recognized this limitation from the start and advised its officials to use their best judgment in applying royal law. In 1602, for instance, Philip III told his viceroys in America that they should consult with local experts before deciding which provisions of the 1584 ordinances to apply and which ones to set aside.[9] The crown accepted that a one-size-fits-all approach was not feasible in a diverse and constantly changing empire. Solórzano captured this understanding in *Política Indiana* when he wrote, "each province needs its own laws and customs suited to it, as justice always teaches us."[10]

On the crucial question of jurisdiction, rules had been worked out in New Spain that differed markedly from the 1584 statute, which had mandated the creation of a special tribunal with exclusive jurisdiction over mining. According to Gamboa, "this ordinance is not observed in the Indies, nor could it be enforced without great damage to the public, particularly to the miners, who would have to maintain at their own expense a mining administrator general and particular administrators in each department and in each mining district."[11] Instead, as he noted approvingly, from the start mining fell into the ordinary jurisdiction overseen by the audiencias. At first instance, mining cases were heard by alcaldes mayores and corregidores, local crown officials. The audiencias of Mexico and Guadalajara supervised their judicial work and handled appeals. Leaving mining within ordinary jurisdiction saved the crown the expense of running a separate mining tribunal while guaranteeing miners the fundamental right of appeal to the high courts of royal justice. This expansion of the jurisdiction of the audiencias beyond what written law mandated was common in America. To deliver justice, the preeminent goal of the Spanish legal system, required flexibility beyond what state law stipulated.[12]

As much as Gamboa agreed that mining should fall within the ordinary jurisdiction, he knew the local administration of justice left much to be desired. Few alcaldes mayores had sufficient knowledge about the industry or the laws to adjudicate complicated mining cases. In addition, many treated their positions as moneymaking opportunities, typically by contracting to distribute goods and credit to people in their districts on behalf of city merchants. Their impartiality, therefore, could easily be compromised. But rather than strip them of jurisdiction, as an exclusive mining tribunal would, Gamboa proposed that the crown just take better care to appoint men in mining districts with prior knowledge of the industry and its laws. They could also be assisted by technical experts, licensed by the government, who would handle such difficult matters as boundary surveys and the design of mines and drainage works.[13] At the audiencia level, Gamboa insisted, the administration of justice was solid. Magistrates, he wrote, "complied, for their part, with the expeditious dispatching of mining cases, in conformity with the Law."[14] More than a decade before the idea of specialized mining tribunal was revived during the visita of José de Gálvez, Gamboa laid out in the *Comentarios* a strong case against it. Justice would best be served by keeping mining within the ordinary jurisdiction overseen by the audiencias.[15]

The Economics of Mining Law

Gamboa may have cited a mountain of old juridical authorities but his analysis was guided primarily by what he perceived as the economic logic of the 1584 ordinances. This is perhaps the most strikingly modern part of the *Comentarios a las Ordenanzas de Minas*. It was less about finding the consensus of opinion on a legal question, the basic methodology of the ius commune, than following the underlying economic rationale of the law. And this was, he declared, "to encourage the labor of the mines, and to excite the vassals to make discoveries for the benefit of the public, the royal treasury, and themselves."[16] Long before Adam Smith coined the term the "invisible hand," people clearly understood the potential social benefits of the private pursuit of profit.[17] The legislation had evidently lived up to its purpose: silver mining in New Spain had flourished since the late sixteenth century, driven by risk-taking entrepreneurs and technical innovators. Gamboa might rhetorically have highlighted the shortcomings of the industry, but he also explained why it was prospering. The historian John Tutino argues that, thanks to its silver mines, New Spain became an engine of global capitalism.[18] Largely because the existing legal treatment of mining, with its bewildering mix of old statutes, new cédulas, local customs, and ius commune, had worked, Gamboa saw no reason to change it.

Did Spanish law neglect the protection of property rights? Not on the evidence of the 1584 ordinances, the most important piece of economic legislation for Spain's most valuable American viceroyalty.[19] The second ordinance stated:

> In order to benefit and favor our subjects, and the natives of these kingdoms, and all other persons whatsoever, though foreigners to these our kingdoms, who shall work or discover any silver mines whatsoever, discovered or to be discovered, it is our will and command that they shall have them, and they shall be their own, in possession and property, and that they may deal with them as anything of their own.[20]

The protection of property rights began with the registry, which the crown maintained in each mining district. According to ordinance seven, prospectors had twenty days to register new claims. They had to provide specific information on the location of the claim and the proposed name of the mine. They then had another ten days to post visible stakes to demarcate the boundaries. This registration was essential, according to Gamboa, since "the mine that is worked without being registered is not a mine nor deserves such a name, even if it yields good metals."[21] To be sure, the registry was far from infallible. Miners were often careless in registering claims, which led to unnecessary disputes over boundaries. But the definition and protection of private property rights was fundamental to the legal regime established by the Royal Mining Ordinances.

The ordinances and local custom also encouraged private enterprise. One way was by limiting the size of mining claims. The discoverer of a deposit could register parcels measuring 160-by-80 *varas* (about a meter), but all subsequent registrants were limited to 120-by-60 varas. According to Gamboa, "the value and rarity of the material requires that mines be distributed with this economy, and even less for gold mines because of their greater value, in order that more vassals can benefit."[22] Despite the attention paid to big operations like the Valenciana mine in Guanajuato or Real del Monte, the majority of New Spain's three thousand or so mines were relatively small scale. Particular customs in New Spain broadened access to the industry even more. For example, Native Americans who found precious metal deposits would be exempt from tribute, the poll tax they paid to the crown. Even their descendants would enjoy this privilege. Although the ordinances prohibited priests from owning mines, in New Spain custom allowed it, as long as clerics refrained from exploiting the labor of their Native parishioners. The ordinances stipulated that the crown operate refining facilities, but in New Spain, private persons did the work of turning ore into silver. The crown just maintained the treasury offices in each district to assay and stamp the metal and collect royalties. This privatization of refining allowed for the development of an important sector of stand-alone refiners, who purchased ore from either small miners or workers who received partidos. Local custom also did away with superfluous privileges inscribed in the law, such as preferential water, grazing, and hunting rights. Gamboa called these unnecessary, "since the only thing that encourages mining, with its immense challenges, is the hope, usually futile, of wealth." [23]

Novohispano custom also vastly simplified the system of collecting royalties. The 1584 law required government inspectors, posted in each mining district, to assess a number of factors, such as the age of the mine and the quality of the ore, in order to calculate the specific amount charged to each miner. Instead, in New Spain all miners were charged the same rate, first 20 percent of production, the *quinto*, and by the early eighteenth century, 10 percent, the *diezmo*. This reduction in the main tax paid by miners illustrated how much the Spanish crown wanted to encourage private enterprise in the mining industry. Gamboa said that the reduction in royalties had worked as intended and had boosted production, in part just by making the temptation to underreport output less enticing.[24]

The legal regime did not protect private property rights for their own sake but as a means to encourage silver production. This meant that in certain instances private rights could be circumvented if they would impede mining activity. Most conspicuously, according to ordinance sixteen, one could "look for veins of metal in other people's land, even against the will of the owner." [25] Gamboa pointed out that this provision went well beyond the ius commune, which, quite sensibly it would seem, required prospectors to seek the permission of property owners before tramping through their land in search of gold and silver. But this curtailment of private property rights made logical sense in a couple of ways. First, the crown still maintained title to subsurface minerals, and thus its right trumped the private rights of surface landowners. In addition, the provision created a strong incentive on landowners to scour their properties diligently for minerals before any outsider could take advantage. In like manner, the 1584 statute allowed miners to follow veins even if they crossed into another's property. The more enterprising miner was rewarded, and society benefited from the increased production. Only when the tunnels of neighboring mines intersected would the miner working the vein have to retreat to his side of the property line.

The government was an active but supportive player in the industry. It maintained the registries for mine claims in each district; operated treasury offices to assay, stamp and tax raw silver; distributed blasting powder and mercury via crown monopolies; and ran the mint in Mexico City, the world's biggest manufacturer of silver currency. The crown's support for innovation—again contrary to the common assumption of Spanish backwardness—was demonstrated in the steps it took to promote mercury amalgamation. The process was pioneered in the 1550s by Bartolomé de Medina, a Spanish cloth merchant and amateur metallurgist, who received crown backing to experiment at Real del Monte. Medina blended finely ground silver ore with mercury, salt, water, and a chemical reagent, like copper sulfate. Piles of the mixture were then allowed to steep in the open air on a stone surface. Workers periodically stirred the mounds to speed up the chemical reaction. Within a few weeks, silver chloride, the main silver compound in the ores, decomposed and bonded with the mercury.[26] Workers then shoveled the piles into vats of water to separate the chunks of silver-mercury amalgam from the rest of the material. The mercury was then vaporized with heat and was recaptured by an ingenious hooded device, a *capellina*, invented by Juan Capellín in Taxco in the 1570s.[27] The whole process, which in New Spain took a month or so, could recover up to 99.99 percent of the silver in ores of just 3 percent silver content. The Spanish government actively supported this innovative new technique. It sponsored Medina's early experiments, rewarded him a patent to collect royalties from those using his invention, and immediately notified Francisco de Toledo, the viceroy of Peru, of the usefulness of this new technique. In chilly Potosí, as Barba described in his 1640 book, innovative miners learned to heat the mixture in cauldrons rather than laying it out on patios in the open air as in New Spain. In mining, far from discouraging innovative practices, the crown promoted them with subsidies and even basic intellectual property protection.

In chapter 22 of the *Comentarios*, Gamboa described the variety of techniques invented in Spanish America to beneficiate minerals, including the many forms of mercury amalgamation. This was presumably a key reason for the book's translation into English seventy years later. Although he made it clear that the crown encouraged research and development, he admitted that there had been lapses. For instance, in the 1640s Pedro González de Tapia and Pedro de Mendoza Meléndez received support from the viceroy of New Spain, Conde de Salvatierra, to test a promising twenty-four-hour process to refine silver in Taxco. Luis Berrio de Montalvo, an audiencia magistrate, was sent to observe the experiments. Gamboa only learned about this episode in Madrid, after he unearthed Berrio's report in the archives. He described the report as "a rare and exquisite work, of singular erudition and clarity, which should be in the hands of all those for whose benefit it was written."[28] Very often, the concern for state secrecy prevailed over the desire to spread the news about useful science; valuable reports sometimes ended up gathering dust in state archives.[29]

The Three Enemies of Miners

Gamboa had a decidedly jaundiced view of miners as a group. "Generally speaking," he wrote, the typical miner "is prodigal, unlimited in his indulgence in expense, luxuries, superfluities and even vices."[30] The *Comentarios* is full of such disparaging words against miners. "More than just prodigious spendthrifts, they lack application. They are happy telling stories of their great pasts and their present troubles but don't follow what the law clearly stipulates."[31] He stereotyped miners as fundamentally irresponsible. "If the miners were capable of overcoming their lethargy, their wastefulness, their spending and adopting a moderate frugality and economy, it would cause admiration and envy, and allow them to undertake larger projects."[32] Gamboa contrasted miners to the hardworking and honorable merchants he knew from the Consulado of Mexico. He could name only a couple of miners who truly deserved the public's acclaim, above all Pedro Romero Terreros, who had saved Real del Monte from ruin and bankrolled missions to the Apache, and José de la Borda, who used the fortune he made in Taxco to build the ornate Santa Prisca Church, for decades the tallest building in New Spain.[33]

Most miners, however, were reckless and irresponsible, according to Gamboa. This was what filled the courts with lawsuits. It started with their failure to survey their mines properly. "Because of negligence or sloth, greed or malice, mines are not measured," Gamboa wrote, even though the "one hundred and twenty varas of each ordinary mine deserves to be measured with greater care and exactitude than one hundred and twenty varas of the finest lace or most expensive cloth."[34] Miners employed no rational excavation method. They followed what has been called the *sistema del rato*, optimizing short-term gains over long-term sustainability. In the evocative words of historian Clement Motten, miners in New Spain followed mineral veins "like a terrier after a rat, they wound and twisted, even corkscrewed, up and down until either they or the veins were played out."[35] Because of the initial failure to measure and stake claims properly, miners were constantly burrowing into each other's properties. Fights would then erupt over where to place underground barriers to delineate boundaries.[36] Miners also dug shafts, so-called *bocas ladronas*, just to access the ore of their neighbors. Partnerships inevitably collapsed in rancor "since the order of business of many is disorder and confusion."[37]

Gamboa did admit that miners faced enemies other than themselves. They had to deal with aviadores. Gamboa colorfully called them "the blood-suckers of the miners, who don't let go until they have sucked them dry and satiated themselves, leaving the poor miners to go in search of new veins, to produce more blood."[38] He claimed they refused to extend credit when it was most needed and charged exorbitant interest rates. There were less than a dozen miners in all of New Spain, he said, who had the financial wherewithal to avoid these petty financiers.[39] Gamboa did not explain why aviadores should willingly lend more money to men he had damned as untrustworthy. And how could he blame miners for prioritizing short term gains if aviadores left them no choice?

Gamboa had greater sympathy for those whom he identified as the third enemy of miners: ordinary workers. These were not, except in rare circumstances, coerced Natives or African slaves, but rather free and mobile men of mixed racial origins. They roamed the mining districts of New Spain looking for opportunity. They could be as heedless in their spending as their employers. As Gamboa described it, "the workmen drink, game and spend all they make; they have no notion of economy, but live for the present moment. They attire themselves in rich cloth or fine linen, and the next day descend into the mine, where their fancy dress serves for wadding or to ease the blow of a pick."[40] They also had a proclivity for thievery. "Against the poor mine owner, already troubled by aviadores and burdened by debt, they conjugate in all its modalities the verb 'to steal.'"[41] Since all mine workers stole anyways, Gamboa suggested that the authorities should send more convicts to labor at mines. Yet in the end, Gamboa believed mineworkers deserved more sympathy than disdain. They risked their lives toiling in caverns that were "damp, suffocating, and dark, where noxious fumes were the only air and the dangers in ascending and descending" were terrifying. Aboveground "the poor smelter workers suffer infinitely in this immensely tiring task, because the oven is hot as hell, the iron bar used is very heavy, and the incrusted matter difficult to dislodge."[42] Those involved in mercury amalgamation ingested poison and only found relief by drinking a tea made from the San Pedro plant. "Mining in short," Gamboa stated, "is attended, according to the grave description of Plautus, by every pain that hell itself can inflict."[43]

A Commentary on Mining Technology

Gamboa was obviously fascinated by the technical processes of mining and used the *Comentarios a las Ordenanzas de Minas* to disseminate what he considered the best practices in the industry. He included several purely technical sections, including a list of all the mining districts in New Spain and a glossary of unique mining terms used in New Spain. In chapter 12, he explained in meticulous detail the proper way to measure and survey mines. He drew upon an unpublished 1706 manuscript by a fellow novohispano lawyer, José Saenz de Escobar, *Geometría práctica y mecánica*, which set out the principles on how to survey land, mines, and water.[44] It was a great pity, Gamboa said, that this work, "a treatise of small size, but great force and substance," had not been published and distributed to the mining camps of New Spain.[45] He also included in this chapter trigonometry tables used by German surveyors to calculate underground dimensions as well as illustrations of tools and methods prepared by Juan Minguet, a young Spanish printmaker and graduate of the fine art academy of San Fernando in Madrid. Gamboa did not expect that miners themselves would master the fine art of measurement; rather he proposed that the crown license a corps of technicians to help them. To qualify, candidates would have to pass "a rigorous examination before one or two magistrates of the Audiencia on the Ordinances and principles of Geometry."[46] Even in scientific matters, it seemed, Gamboa trusted the authority of audiencia judges above all else.

In chapter 22 he described all the different methods used in New Spain and Peru to turn ore into metal.[47] He explained how to construct and operate smelting ovens. He explained the patio method of mercury amalgamation of New Spain and the cauldron method of Peru. The key to success in both operations was to employ an experienced *azoguero*, or mercury mixer, to oversee the amalgamation process. Gamboa thought these skilled technicians should be examined and licensed just like mine surveyors.[48] He gave credit to recent innovators in Spanish America, like Lorenzo Felipe de la Torre Barrio y Lima, who wrote a book, *Arte del nuevo beneficio de la*

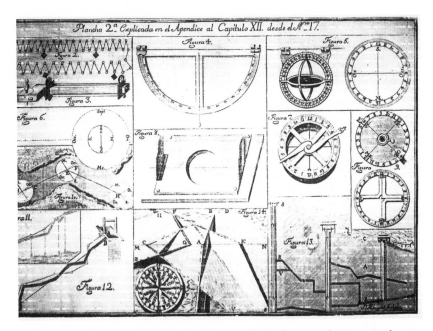

Figure 5. Gamboa included in the *Comentarios a las Ordenanzas de Minas* mathematical tables and illustrations of instruments to help miners survey their mines better. The illustrations were prepared by Juan Minguet, a graduate of the San Fernando academy of fine arts in Madrid.

plata, to describe the use of copper sulfites in the mercury amalgamation process.[49] This book caught the eye of Benito Feijóo, who wrote, "what Spaniard would not feel the same pleasure I do in seeing printed the news of an invention so extraordinarily useful for all of Spain?"[50] Gamboa also mentioned the mercury experiments of Juan Ordóñez Montalvo, the director of mines for the Valle Ameno family in Real del Monte. Ordóñez published his book in 1758, although Gamboa might have learned of his experiments before leaving New Spain in 1755, thanks to his legal work on behalf of the family.

Gamboa stressed that the greatest technical challenge facing operators was keeping water out of their mines.[51] The basic instrument they used was the *malacate*, a mechanical winch usually powered by horses or mules that extracted water from the depths of the mines in buckets or leather bags. These devices were slow and cumbersome, especially when employed at deep mines. Nor surprisingly, miners in New Spain were always looking for new ways to fight flooding. Gamboa knew of the efforts made in the late 1720s by mining entrepreneur Isidro Rodríguez de Madrid to import an English steam pump, the Newcomen fire engine, to drain his mines at Real del Monte.[52] Invented by Thomas Newcomen around 1712, this pump was already installed in many coal and tin mines in Britain. Rodríguez de Madrid sent an agent to Britain to investigate. After visiting mines throughout England and Wales, the agent concluded, however, that Newcomen's pump would not work in New Spain. It was too heavy to ship across the ocean; it could not be assembled from a blueprint since New Spain lacked the steel fabrication facilities; and, in any case, the pump lacked the power to draw water from the exceptionally deep novohispano mines.[53] The only sure way to drain mines, where possible, was to excavate adits or drainage tunnels beneath the working galleries. This is what Pedro Romero Terreros accomplished, after immense expense and toil, at Real del Monte in the late 1750s. The cost of digging adits was generally so high that Gamboa thought the crown should provide financial assistance to miners engaged in such projects.

Gamboa also addressed the problem of ventilating mines. He mentioned the mechanical bellows invented by the English scientist Stephen Hales in the early eighteenth century. "But of all the inventions and contrivances for renewing the air and extracting the foul vapors from the mines," Gamboa pronounced, "none is comparable to the Fire Engine."[54] This was not Newcomen's fire engine, of course, but an invention he learned from reading the French translation of Johann Gottlob Lehmann's mining text. It consisted of an oven located aboveground connected to tubes that sucked noxious air from below.

Even in the 1790s, thirty years after its publication, the technical sections of the *Comentarios* continued to circulate in manuscript form in the mining camps of New Spain.[55] In 1794 Alzate said Gamboa's book allowed one to understand all the technical processes of mining "without having to go down into the terrifying caverns of the mines, without having to face the insufferable heat of the smelting ovens, without having to breath in the poisonous vapors of mercury."[56] And it was the technical content in the *Comentarios* that most attracted the attention of the English lawyer Richard Heathfield, who translated the book in 1830 for British miners arriving in newly independent Mexico.

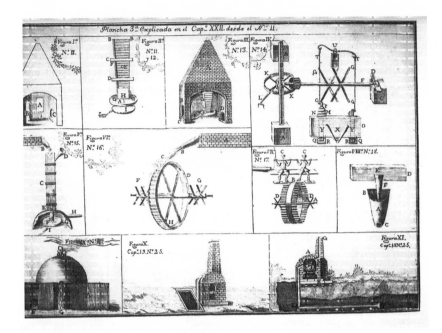

Figure 6. Gamboa described in the *Comentarios a las Ordenanzas de Minas* various useful devices used in mining, including systems to ventilate mines, with illustrations by Spanish artist Juan Minguet.

Silver Mining and the Economic Autonomy of New Spain

Consistent with his submissions on behalf of the consulado, the *Comentarios a las Ordenanzas de Minas* served Gamboa's agenda to expand New Spain's economic autonomy within the Spanish Empire. He argued that silver mining deserved the crown's support primarily because it anchored the economy of New Spain, not because it enhanced the splendor of the Spanish monarchy. As he wrote, "mineral districts of gold and silver give rise to towns, which then promote the civilization and settlement of the Indians; from there follow consumption, agriculture, and taxes, as well as many other consequences, of the greatest importance to religion and the state."[57] But he had to contend with the feeling in Spain that American precious metal mines had been more of a curse than a blessing. As early as 1600, the *arbitrista* Martín González de Cellorigo declared that "if all the gold and silver that the natives of the New World have found, and go on finding, were to come to [Spain], they would not make it as rich or powerful as it would be without them."[58] Gamboa also quoted the famous condemnation of Feijóo:

> The gold of the Indies makes us poor. But this is not the worst of it, as the gold enriches our enemies. For having mistreated the Indians, we Spaniards are now the Indians of the Europeans. For them we dig our mines and for them we bring our treasures to Cadiz.[59]

Many eighteenth-century Spaniards shared this view. They believed the silver and gold of America caused emigration, ruined Spanish factories, and benefitted Spain's rivals. Gamboa countered that if Spain had squandered the precious metals of America, it was hardly the fault of Americans.[60]

Gamboa made three specific policy proposals to advance this vision. First, as already covered in the previous chapter, he proposed the creation of a mining bank chartered by the crown and controlled by the merchants of the consulado to finance large-scale mining projects.[61] In stark contrast to the scorn he showed miners and aviadores, he heaped praise on the big merchants of Mexico City. "The management of the consulado is beyond the hint of suspicion, from being made up of subjects with intelligence, judgment, maturity, and capital, the last of which they have known how to earn through prudent and well-governed economy."[62] He said they already enjoyed the trust of outside investors, like religious communities and landowners, and thus would easily be able to raise millions of pesos in capital to pour into expensive rehabilitation projects beyond the capacity of individual miners or private silver banks. This was not just, as historians have portrayed it, Gamboa's bid to please his employers, the merchants of the consulado and especially Manuel Aldaco, his old Basque patron and a leading silver banker.[63] This was a serious and practical plan that remained under consideration in Mexico City and Madrid until the early 1790s.

Gamboa's second proposal was even more overtly autonomist. He recommended the abolition of the Spanish monopoly on the supply of mercury. The Almadén mine had been worked since Roman times, mainly to produce vermillion from its cinnabar ore. In the sixteenth century, driven by demand from refiners in New Spain, workers at Almadén began to process the cinnabar to produce mercury. Special ships then ferried this valuable material to New Spain. In Peru mercury came from the government-owned Huancavelica mine in the mountains north of Potosí.

Gamboa argued strongly that the crown should permit mercury mining in New Spain. This was consistent, he said, with the spirit of the 1584 ordinances to promote the liberty of mining. He mentioned two known deposits in northern New Spain, el Carro and Picacho. They "are not only high-grade, abundant, easy to work, and sufficient to supply the entire kingdom of New Spain, but would only cost twenty-two to twenty-three pesos for every hundredweight," one quarter of the price the crown charged novohispano miners and refiners.[64] Gamboa accepted that the crown should still control the distribution of mercury through treasury offices. He did not even think it was necessary to lower the official price, as both the 1727 Casafuerte committee and Manuel Aldaco himself had recommended in 1743.[65] More important was assuring a stable supply, and mercury mines in New Spain would do the job better than Almadén. Gamboa's plan, if it had come about, would have severed one of the most important economic links between New Spain and Spain: the mercury supply from Almadén.

Thirdly, Gamboa proposed the establishment of a second mint in New Spain in Guadalajara. He claimed he was "only considering the public good, not motivated by my passion for my hometown."[66] A new mint in Guadalajara would help alleviate a chronic problem in New Spain, identified in his 1756 filing for the consulado: the country might be full of silver mines, but it lacked silver currency. Gamboa had argued in favor of the fleet system over registros sueltos because he said it would allow money to circulate longer in New Spain. Building a second mint closer to Zacatecas, Bolaños, and other northern mining districts would increase the supply of legal tender and thus deter the use of unminted silver in transactions. It would boost commerce and economic activity in areas still vulnerable to attacks by hostile Natives. A second mint in New Spain had been the subject of discussion for decades. In 1727 the Audiencia of Guadalajara had endorsed the idea, as had Matías de la Mota, a crown official in Guadalajara and the author of a 1742 history of New Galicia. More recently, Tomás Ortiz de Landázuri, an experienced Spanish official in New Spain who later became the accountant-general of the Council of the Indies, had proposed the establishment of a Guadalajara mint to the crown.[67] Gamboa added that the government need not fear that a second mint would detract from the preeminence of the Mexico City mint; there was plenty of silver for both to process.

The Arrival of Charles III

In the spring of 1761, Gamboa presented his manuscript to the crown. The Council of Castile vouchsafed it for the king, assuring that it did not propose anything contrary to royal laws. Charles III gave his official consent for publication on September 19, 1761. The church also reviewed the book, not finding anything in it offensive to religion. Gamboa contracted Madrid's finest printer, Joaquín Ibarra, to publish it in a single volume of 534 pages.[68] A notice appeared in the *Gaceta de Madrid* on May 25, 1762—right beside an advertisement for a new open course on experimental physics at the Jesuit Imperial College—announcing that the *Comentarios a las Ordenanzas de Minas* by Don Francisco Xavier de Gamboa was now available for purchase at Angel Corradi's bookstore on the Calle de las Carretas.

Since Gamboa began work on the *Comentarios* in the late 1750s, much had changed in Madrid. King Ferdinand VI died in August 1759. He was succeeded by his half-brother, Charles, who had already served a long apprenticeship as the king of the Two Sicilies. He arrived in Madrid in early 1760, eager to implement administrative reforms already rolled out in Naples. He brought with him two Italians to head his government, Pablo Jerónimo Grimaldi, ennobled as the Duke of Grimaldi, and Leopoldo de Gregorio, the Marqués de Esquilache. He put another Italian, the architect Francesco Sabatini, to work modernizing his new capital city. Gamboa probably applauded the new government's efforts to pave the streets, erect streetlights, lay out new parks, and collect the garbage regularly. But as a former student of the Jesuits, he must have shared their concern over the new king's well-known hostility towards the order.[69] Portugal had expelled the Jesuits from its territories, including Brazil, in 1759, and Charles seemed to be considering the same drastic action in the Spanish Empire. He had signaled his attitude towards the Society of Jesus by breaking with royal tradition by choosing a Franciscan rather than a Jesuit as his personal confessor. He also supported the publication of the writings of Juan de Palafox, the seventeenth-century bishop of Puebla and famous enemy of the Jesuits.

The biggest stir in the political scene came in foreign policy. Charles broke decisively with Ferdinand's policy of neutrality between Britain and France. On August 15, 1761, he signed the Third Family Compact, swinging Spain into alliance with France against Britain in the midst of the conflict later known as the Seven Years' War. Britain retaliated immediately. It declared war on

Figure 7. Painting of Charles III
by Ramón Torres, ca. 1762.
Charles III brought his experience as monarch of the Two
Sicilies and his reformist incli-
nations to the throne of Spain
in 1759. Reproduced by permission of the Instituto Nacional
de Antropología e Historia.

Spain in January 1762 and attacked and occupied Havana and Manila a few
months later. After peace was restored in 1763, the Spanish crown did recover
its territories and even won Louisiana from France. But it remained shocked
by the ease with which Britain had seized Havana, arguably its most important American port. Long gestating plans to strengthen Spain's grip on its
American territories thus moved to the top of the government's agenda. In
such a climate, Gamboa's argument in favor of more relaxed links between
Spain and New Spain did not stand much of a chance in Madrid.

The Appointment to the Bench

Gamboa wrote the *Comentarios a las Ordenanzas de Minas* not just to help
make the novohispano silver-mining industry stronger but also to impress

the ministers of the Council of the Indies responsible for judicial appointments. Writing a useful juridical text was a tried-and-tested way to gain official favor. Gamboa had in fact launched his candidacy in 1757 when he first submitted to the crown his relación de méritos, along with letters of recommendation from the top authorities of New Spain, including the former Viceroy Revillagigedo, the audiencia, the consulado, and the college of canons of the metropolitan cathedral. Very likely members of Congregation of San Ignacio, who were bound by honor to assist their Basque brothers from New Spain at court, also lobbied for his appointment. Still, it was not until April 1764, almost seven years after he first put his name forward and more than two years after the publication of the *Comentarios*, that the Council of the Indies finally awarded him a judicial posting. He would be returning to Mexico City to sit on the Sala de Crimen, the criminal law chamber of the Real Audiencia of Mexico, as an alcalde del crimen.[70] He would be taking the place of his former mentor, José Mesía de la Cerda, who had died in 1760. Gamboa was the first local lawyer to be appointed directly to his home bench, without having to purchase the seat, since 1705.[71]

Gamboa left Cadiz in September 1764. Accompanying him were three young Basques, the brothers Manuel and Antonio de Perón and José de Ayarzagoitia, the young nephew of Gamboa's good friend, Ambrosio de Meave.[72] The party also included Gamboa's two servants, his black slave Nicolás Márques, who had spent the entire decade with Gamboa in Madrid, and an Asturian cook, Juan Antonio Fernández Mastache. They crossed the Atlantic without incident in the fall of 1764. From the port of Veracruz, Gamboa and his entourage set off for Mexico City. They passed through Jalapa, crossed over the Sierra Madre Oriental, and descended into the central plateau. From Puebla, they climbed again, near the snow-covered volcanoes of Popocatepetl and Iztaccihuatl, and reached the edge of the Valley of Mexico. From there, Gamboa and his travel companions could look down at last on Mexico City, still partially surrounded by lakes.[73]

We can imagine a jubilant reception for Gamboa when he stepped into his house for the first time in over nine years. His wife Maria Manuela was now thirty-five years old. Juan José, his eldest son, was studying at his father's old school, the Jesuit college of San Ildefonso. His four daughters ranged in age from ten to seventeen. At least the family had not suffered financially in his absence. The consulado had advanced his wife a share of his salary as deputy and Gamboa himself had invested wisely in the trading house of the Conde de San Pedro del Alamo, which yielded an annual income of around 700 pesos. He was now ready to assume a new set of tasks, no longer representing private clients at the bar or rich merchants at the royal court but rather working to keep the streets of Mexico City safe from criminal riffraff.

CHAPTER FIVE

Bourbon Crime and Punishment

He comes to govern societies he does not know, to administer laws he
has not studied, to immerse himself in customs he has not experienced,
to deal with peoples he has never seen, and look for answers to the equally
inexpert family that usually surrounds him. He comes full of the maxims
of Europe unsuited for these places.

—"REPRESENTACIÓN VINDICATORIA" OF MEXICO CITY, 1771

⚜ FRANCISCO XAVIER DE GAMBOA, ONE OF THE TOP LETRADOS IN
Mexico City in the 1740s and 1750s, took on a radically new set of responsibilities upon his return from Spain in 1764. Now a member of the Real
Audiencia of Mexico, albeit in its less prestigious criminal chamber, the Sala
de Crimen, Gamboa was tasked with cracking down on crime and disorder
in the viceregal capital. This chapter examines his years as an alcalde del crimen in the rough-and-tumble world of criminal justice in New Spain of the
1760s. Gamboa took part in a wide range of activities as a criminal magistrate, from investigating the mistreatment of Native workers confined to the
bakeries of Mexico City to breaking up violent melees in front of pulquerias
to mediating the first industrial strike in Mexican history, the uprising by
mine workers at Real del Monte in 1766. Despite the commendations he
received for his handling of these matters, he quickly fell out of favor with
the viceroyalty's top officials, the viceroy, Carlos Francisco de Croix, and the
visitor general, José de Gálvez. The main problem was his uncompromising
defense of the established system of criminal justice, especially the jurisdiction and independence of the audiencia. As part of an ambitious program to
reassert Spanish authority in New Spain, Croix and Gálvez wanted to trim
the sails of the high courts in matters of crime and punishment. They saw the

Sala de Crimen especially as an obstacle to reform. Gamboa, on the other hand, while admitting its weaknesses, still thought it a vital institution to protect the administration of justice in New Spain.

In November 1766, Viceroy Croix extinguished the jurisdiction of the Sala de Crimen over the police outside of Mexico City. This was the result of a police corruption scandal in Puebla that implicated the captains and lieutenants appointed by the sala. Croix, with the backing of Gálvez, transferred policing throughout New Spain to the Tribunal of the Acordada, a quasi-independent constabulary created in the early eighteenth century to fight rural banditry. The Acordada had been effective in this mandate but at a significant cost: it ignored basic rules of criminal procedure, such as the substantiation of charges with sworn testimony. It carried out summary trials and frequently mutilated the bodies of those it found guilty. There was no appeal of its sentences to a higher court. A few months later, in May 1767, Croix, again backed by Gálvez, ordered that all the criminal courts of New Spain, including the Sala de Crimen and Acordada, send their convicted prisoners to serve terms of forced labor at the presidios, or fortresses, of Veracruz, Havana, and Manila. This meant the effective end of the *collera*, the practice of sentencing convicts to labor for private employers at obrajes, butcher shops, and bakeries.[1] The Sala de Crimen profited from the collera: it charged the private employers for the convict labor it supplied and used the proceeds to pay its support staff. In one year, therefore, soon after Gamboa had joined the court, the Sala de Crimen lost not only jurisdiction over the police outside of Mexico City but an essential source of income.

In the *Comentarios a las Ordenanzas de Minas* of 1761, Gamboa had endorsed the existing juridical order of New Spain. In particular, he defended the pluralistic legality of New Spain, the force of local custom, and the expansive jurisdiction of the audiencias. After 1764, as an audiencia magistrate, he could act upon these convictions. He thought the criminal justice reforms of 1766 and 1767 were abominable. In his view, the officers of the Acordada, unconstrained by formal procedure, would inevitably harm ordinary, law-abiding people. Meanwhile, the presidio decree would weigh heaviest on the Native population of New Spain, who would be forced from their highland villages to serve their sentences in distant and insalubrious coastal fortresses. He considered both measures part of an ill-considered scheme to strip power from the judiciary and shift it to executive officials, like the visitor general himself, who lacked experience and knowledge of American conditions. Although the most junior member of the Real Audiencia of Mexico,

Gamboa's opinion carried weight. He had a depth of knowledge about New Spain and its legal culture that only the most veteran audiencia magistrates could match.

Gamboa's outspoken opposition to the criminal justice reforms and, more generally, the visita itself did not sit well with top policymakers in Madrid. They wanted no obstacles to the success of the reform mission. During the tumultuous summer and fall of 1767, when the expulsion of the Jesuits threatened to set New Spain aflame, the Spanish crown began to see Gamboa as a threat to peace and security. He was ordered to leave New Spain as a supposed opponent of the government. Just five years after returning home in triumph, the first locally born jurist appointed directly to the Real Audiencia of Mexico in decades, Gamboa sailed back to Spain in despair in the fall of 1769.

The Sala de Crimen

On December 6, 1764, Gamboa took his oath of office as an alcalde del crimen before the viceroy of New Spain, Don Joaquín de Montserrat, the Marqués de Cruillas.[2] He was just shy of his forty-seventh birthday, relatively old for a new audiencia magistrate. On the bench of the Sala de Crimen, he joined Antonio de Rojas y Abreu and Diego Antonio Fernández de Madrid. Rojas y Abreu, born in Tenerife in 1703, had been an alcalde del crimen since 1742 and by 1764 his health no longer allowed him to carry out his duties.[3] Fernández de Madrid, born in Guatemala in 1726 and educated in Mexico City, was just twenty-five when the crown appointed him in 1751 but he too was frequently incapacitated by ailments.[4] The sala's crown attorney at the time of Gamboa's appointment, Miguel José de Rojas Almansa, was in no better shape and would die in 1767.[5] One seat remained vacant on the court, not filled until early 1768 when Francisco Leandro de Viana, a healthy Basque judge, arrived from Manila. Gamboa was thus the only truly able-bodied member of the sala during the crucial years of 1766 and 1767.[6]

The Sala de Crimen was the highest court of criminal jurisdiction in the viceroyalty. The Spanish crown authorized it in 1568, some forty years after the Real Audiencia of Mexico itself. Its main responsibility was the maintenance of public order in the capital. The alcaldes del crimen were expected to patrol the city streets at night, assisted by the sala's sheriff and its volunteer police officers. They heard in first instance serious criminal cases within a five-league radius of Mexico City, as well as so-called *casos de corte*, serious crimes against vulnerable people like widows and orphans from anywhere in the Real Audiencia of Mexico's judicial district.[7] They also heard local civil cases in their capacity as *jueces de provincia*. The two *alcaldes ordinarios* elected annually by the municipal council of Mexico City handled lesser criminal matters. In theory the sala could hear appeals from lower-level judges, alcaldes ordinarios in the cities and alcaldes mayores in small towns, although in practice this meant, at most, reviewing death sentences. The sala operated one of Mexico City's six jails, which was located, like its chambers, in the viceregal palace.[8] Besides their regular judicial duties, the sala's magistrates handled special commissions at the request of the viceroy, such as the pacification of village riots. Unlike the oidores, the more senior civil court magistrates of the audiencia, the alcaldes del crimen did not take part in the Acuerdo, the viceroy's advisory council.

The Sala de Crimen followed formal procedures in criminal cases, derived from Roman law, transmitted to Spain through *Las Siete Partidas*. The standard procedural text in the eighteenth century for both civil and criminal proceedings was the *Curia Philipica*, written in 1603 by Juan de Hevia Bolaños, a former scribe on the Audiencia of Lima.[9] The formality of proceedings offered parties a modicum of due process. A criminal process began with a simple statement filed before a judge, which set out the alleged offense and a plea for justice. In a typical case before the sala, after the complainant filed the accusation and paid the required fee, the court's staff attorneys would prepare the formal charge. A prosecution could also commence ex officio, at the instigation of the crown. On the basis of the *sumaria*, the court could then send one of its police officers to arrest the accused. If the accused then confessed, the court proceeded directly to sentencing. Otherwise, court personnel would begin to substantiate the case by gathering evidence from witnesses, who typically answered a set of questions under oath prepared by the court's attorneys and recorded by its scribes. All of this material made up the *sustancia*. If the accused was indigent, the court might appoint an attorney to assist them at no cost. Once the evidence was compiled in written form, the parties could submit legal arguments. To be sure, the vast majority of criminal cases in New Spain, including before the sala itself, were handled with much less formality. Judges, including the alcaldes de crimen, were encouraged to resolve cases expeditiously, to save everyone time and money.[10]

Formal, paper-based proceedings required a large staff, including scribes, attorneys, fee collectors, jail guards, and even a doctor and pharmacist to look after sick prisoners.[11] Some positions, such as scribes, could be purchased from the crown with the expectation that the officeholder would recoup his investment through court fees.[12] Income from fees, however, was never enough to cover the salaries of all staff members. Employees of the sala could be tempted by the gifts and gratifications offered by parties with business before the court. Deep-pocketed individuals could launch vexatious actions against their enemies by putting enough money into the right pockets.[13]

The Sala de Crimen also needed men for the more physical aspects of law enforcement. Besides the sheriff, the sala commissioned private citizens to patrol the streets, break up brawls, search homes for stolen goods, arrest suspects, and escort convicted prisoners to obrajes and other places of punishment. These appointed police captains were typically small businessmen or the trusted dependents of big merchants or landowners. They would have the interest in maintaining public order and the wherewithal to manage unruly plebeians. They could appoint their own subordinates.[14] The captains and their lieutenants received no official salaries but could be compensated from the proceeds of fines or the sale of sequestered property. The sala's police received no special training and were quick to use strong-armed methods, such as beating up apprehended delinquents. This was hardly remarkable for the period. Even London had notoriously rough volunteer cops, at least until the Metropolitan Police Act of 1829 created its first professional force.[15]

To be sure, it was not easy to enforce the law in Mexico City or elsewhere in New Spain. First, the commissioned police of the Sala de Crimen were expected to oversee the prohibition on domestic alcoholic spirits. To protect Spanish brandy imports, the crown outlawed in New Spain the manufacture and sale of distilled liquors like *chinguirito* (rum) and mezcal. The only locally produced alcohol sold legally was pulque, fermented agave juice. This popular beverage, consumed in Mesoamerica for thousands of years, generated considerable tax revenue for the government as well as steady profits for a number of big landowners who grew the agave, produced the pulque, and often operated the pulquerias as well. Despite the wide availability of pulque, demand was still strong for more potent drinks, and there were plenty of places to buy prohibited alcohol.[16] You could even enjoy chinguirito in la Botellería, a tavern located within the walls of the viceregal palace.[17] Besides the impossible challenge of controlling the sale of illegal booze, the police of the Sala de Crimen were also called upon to suppress illegal gambling. This was another futile endeavor in a colonial society full of risk-takers and fortune seekers. Under such circumstances, what could the unpaid and part-time police officers reporting to the sala realistically do? No wonder many sought to profit from activities they had no chance to suppress. The Sala de Crimen's poice force in Mexico City had a terrible reputation. In 1755 Viceroy Revillagigedo complained that they were a bunch of rogues, "more inclined to swindle, injure and extort than to fulfill their legal duty."[18]

The Case of the Natives and the Bakers

In February 1765, in his first major initiative as an alcalde del crimen, Gamboa ordered the release of over one thousand Natives confined to the bakeries of Mexico City. In a letter to Viceroy Cruillas, Gamboa said he acted because "there is not in all of the *Recopilación de las Indias* laws and ordinances more emphatically recommended than those that look to the liberty and good treatment of the Indians, excusing them from personal service, from being abused for protracted periods, defrauded of their just labor, or tormented by confinement, deprivations, and whippings."[19] Gamboa accused the bakers of flogging their indigenous workers, depriving them of adequate food and shelter, and forcing them to take on debt they could never hope to repay. Perhaps the oath of office he took just weeks earlier was still fresh in his mind. It enjoined him not "to cause [Indians] any harm or vexation, since it is necessary to attend to their comfort and conservation."[20]

Why were Natives locked up in the city's bakeries in the first place? In the eighteenth century, bakeries served as places of punishment. Since the 1560s, the Sala de Crimen and lower-level courts had sentenced convicts to labor for private businesses such as the obrajes; the textile mills found in Mexico City, Puebla, Querétaro; and other places of cotton and wool production. This system, known as the collera for the yoke that shackled prisoners together in public, alleviated labor shortages brought on by the postconquest collapse of the indigenous population. By the eighteenth century it was the standard punishment for serious offenders, Natives, and non-indigenous alike. It supplied businesses with cheap labor; it allowed Natives and people of African descent to keep up with tribute payments to the crown while in custody; and it spared the government the expense of building prisons. The collera also served another important function: it provided a regular source of income to the Sala de Crimen and other courts of criminal jurisdiction. Yet as Gamboa recognized in 1765, the system was rife with abuse. In 1716 the Viceroy Fernando de Alencastre Noroña y Silva, Duque de Linares, accused owners of obrajes of forcing their convict laborers to rack up debt on such items as food, clothing, and even religious services as a way to keep them in bondage long after their official sentences expired. If prisoners escaped or died, obraje owners sometimes even seized their wives or children to complete their terms.[21] On the other hand, business owners had their own complaints. They accused the sala of forcing them to buy workers they did not need just to make money for the court.

While Gamboa justified his writ to release the Native prisoners on humanitarian grounds, he did not try to conceal an ulterior motive. He wanted to punish the bakers for their audacity in proposing a plan to create their own artisanal guild, which would allow them to restrict the bread market to the detriment of consumers and also exempt them from the ordinary jurisdiction of the Real Audiencia of Mexico. According to Gamboa, bakers would then be able to "resist the rulings of the Justices, even when they were so well-grounded in the Laws of the Indies as those that protected the liberty and good treatment of the unhappy Indians."[22] His liberation order thus served notice to the bakers that the audiencia would not surrender its authority lightly.[23] This concern for the jurisdictional integrity of the audiencia appeared to outweigh his concern for the well-being of the Natives. Despite condemning the abuses the bakers inflicted on their convict labor, he did not recommend the abolition of the collera. He knew it was too important for the financial health of the Sala de Crimen. He just called for stricter enforcement of existing rules to protect prisoners, such as the requirements that business owners pay cash wages and provide adequate food and shelter.

The Arrival of José de Gálvez

José de Gálvez arrived in Veracruz in July 1765, eager to get to work on the most ambitious reform project in New Spain since the sixteenth century. The case for a general *visita* to New Spain had first been floated by government minister José Campillo in 1743. He saw it as a way to kick-start a radical remaking of the entire colonial system, which would include the abolition of the fleet system, the appointment of intendants for regional government, and land reform to help turn Natives into profit-seeking farmers.[24] But it took the shock of the British occupation of Havana in 1762 for the crown finally to authorize the ambitious undertaking. The first candidate for the position of visitor general, Francisco Carrasco, a veteran treasury official, declined the assignment. The second, Francisco Anselmo Armona, the intendant of Murcia, agreed reluctantly but then died en route to New Spain.[25] Finally, on the recommendation of Carrasco, the crown turned to José de Gálvez, a crown attorney in the treasury department without any colonial experience.

Gálvez carried with him from Madrid a long list of instructions. His main tasks were to crack down on abuses in the treasury and judicial branches, establish a crown tobacco monopoly, take measures to spur silver mining, implement the intendancy system, and secure the viceroyalty's northern frontier. Besides visitor general, with the authority to initiate legal proceedings against anyone accused of wrongdoing, Gálvez was also named the intendant of the army in New Spain, which allowed him to supervise the military reforms begun the previous year by General Juan de Villalba. The objectives here were to station more regular Spanish troops in New Spain, increase the size of local militias, and refurbish the presidios, especially the fortress of San Juan de Ulúa off Veracruz. To enhance his status further, the crown named Gálvez to the Council of the Indies before he left Spain. As visitor general, he outranked the viceroy for the duration of his mission.

Born near Málaga in 1720, Gálvez had studied law in Salamanca and Alcalá before starting a legal practice in Madrid. Like many young lawyers at the time, including his contemporary Gamboa, Gálvez aspired to enter royal service. And like Gamboa, he wrote something on his own account that he hoped would attract the attention of ministers of the government. The title alone of this 1759 policy paper on colonial affairs gave away his general thinking: *Discurso y reflexiones de un vasallo sobre la decadencia de Nuestras Indias.*[26] Gálvez simply assumed that the Spanish colonial system was in a state of advanced decay. The tract reflected more the thinking of the men in Madrid he wanted to impress than the reality of America, which Gálvez had never seen.[27] He drew upon several of the critical reports on America that had been circulating in royal offices for decades, such as the so-called *Noticias secretas.* This scorching indictment of government in Peru was written in the late 1740s by the young naval officers Jorge Juan and Antonio de Ulloa, the official Spanish representatives on a French scientific expedition to South America to determine the sphericity of the earth.[28] According to historian Colin MacLachlan, Juan and Ulloa, who went on to distinguished naval and scientific careers, had little understanding of the colonial system at the time, particularly the negotiated quality of Spanish rule in America: "Their rational, economically oriented frame of reference was narrow and the degree of flexibility and accommodation they believed proper correspondingly narrow."[29] Yet they helped to buttress an assumption of colonial decadence that Gálvez gladly accepted. Only the energetic assertion of royal authority could correct the worrisome drift in Spanish America. As he put it, "it is not possible to summarize all the abuses introduced into Spanish America, since they have been multiplying over time and at such great distance from the beneficial influences of the throne."[30] Gálvez naturally viewed with suspicion any American custom or practice that deviated from metropolitan norms or any instance of locals dominating Spaniards in America. He worried that the recently restored fleet system gave too much power to American-based merchants over their Spanish counterparts. He criticized manufacturing in America, even the obrajes that produced rough cloth for domestic use, as inimical to Spanish industry. The worst example of the decay of the colonial system was the inordinate role played by creoles in American government. He warned of the danger of appointing American lawyers to their local audiencias. "Experience in the handling of various matters has taught me that it would always be best to place them in positions far from their place of origin, since in the Indies the spirit of party and partiality reigns so strong."[31]

In his *Discurso y reflexiones de un vasallo sobre la decadencia de Nuestras Indias*, Gálvez made the unusual recommendation for wholesale law reform in America. He proposed a revision of the 1680 *Recopilación de las leyes de Indias*, the massive compendium of royal legislation. Experts should comb through this text, he said, striking out obsolete provisions, inserting new ones in their place, and putting the whole thing in a clear and orderly manner. This would create in his words a "decisive law code" for America. This would mean there would no longer be a need to look to the ius commune or local custom to determine the applicable rule in a given situation. Codification would strike at legal pluralism and casuistic adjudication; judges would just have to enforce the written code, not scour juridical materials to find just solutions to particular cases. To be sure, Gálvez later discovered, as the minister of the Indies, that law reform was much easier said than done. The committee he appointed in 1776 to undertake the project was disbanded in the early 1790s, having made scant progress in the effort to replace the 1680 *Recopilación de las leyes de Indias*.

From the moment Gálvez arrived in Veracruz in July 1765 he took actions that alarmed officeholders in New Spain. For example, without first notifying the viceroy, the Marqués de Cruillas, he ordered the seizure of British

Figure 8. Painting of José de Gálvez, the visitor general of New Spain and later secretary of state for the Indies. Reproduced by permission of the Instituto Nacional de Antropología e Historia.

vessels suspected of contraband trading off the coast of Campeche.[32] Cruillas, an aristocrat of the old school, found Gálvez a "hot-headed and resentful official," who was determined "to take for himself unlimited authority."[33] The viceroy was particularly perturbed by Gálvez's plan to examine his conduct in the investigation of treasury operations.[34] Juan Antonio de Velarde, the crown attorney of the audiencia and Cruillas's official legal advisor, argued that Gálvez's mandate was dangerously broad. Velarde told the visitor general to his face that the visita was bound to fail.[35] Madrid however was determined to make sure it succeeded. One decision already made but not yet implemented was to replace Cruillas with a more pliant viceroy. In October 1765 the crown named Carlos Francisco de Croix, a French-born army officer, as the next viceroy to New Spain. He received strict instructions to support the work of Gálvez.

The Troubles of 1766

On Palm Sunday 1766, an angry crowd congregated in the Puerta del Sol in central Madrid. They proceeded to loot the homes of government ministers, including that of Leopoldo de Gregorio, the Marqués de Esquilache, the Sicilian-born chief minister of Charles III. People were incensed by high food prices, caused by bad harvests and a poorly implemented liberalization of the grain market. They also resented recent urban and cultural reforms in Madrid, notably a ban on wearing long capes and broad-brimmed hats. The next day twenty-five thousand protestors gathered outside the newly completed royal palace to demand, among other things, the ouster of Esquilache. The king's Walloon Guards charged the crowd, killing several dozen people.[36] That night Charles, fearing that the mob could turn on him, fled the palace with his family. He also acceded to the main demands of the protestors: he disbanded the Walloon Guards, revoked the hat and cloak ban, authorized food subsidies, and dismissed Esquilache as his chief minister. The king turned to Pedro de Abarca y Bolea, Conde de Aranda, a tough but well-educated military man from a distinguished Aragonese family, to head the government and restore order.[37]

New Spain faced its own spate of unrest that same year. In July 1766 thousands of mine workers marched into Guanajuato, demanding that the city council rescind new taxes on maize and tobacco ordered by the visitor general. To avoid violence, the council agreed not to collect the new taxes. There was also unrest in San Luis Potosí and Michoacán. Just like Madrid, people in New Spain were upset by government reforms that disrupted accustomed routines and dug into their pockets. In particular, they were angry with measures implemented by Gálvez, such as forced recruitment into the local militias, stricter enforcement of tribute collection, the end of tax exemptions on maize, and the establishment of new crown monopolies for tobacco and playing cards.[38]

In August 1766 mine workers rioted at Real del Monte, the most important mining district close to Mexico City. They were protesting local working conditions more than the impositions of the visita. Their main grievance was the decision of their employer Pedro Romero Terreros, perhaps the richest man in New Spain at the time, to cut the partido, the distribution of ore that went to underground mine workers.[39] They had already drawn up a petition, with a thousand names attached, which they submitted to the alcalde mayor of the nearby town of Pachuca and sent as well to Viceroy Cruillas in Mexico City. By drafting a petition and addressing authorities, the disgruntled workers were following correct legal procedure. But the alcalde mayor of Pachuca, Miguel Ramón de Coca, a recent arrival from Spain, refused to hear their plea. He even arrested the spokesmen of the workers on the charge of inciting rebellion.

Ilarione da Bergamo, an Italian Capuchin friar collecting alms in the district, reported what happened next:

> On August 15, 1766, the day set by the rabble for the total destruction of Real del Monte, many of them gathered in the mine of San Cayetano. There, after some quarrels between them and a mine foreman, they stoned him so that he died a few hours later. When the alcalde mayor of Pachuca, a young man recently arrived from Spain, attempted to bring these people to a halt by drawing his sword, they flung themselves on him with such ferocity and cruelty that they left him there dead, completely crushed by stones. Señor Terreros, having heard about the uprising and the two fatalities that had already occurred, hid in a room where he kept plenty of fodder for his horses, burying himself up to his neck. However much the rebel Indians tried to hunt him down and kill him, they could not find him. It was necessary for the parish priest to lead a procession with the Blessed Sacrament, which I also accompanied, to convey Señor Terreros from his hiding place and guide him to the church.[40]

Riots were also a common if unwelcome part of the system of righting wrongs. If a plea for justice was ignored by local authorities, people felt entitled to take to the streets to get the government's attention. Attacking symbols of authority, such as treasury offices and jails, was also part of the ritual. As long as rioters did not go too far, did not for instance question Spanish sovereignty, the government was usually prepared for reconciliation rather than vengeance.[41]

The riot in Real del Monte certainly got the attention of Mexico City. The mines there were too important to lose to a prolonged work stoppage. Viceroy Cruillas, in one of his last acts before leaving Mexico City, appointed Gamboa as mediator of the conflict. The alcalde del crimen was the obvious man for the job, both an expert in mining law and experienced, after two years as a criminal magistrate, in handling plebeian disturbances.[42] He set off for

Pachuca immediately, accompanied by a company of Spanish grenadiers. Although he had the authority to order a military attack on the workers, he refrained. Instead Gamboa initiated a legal process by inviting all members of the community, including the rebellious workers, to give sworn testimony before him. The goal was not to punish the rioters but to come to a solution that would restore order and harmony in the district. As he put it, he needed to figure out "the best arrangement of the labor of the mines to serve the interests of the owners and workers in equal measure." [43]

The main question for him was whether the partido, the distribution of ore to the workers as a form of compensation, was a custom that should be enforced with the power of law, as the workers argued. Gamboa consulted with many members of the community, including his old mentor Manual Aldaco, who had spent thousands of pesos in a futile attempt to rehabilitate a flooded mine along the Vizcaína vein. [44] Aldaco, like all financiers and mine owners, resented the partido but admitted there was no alternative: it was the only way to maintain a stable labor force. Gamboa already knew the utility of the partido. In the *Comentarios* he had written that no one undertook hazardous mine labor, "for a daily wage, which could be found anywhere, but for the partidos." [45] It more than supplemented the regular wage; it offered humble workers the chance of a small windfall, if the ore they sold to third-party refiners was high in silver content. It also benefitted the owners of small or fledgling mines as it relieved them of much of the cost of paying cash wages.

After just a few weeks, Gamboa concluded his work at Real del Monte. After hearing from all parties to the conflict, he drafted a new labor code for the district, which explicitly recognized the legality of the partido. Mine work should proceed, he said, "with such justice and equity that, without fraud, the owners should receive the first fruit of their mines while the miners receive the moderate gratification of the partido, by virtue of the custom observed in this district." [46] To address the legitimate complaint by owners that workers stole everything they could get their hands on, Gamboa included in the code strict penalties against theft, including corporeal punishment. He also issued arrest warrants for the ringleaders of the August violence but offered amnesty for the rest of the laborers as long as they returned promptly to work. This too was standard procedure in the mediation of riots: leaders were punished, often with exemplary cruelty, but their followers were forgiven. With his commission apparently completed in Pachuca and Real del Monte, Gamboa returned to Mexico City in late

September 1766. While he was away, Cruillas had left office and Croix had been sworn in as the new viceroy. Both Croix and Gálvez commended Gamboa for his success in quickly settling the violent dispute in Real del Monte.[47]

The Puebla Police Scandal

To support the visitor general, Croix turned his attention to public order. He knew from the events in Spain and New Spain in the spring and summer of 1766 that plebeian unrest could easily upend government reform initiatives. Croix was thus determined to crack down on all potential sources of trouble in New Spain, including the vagrants, drunks, and common criminals of the capital. In some of his first letters as viceroy he admonished the Sala de Crimen to do more to prevent crime in the capital. He wanted more of the city's troublemakers sent to hard labor at the presidios.[48] A few months later, Croix would issue a draconian decree against vagrancy: anyone in Mexico City without regular employment would have to find a job within one month or face either obligatory militia service or banishment to the presidios. He blamed the Sala de Crimen and the other judicial authorities for tolerating vagrancy, "one of the dominant vices of this kingdom, and the cause of so many fights and quarrels in gambling houses and pulquerías."[49] A military officer without experience in America, disturbed by the unruliness of Mexico City, as newcomers typically were, Croix seemed to believe that he could simply decree away long-standing social problems.

In September 1766, his first month in office, Croix received an alarming letter from Puebla, the second largest city in the viceroyalty. It accused the captains that the Sala de Crimen had appointed to police the city of rampant corruption. According to the anonymous author, the sala's captains profited from prostitution, gambling, and bootlegging. The worst of the bunch, Ignacio Soto, reportedly lived in a brothel and hosted raucous gambling parties popular with the dissolute sons of the poblano elite. Soto had also killed a man in custody but had been exonerated, without trial, by the sala. The whistleblower pointed out that Soto and the other eight captains of the sala commanded a force of over sixty lieutenants, who did little more than harass people in the streets. The city lived in fear, the informant claimed, not of common criminals but of the Sala de Crimen's police force.[50]

Croix asked the top Spanish officials in Puebla, its bishop, Francisco Fabián y Fuero, and the head of its military garrison, Francisco Fernando Palacios, for advice. They corroborated the allegations and added new details. Fabián y Fuero, most famous for his campaign to impose discipline in the city's convents, agreed that the Sala de Crimen's men were more inclined to commit than fight crime. He named two other corrupt captains, Manuel Pacheco, the excommunicated owner of a pulqueria, who was neck-deep in gambling and prostitution, and Juan José Leal, who had killed a young man seized unlawfully on church property. The bishop found the police's involvement in gambling particularly disturbing, perhaps because it was a vice that tended to undermine the honor of elite families.[51] For Palacios, the military commander, the bigger concern was the illegal liquor trade, which affected military discipline. Palacios told Croix, "I believe that if your Excellency rids this city of all the commissioners of the Sala de Crimen and their dependents you would do a great service to God and the King, to this community, and even to the Royal Audiencia itself, whose reputation suffers for its tolerance of such men."[52] Both the bishop and the general had the same recommendation for the viceroy: disband the sala's police force and invite the Tribunal of the Acordada to take over policing in the city.

Croix then turned to the Sala de Crimen. By what right did it appoint police captains not only in Puebla but throughout New Spain when laws contained in the *Recopilación de las leyes de Indias* clearly limited its first-instance jurisdiction to Mexico City?[53] Gamboa, recently returned from Real del Monte, answered for his colleagues on the bench.[54] The court's authority over the police in Puebla rested, he said, on "practice, custom and use, rooted by the force of the superior authority of the Tribunal, supported by the Laws, for the exercise and handling of the entire universe of criminal actions."[55] In other words, the court's jurisdiction was based on custom, not statute. The practice originated in the early seventeenth century when the sala first named captains to fight rural bandits. At the time, no other institution in New Spain could handle this necessary job. When the Santa Hermandad, comprised of volunteer companies that patrolled rural areas in Spain, was set up in New Spain later in the seventeenth century, it also fell under the jurisdiction of the sala. In fact, according to Gamboa, for almost 150 years no superior authority had questioned the sala's right to appoint men outside of Mexico City. Indeed, as recently as 1740 the viceroy had expressly endorsed the power. The five-league jurisdictional limit, Gamboa claimed, applied only to adjudication. Alcaldes del crimen could not hear cases in first instance arising outside of Mexico City since these fell to local justices.[56]

In the *Comentarios*, Gamboa had analyzed a similar situation. Even though written law prohibited the audiencias from hear mining cases, they did so anyways since no other institution could do it. The crown had never established the separate mining tribunal contemplated in the 1584 ordinances. Gamboa wrote that the audiencias' assumption of jurisdiction beyond the scope of royal law was not only necessary but desirable. It saved money and guaranteed miners the right of appeal to authoritative royal courts.[57] The Sala de Crimen's authority over the police was analogous: it too rested on well-founded custom that might conflict with statute but nevertheless served the greater cause of justice. Gamboa could have cited here both Jerónimo Castillo de Bobadilla's *Política para corregidores* (1597) and Juan de Hevía Bolaños's *Curia philipica* (1603), two authoritative law books that advised officials always to respect local custom, even if it contradicted written law.[58]

Gamboa concluded the Sala de Crimen's letter to the viceroy by challenging the allegation of widespread misconduct among the police of Puebla. Sure there were some bad apples, as occurred with any group of men, but the majority, he asserted, fulfilled their duties honorably. Since the sala's jurisdiction over them was founded on unimpeachable custom, the viceroy should defer to the court. It would discipline any men found guilty of abuse, but only after a proper investigation and legal process. The wild claims of an anonymous letter writer had to be substantiated with evidence before final action could be taken.

Croix also asked his official legal advisor, Diego de Cornide, for an opinion.[59] A Spanish lawyer new to Mexico City, Cornide's advice to the viceroy reflected the thinking of Bourbon reformers, not that of jurists familiar with colonial legal culture.[60] First, he read the provisions in the *Recopilación de las leyes de Indias* narrowly; they clearly barred the magistrates of the sala not just from adjudicating cases beyond a five-league radius but from appointing police officials as well. There was no need then to consider Gamboa's argument about custom; royal law on the matter was clear and should prevail. This insistence on the supremacy of state legislation echoed what several reformist jurists in Spain were writing at the time. In 1765, Juan Francisco de Castro, an audiencia magistrate in Galicia, argued in his *Discursos críticos sobre las leyes y sus interpretes* that lawyers and judges should decide cases solely on the basis of legislation, not on Roman law or unwritten custom.[61] In fact, he wrote, "it would serve the public peace to eradicate completely all custom that derogates from the law."[62] The main problem with custom, according to Castro, was that it was inherently vague. It was impossible to determine with certainty when it arose or how much community support it enjoyed. For him and other legal rationalists of the time, certainty was a higher value in the legal order than flexibility and royal legislation was its best guarantee.[63]

Cornide's opinion also nodded in the direction of the long-standing Bourbon desire to standardize administration throughout the empire. In 1713 Philip V, the first of the Spanish Bourbons, abolished the separate legal regime of the kingdom of Aragon to extend the reach of Castilian law and institutions. Then in the second half of the eighteenth century, the crown pushed for greater uniformity in regional government through the implementation of the French-style intendancy system. This was one of Gálvez's main directives for New Spain, the replacement of alcaldes mayores with a new class of officials, the intendants, who would report directly back to Madrid. Consistent with this preference for standardization based on Castilian norms, Cornide wondered why the Real Audiencia of Mexico, through its Sala de Crimen, exercised powers unknown to the Chancelleries of Valladolid and Granada, the highest courts of royal justice in Spain. They did not appoint police captains outside of their home cities; why should the Sala de Crimen? Solórzano had an answer for this in *Política Indiana*. The magistrates of the audiencias in America exercised more powers than their counterparts in Spain because they were much farther from the king, the ultimate font of justice. To prevent delays that could cause injustice to the American vassals of the king, audiencia magistrates needed additional powers.[64] In addition, Solórzano had recognized that the government of the Indies could not be squeezed into a peninsular mold.[65] Reformers in the eighteenth century, however, did not share Solórzano's equanimity with local variations.

In late November 1766, Croix, after consulting with Gálvez, who had final say in New Spain, announced his decision. All police serving the Sala de Crimen outside of Mexico City would immediately be stripped of their commissions. He invited the Acordada to assume the responsibility for patrolling New Spain's cities. This force, authorized to ignore formal proceedings and operating independent of outside judicial supervision, would become, in effect, Mexico's first national police force.

The Tribunal of the Acordada

The Acordada was created in the early 1700s to combat an outbreak of banditry in rural New Spain.[66] The Santa Hermandad, the volunteer companies of horsemen who patrolled the roads, could not cope with the problem; its captains complained that their hands were tied by their obligation to report to the Sala de Crimen before punishing miscreants. In the early 1710s, Viceroy Linares gave Miguel Velázquez Lorea, the Hermandad captain in Querétaro, free rein. He could pursue bandits anywhere in New Spain and act on his own initiative. There were certainly precedents for this in Spanish law. The medieval *Las Siete Partidas* basically authorized vigilante justice against bandits, stating that individuals who killed "any robber who publicly frequents the highways . . . shall not be liable for punishment."[67] The prescribed penalty in *Las Siete Partidas* for bandits and livestock rustlers was death.[68]

The Real Audiencia of Mexico, much to its later regret, consented to this derogation of its authority, evidently believing it would be temporary, until Velázquez managed to restore security to the roads of New Spain. In 1722, the crown endorsed the agreement between the viceroy and the audiencia that gave Velázquez his extraordinary powers. This accord provided the legal foundation and the name for what thereafter was known as the Tribunal of the Acordada. This was a peculiar institution. It operated outside ordinary jurisdiction, completely exempt from the authority of the audiencias. Audiencia magistrates could not hear appeals of its sentences or even inspect its jails, the basic mechanism by which the courts ensured that people were not held arbitrarily without legal charge. The Acordada had the freedom to practice summary methods of law enforcement. In addition, the first judge of the Acordada, Miguel Velázquez, exercised propriety control over the new tribunal. He could choose his own regional commanders and even select his successor. The merchants of the consulado, early cheerleaders of the Acordada because of their interest in keeping the roads safe for commerce, provided an annual sum to fund its operations.[69]

Velázquez and then his son and successor José Velázquez did manage to turn back the tide of banditry. Free to disregard the formal procedures observed by the Sala de Crimen, members of the Acordada acted decisively against suspected criminals. They frequently garroted apprehended bandits on the spot and then displayed severed body parts in public. The head of the gang leader who had tormented Celaya was stuck on a pole in the town's main square.[70] José Velázquez, who succeeded his father Miguel in 1732, became known in the next twenty years as the "general terror of the whole kingdom."[71] In a three-year span in the 1740s, when capital punishment was declining in Mexico City, the Acordada executed fifty-five prisoners.[72] According to the admiring Viceroy Revillagigedo, the younger Velázquez "managed with inflexible justice, tenacity, and integrity to exterminate execrable crimes, condemned to death or presidios innumerable criminals, for which his commission has earned all the protection of my predecessors."[73]

In the late 1740s and early 1750s, with the support of Revillagigedo, the Acordada began to expand its operations. In 1747, the viceroy assigned it control over the Guarda Mayor de Caminos, a separate security branch that operated fixed garrisons with salaried troops along the major roads of New Spain. In 1749 Revillagigedo wanted to give it responsibility for prosecuting prohibited liquor offences but Velázquez refused, claiming his men were too busy chasing down bandits.[74] In the early 1750s Revillagigedo invited the Acordada to patrol the streets of Mexico City, a decision that outraged the Sala de Crimen.[75] The viceroy dismissed the complaints of the magistrates and praised Velázquez, whose "energy, diligence and zeal have filled delinquents with terror, which the alcaldes, for all their position and power, have not achieved."[76] When José Velázquez died of illness in 1756, command of the Acordada passed to one of his trusted lieutenants, Jacinto Martínez de la Concha, since his own son was too young to take over.[77]

The decision to extend the jurisdiction of the Acordada to all of New Spain posed an existential threat to the Sala de Crimen. In a letter to the Council of the Indies, Gamboa, again writing on behalf of the court, complained that Croix, lacking knowledge and experience, had acted contrary to both law and custom.[78] The viceroy had no legal power to create or expand exemptions to the ordinary jurisdiction, as his decision to expand the Acordada effectively did. Only the king had such authority. Furthermore, by dismissing the sala's police on the basis of an anonymous letter, the viceroy had ignored basic procedures of justice. As for Soto, whom Croix charged with murder, Gamboa pointed out that the sala had already absolved him on the basis of self-defense. If that was not enough, Soto was eligible for the royal pardon issued in 1762. Gamboa demanded that the Council of the Indies reverse Croix's decision and reaffirm the sala's jurisdiction over the police outside of Mexico City. In return, the sala would undertake to discipline any captains found culpable of misconduct.

Gamboa also wrote—in far from deferential tones—to Croix himself. He accused the viceroy of acting "unilaterally, without consultations, against the Laws, with their effects not corresponding to their purposes but rather with unavoidable and manifest harm to the vassals" of New Spain.[79] He warned that expanding the powers of the Acordada would threaten the well-being of ordinary novohispanos. With unlimited authority to take action against every class of criminal offense in the viceroyalty, the men of the Acordada "would live without restraint, harassing and destroying the vassals of His Majesty without recognizing another superior in the midst of these distances than the Judge of the Acordada, with scorn for the Audiencias, Governors, and Judges, against the Laws, practice and style always observed and the determinations of this government."

The Council of the Indies, despite the recommendation of its crown attorney in support of Gamboa's plea, refused to reverse Croix's decree.[80] Indeed, in a royal cédula dated December 16, 1767, the council endorsed it. And it is not hard to see why. The Sala de Crimen, if we accept the evidence at hand, had abjectly failed to supervise its commissioned captains. It had appointed men of dubious moral quality and ignored their corrupt behavior. The Acordada, on the other hand, was fast, effective, and cheap. Why not give it a chance to impose order in the cities as it had in the countryside?

The expansion of the Acordada was admittedly not part of the instructions Gálvez carried with him from Spain. The measure nevertheless enjoyed his full support since it served the essential purposes of his reform mission. First, the move reinforced executive authority at the expense of the judiciary, which was much more likely to resist than welcome structural reforms. Secondly, the decision affirmed the sanctity of royal legislation over contrary local custom. How else would the crown restore order in America if not by insisting that vassals obey the written law? And thirdly, shifting responsibility to the Acordada saved the government money. Without the obligation to hold formal proceedings, the tribunal was much cheaper to operate than the Sala de Crimen. Funds were needed for military purposes, not formal trials for New Spain's troublemakers.

It did not take long, however, for the problems forecasted by Gamboa to emerge. Bishop Fabián y Fuero of Puebla, who had welcomed the arrival of the Acordada in 1766, complained two years later that their jail in the city was full of prisoners held without charge.[81] Without any court personnel and the habit of proceeding summarily, the Acordada was depositing people in the jail without even recording their names or offenses. The Sala de Crimen told Croix the same thing was happening in Oaxaca, which the Acordada took over in 1767.[82] In Mexico City, Croix's decision to deploy regular troops to police the streets led to similar problems, as the city's jails filled up with prisoners whose guilt or innocence could not be ascertained since no one had bothered to collect evidence against them.[83]

As the Acordada became the busiest agency of criminal law in New Spain, it stuck to its old ways.[84] While it did adopt a code of formal procedures in 1776, the new rules were "too refined for an organization like the Acordada," in the words of historian Colin MacLachlan.[85] By the late 1780s, it employed almost 2,500 men throughout the viceroyalty, handling four times as many cases as the Sala de Crimen. From 1782 to 1808 the Acordada handled over forty thousand cases, sentencing 246 people to death and over 10,000 people to terms of labor at presidios.[86] In the late 1780s, after decades of complaints by the audiencia, the crown did authorize a panel to review Acordada death sentences. It consisted of an independent lawyer, the viceroy's legal advisor, and a member of the Sala de Crimen. But this panel lacked teeth and rarely reversed an Acordada decision.[87] In the late eighteenth century a sign hung above the door of the Acordada's jail in Mexico City that proudly advertised its approach to law and order: "Passerby, be wary of this place / And see that you avoid entering / Since once its hard door closes / It will only open again for your execution."[88]

Punishment by Presidio

The Sala de Crimen lost jurisdiction over the police outside of the capital in November 1766. A few months later, in May 1767, it lost a principal source of funding. Under pressure from Madrid to contribute more manpower to the refurbishment of coastal fortifications, Croix, again with the enthusiastic backing of Gálvez, ordered that all courts in New Spain, including the Sala de Crimen and the Acordada, send convicted prisoners to the presidios in Veracruz, Havana, and Manila.[89] The prisoners would supplement the black slaves and free laborers engaged in construction work and even serve as auxiliaries in the event of enemy attack. Mandating presidio labor as punishment would obviate the collera, the practice of selling convict labor to owners of obrajes and other private employers, by which both the sala and Acordada made money. Rather than question the inherent abusiveness of a system that consigned convicts to a form of slavery, Bourbon reformers considered the collera an illegitimate subsidy that helped American textile manufacturers compete against Spanish imports.[90] The viceroy agreed to compensate the Acordada for its loss of collera income by assigning it a share of pulque revenue. But for the Sala de Crimen, far more dependent on the income since it employed a much larger staff, Croix did nothing.

Gamboa and his colleagues on the bench fired off a fifty-seven-page letter to Madrid protesting the viceroy's move.[91] Gamboa, again the lead author, began by arguing that the viceroy had no right to interfere in such basic judicial matters as the sentencing of criminals. This was a matter solely for the courts to decide. Croix could certainly request that the sala send more convicts to the presidios, as previous viceroys had done, but he had no legal power to compel it. Gamboa also invoked, as he had done in liberating prisoners from Mexico City's bakeries in February 1765, the Spanish crown's duty to care for the Native population. "Sentencing an Indian to a presidio would indeed punish his offence," he wrote, "but it would also gradually consume his race and impede its reproduction, very important matters since without the Indians, there would be no Indies, no Agriculture, no Mines, no Irrigation, no work of any sort."[92] The law had always been clear on this point: Natives should not be subject to either banishment or presidio labor. It was considered too harsh for them and would separate them from their families and fields.[93]

The best way to punish wayward Indians, according to Gamboa, was to sentence them to labor at private workplaces. Two years earlier he had criticized the collera when he liberated Natives held in inhumane conditions in Mexico City's bakeries; now he argued in favor of it. He could at least pretend that his 1765 intervention had improved conditions in the obrajes and the like. But if the reason for freeing Indians in 1765 was to protect the audiencia's jurisdiction from the possibility of a bakers guild, the reason to defend the practice in 1767 was to protect the audiencia's income. Without the money from the collera, the Sala de Crimen would not be able to pay the salaries of the auxiliary staff it needed to carry out formal proceedings.

In practice, the presidio decree was not as draconian as it first appeared. Many convicts, including the indigenous, were sent to urban work crews close to home rather than to the coastal fortifications. In addition, some obraje owners contracted secretly with the Sala de Crimen for convict labor even after it was outlawed.[94] But the financial impact on the sala was real. Over the next few years, the court complained repeatedly of its financial distress. In December 1767 the court told Croix that the abolition of the collera had wiped out "the funds that the Sala had used for the administration of Justice and the processing of cases."[95] In July 1768 the magistrates claimed they lacked the money to buy paper.[96] In March 1769 they reported they owed their staff over 15,000 pesos in back pay. The pharmacist who treated sick prisoners in the Sala de Crimen's jail resigned after not being paid for two years. This departure may have exacerbated the effects of an epidemic that hit the sala's jail in early 1769.[97] With underpaid employees, delays in the sala's business undoubtedly increased, as did the temptation to accept under-the-table payments.[98]

Expulsions from New Spain

On June 25, 1767, top crown officials, backed by companies of Spanish soldiers, fanned out across Mexico City to enforce the royal order of Charles III to round up and expel the Jesuits. They had already been forced to leave Spain. The crown was acting on the recommendation of Pedro Rodríguez de Campomanes, crown attorney of the Council of Castile, who accused the Jesuits of instigating the Easter Riots of 1766 in Madrid. He provided no concrete evidence of their guilt, just the usual litany of Jesuit sins in the eyes of regalists.[99] According to Campomanes, the order disregarded secular laws, refused to pay taxes on the profits of their numerous properties, and taught suspect theology and philosophy in their extensive network of schools.[100] They thus made convenient scapegoats for the troubles of 1766. Charles had been wary of the Jesuits since his years in Naples under the tutelage of Bernardo Tanucci, an Italian jurist and harsh critic of the order. The basic problem, which the monarchies of Portugal and France had already recognized, was that the Society of Jesus was simply too powerful for monarchies, no matter their adherence to Catholicism, that were determined to expand their authority.[101]

In New Spain, Visitor General Gálvez and Viceroy Croix oversaw the expulsion. They sent Jacinto Martínez de la Concha, the head of the Acordada, to enforce the order at the Colegio de San Ildefonso, the Jesuits' most important college in New Spain. Gamboa was ordered to accompany the Acordada boss and read out the royal order before the assembled priests.[102] This was a cruel assignment for the proud alumnus of San Ildefonso. Gamboa reportedly broke down before he could finish reciting the order.[103] Once the Jesuits abandoned their magnificent college, built at enormous expense in the 1730s, Croix turned it into an army barracks. Its library, the best in New Spain, was scattered and lost.[104] The ouster of the Society of Jesus decimated higher education in New Spain, forcing the closure of twenty-six schools and twelve seminaries. The almost seven hundred Jesuit priests and novices forced to leave, the vast majority born in America, included twenty-five professors of theology, twenty-four of philosophy, and forty of Latin.[105] Dozens of Jesuits died even before they disembarked from Veracruz in October 1767, headed for an uncertain exile in Italy.[106]

In the Bajío, the expulsion of the Jesuits gave many discontented groups— Natives, mulattoes, and mestizo mine workers—another reason to rise up against the government. To be sure, the Jesuits themselves did nothing to whip up support. They accepted their fate with resignation. One hot spot of unrest was Guanajuato, where mine workers had already marched against higher taxes in the summer of 1766. Another was Michoacán, where mulattoes had rioted in Pátzcuaro and Valladolid in September 1766 on account of the intensified collection of tribute. A third was San Luis Potosí, where measures to enforce labor discipline at mines, including a prohibition on firearms, had riled up the lower class. Local militias led by landowners and mining entrepreneurs quickly suppressed these plebeian uprisings. Then Gálvez arrived on the scene, escorted by six hundred regular Spanish soldiers. In stark contrast to how Gamboa handled the August 1766 revolt at Real del Monte, Gálvez did not seek to reconcile the protestors. Instead, he held summary trials that condemned eighty-five people to death and dozens more to the whipping post or forced labor at the presidios. He ordered the demolition of the homes of rebel leaders and their farms sown with salt. Even their wives and children were banished.[107] According to historian William Taylor, Gálvez's harsh response "amounted to punishment for the sake of punishment as the unbending response of a leading peninsular reformer who had little understanding of the delicate divide-and-rule policies that had governed the Mexican countryside for two centuries."[108]

Meanwhile, in Mexico City the move against the Jesuits further upset local elites already fed up with the visita. By July 1767 anonymous pro-Jesuit and anti-government pasquinades circulated in the city, ridiculing Gálvez, Croix, and members of their entourage.[109] Croix then issued another one of his decrees, this time imposing "perpetual and absolute silence" on any discussion of the Jesuit expulsion, "whether in favor of it or not."[110] Anyone caught writing or distributing pro-Jesuit propaganda would be considered an enemy of the state.[111] In August the German-born chaplain of the visita,

Adolfo Falembock, reported to Croix and Lorenzana a rumor that creoles from New Spain and Peru, together with agents of a foreign power, presumably Britain, were conspiring against Spanish rule.[112] This prompted the viceroy and bishop to gather names of civil and ecclesiastical officials considered hostile to the government. Gamboa, along with his fellow alcalde del crimen Diego Antonio Fernández de Madrid and crown attorney Juan Antonio de Velarde, appeared on the list.

Gamboa had been in the bad books of the viceroy and visitor general at least since November 1766. He had offended the viceroy with the harsh tone of his letters protesting the extension of the Acordada and the abolition of the collera in favor of presidio labor.[113] He also had been overheard criticizing Gálvez and his visita. Croix had already reported to Madrid that Gamboa and Velarde were "inseparable companions in official occasions, meetings, and evening strolls," and welcomed into their circle all those opposed to the visita.[114] Gamboa even had the gall, Croix reported to Julián Arriaga, the aged minister of the Indies, to have accused Gálvez of hosting illegal gambling parties in his house. He made these charges, Croix said, "with such vivid descriptions that I assure Your Excellency that he almost persuaded me that it was true."[115] Circumstantial evidence also linked Gamboa to anti-government writings. A scribe working for Gamboa, Tiburcio Martínez, testified under oath to Lorenzana that in the house of Antonio López Portillo, a pro-Jesuit diocesan priest, he had read part of a libelous manuscript, *Crisis Divertida*.[116] Croix also suspected that Gamboa, with the aid of Velarde, had written a satirical piece against Gálvez.[117] Indeed, even before the viceroy had sent his list of anti-government officials to Madrid at the end of 1767, Croix had asked the crown to reprimand Gamboa and Velarde for the "hostility with which they seem to look upon the present government of New Spain and for the damage caused by their criticisms, attacks, and conversations, rash and offensive to the decorum and subordination owed to authority and capable of producing disturbances."[118]

Gamboa was mortified to receive a letter of censure from the crown before the whole audiencia on February 5, 1768. He immediately wrote to Madrid to defend himself.[119] He highlighted his accomplishments as an alcalde del crimen, claiming to have had no time for anti-government conspiracies. He cited his work suppressing two street fights in Mexico City in January 1766 and his resolution of the August 1766 labor conflict at Real del Monte. He reminded Arriaga, the minister of the Indies, whom he knew from his days in Madrid, of the success of the *Comentarios a las Ordenanzas de Minas*, which had been "accepted in all the mining districts and tribunals as useful and beneficial, not only for the miners themselves but also for the Royal Hacienda." Despite appearances to the contrary, Gamboa insisted he enjoyed a good relationship with Croix, regularly visiting him in his private quarters to discuss government business. Any doubts about his loyalty to the government must have come from the "shadow of envy and resentment that always accompanied alcaldes in the court." Solórzano, who counseled against visitas, had warned in *Política Indiana* that they inevitably threw dirt on innocent officials, "who, trusting in the security that their good consciences give them of their conduct, do not take any measures to counter what bad-intentioned people say during visitas."[120] Gamboa had a clear conscience. He knew that his harshly worded representations on behalf of the Sala de Crimen had angered Croix, but they had been written, he told Arriaga, "consistent with my duty and ministry . . . in fulfillment of the responsibility with which the king entrusted me."[121]

By the time Gamboa was writing to the minister of the Indies to defend himself, the two crown attorneys of the Council of Castile, Campomanes and José Moñino, were already meeting to decide his fate. It was a sign of how seriously the crown took the threat from New Spain that the more senior Council of Castile took responsibility rather than the Council of the Indies, which properly held jurisdiction. In March 1768, Campomanes and Moñino released their report. It made several recommendations, starting with the immediate dispatch of troops to New Spain. The crown attorneys also recommended that the authorities remove from New Spain as soon as possible any officeholder considered hostile to the government. Although they did not mention Gamboa by name, they did note that audiencia magistrates were "the most pernicious for the authority they hold in their hands and the obstacles they can put before the orders of the Viceroy."[122]

Campomanes and Moñino did, however, acknowledge the legitimacy of creole grievances.[123] "How can they love a Government that they blame for mainly trying to extract from there profits and taxes, and which does nothing to promote love for the Nation; and when everyone who goes there from here has no other purpose than to enrich himself at their expense?"[124] But with the exception of a moratorium on new taxes, they proposed nothing that directly assuaged Americans. Rather, Campomanes and Moñino took the opportunity to advocate once again for the abolition of the Cadiz trade monopoly, hardly at the top of the list of creole complaints.[125] They also suggested that Americans complaining about Spaniards crowding them out of jobs in New Spain should seek employment in Spain. They could attend Spanish universities, serve in the military, and even represent their regions on royal councils. Americans in Spain would then act like "hostages in order to keep those countries under the gentle dominion of His Majesty." Although they admitted their plan to encourage Americans to come to Spain needed further study, it was in fact wholly impractical from the start. Spaniards went to America because they lacked opportunities at home; how could Americans compete for scarce positions in Spain? In addition, the high cost of transatlantic travel meant that even viceroys arrived in America in debt; how could young Americans afford the journey in the opposite direction?

A few years later, as Gálvez's visita was drawing to a close, the city council of Mexico City sent a famous representation to the crown on the plight of Spanish Americans. The 1771 report claimed it was a great injustice to deny locals the opportunity to fill offices in their own countries. It would lead, the council predicted, "not only to the loss of this America but to the ruin of the monarchy."[126] One of the most important reasons for the crown to trust Spanish Americans was that they understood the unique legal culture of the Indies. In contrast, the typical Spanish office holder in America

> comes to govern societies he does not know, to administer laws he has not studied, to immerse himself in customs he has not experienced, to deal with peoples he has never seen, and look for answers to the equally inexpert family that usually surrounds him. He comes full of the maxims of Europe unsuited for these places.[127]

Here was the crux of the case against the Bourbon reform effort spearheaded by Gálvez. America was indeed different than Spain, and only people who took the time to understand its customs and institutions could govern it in a just manner. One American named in the city council's representation as an exemplary royal official was Gamboa.[128]

Gamboa was no longer in good standing with the crown when the Mexico City council praised him in its letter defending creole officeholders. The crown had issued orders for the removal of Gamboa and the other suspect officials in March 1768. The operation, however, was bungled in Mexico City as news leaked before the orders could be delivered. Fearing a public scandal with the destitution of audiencia magistrates, Croix and Lorenzana held off and asked for further instruction from Madrid.[129] Campomanes and Moñino still believed it was necessary to remove Gamboa, Velarde, and Fernández de Madrid from Mexico City but suggested it could be presented not as punishment but as invitations to serve the king in Spain. "These three ministers," the crown attorneys wrote, "should not suffer any prejudice in their placement in Spain in equivalent positions, especially the first two [Gamboa and Velarde] who are disposed to serve."[130] Fernández de Madrid, whose health was bad, was allowed to retire. The crown issued new orders on January 29, 1769. Gamboa received what he had long been dreading on August 7, 1769, a summons to report for duty in Spain in a yet to be determined position.

Despite the benign wording of the invitation, Gamboa knew he was being punished for his criticism of Croix and Gálvez.[131] He informed Madrid that he was "blindly and humbly resigned to comply with the sovereign will of the king, even in the midst of the great difficulties of his family."[132] The poor health of his wife and daughters prevented them from accompanying him, even if the crown had provided the necessary funds. To pay for his own travel and provide for his family, Gamboa sold his most valuable possessions, including "the best editions from one of the most complete libraries in Mexico, built over many years from my sweat."[133] Gamboa also transferred to his merchant friend Ambrosio de Meave his stake in a trading company.[134] In late November 1769, exactly five years after returning home in triumph, the first local lawyer appointed directly to the Real Audiencia of Mexico in decades, Gamboa was heading back to Spain under a black cloud. He and his teenage son Juan José boarded the *El Aquiles* in Veracruz.[135] In Havana they transferred to the *Santisima Trinidad*, bound for northern Spain.[136]

Gamboa paid a very heavy price for doing what audiencia magistrates had always done: vigorously defend the jurisdiction of the court. Writing harsh letters to the Council of the Indies or the minister of the Indies accusing viceroys of acting contrary to law and custom was simply part of the job. This was the way the governing system of America operated to check abuses of power and maintain balance between institutions. Speaking up frankly against government policies would normally have been tolerated in an audiencia magistrate, who enjoyed the benefit of the court's independence. But the mid-1760s was an extraordinary time in New Spain. Under Visitor General Gálvez, assisted by the deferential Croix, the Spanish crown was attempting radical reform, based on the assumption that the old system was decripit. Locals had too much power and autonomy, protected by cherished customs that made a mockery of royal legislation. The centerpiece of the restructuring of colonial government was the intendancy system, the plan for which Gálvez unveiled in 1768. How could the crown implement this new, more direct form of government if powerful audiencia magistrates continued to put up roadblocks at every turn? Punishing Gamboa, a smart and well-connected American jurist with decades of experience in legal combat in New Spain, would send the message the crown meant business in New Spain.

CHAPTER SIX

The Underground Enlightenment

Being that Mining is the Origin and unique source of
the monetary wealth that gives spirit and movement to the other
occupations of men and to universal commerce of the known world,
justice demands that it receives the principal attentions of the
Government; and that it should always be treated with the particular
care and attention that Our Majesty the King is showing it today.

—JOSÉ DE GÁLVEZ, 1771

✦ WHAT SHOULD THE GOVERNMENT HAVE DONE TO REVITALIZE SILVER
mining in New Spain? In 1761 Francisco Xavier de Gamboa painted a depressing picture of the industry in his *Comentarios a las Ordenanzas de Minas*. Due to backward technical practices and shortages of capital, promising veins of silver ore remained unexploited, submerged by flood waters or simply abandoned by helpless miners. Gamboa set out a few ideas to restore vigor to the industry, starting with a mining bank managed by the merchants of the consulado. He also proposed the liberalization of the crown mercury monopoly, the establishment of a second mint in Guadalajara, direct state aid for those excavating drainage tunnels, and the creation of a corps of licensed mining technicians. He did not call for radical reforms to the legal or financial structure of the industry. He endorsed the old Royal Mining Ordinances of 1584 and the jurisdiction over mining by the audiencias. José de Gálvez brought Gamboa's book with him to New Spain in 1765.[1] One of his instructions as visitor general was to stimulate silver mining, whose revenue, after two hundred years, remained indispensable to the financial health of the Spanish crown.

If Gálvez found time to read the *Comentarios* of Gamboa, he did not agree with its conclusions. For instance, Gamboa lamented the irresponsibility of miners, a bunch of spendthrifts who ignored the law and rational mining techniques. Gálvez, on the other hand, saw miners as an oppressed professional group, who would thrive only if they were freed from the clutches of merchant-financiers and audiencia magistrates. The visitor general backed the creation of an independent guild for miners, with its own adjudicative system, bank, and technical college. The so-called Mining Tribunal, officially authorized by the Spanish crown in 1776 after Gálvez became minister of the Indies, has generally been considered by historians as a paradigmatic case of enlightened Bourbon reform in New Spain and a main reason for the increase in silver production in the remaining decades of Spanish rule.[2]

In this chapter, I present the case against the Mining Tribunal from the perspective of Gamboa and his allies. The tribunal went against everything he had recommended in the *Comentarios*. Undoubtedly one reason he opposed the tribunal was that it blocked his own scheme for a consulado mining bank. But that was not the principal reason for his hostility. Since 1764 he was no longer the paid advocate of the consulado but a magistrate on the Real Audiencia of Mexico. Gamboa attacked the tribunal primarily for the harm he believed it would cause to the administration of justice in New Spain. Endowing miners with exclusive jurisdiction over the adjudication of their own disputes was to him a terrible idea. In the *Comentarios*, while acknowledging problems at the local level of justice, he strongly defended the role that the audiencias of Mexico and Guadalajara played in administering mining justice. They provided impartial, expert adjudication and offered all miners the opportunity to appeal unfavorable local decisions to the most authoritative courts in the viceroyalty. For Gamboa and many other veteran officials, the Mining Tribunal was yet another of the poorly conceived reforms championed in New Spain by Gálvez. It would disrupt institutions and practices that, however imperfectly, had served the interests of both New Spain and the Spanish monarchy.

This chapter also surveys Gamboa's career as a civil court magistrate in the Real Audiencia of Mexico. He returned to New Spain in 1773, after three years of exile in Valladolid. He quickly put behind him the ignominy of his 1769 forced departure from the Sala de Crimen and, over the next decade, emerged as a leader on the Real Audiencia of Mexico. He became a trusted collaborator of Viceroy Antonio María de Bucareli, the veteran colonial official who headed New Spain's government from 1772 to 1779. But largely due to the controversy over the Mining Tribunal, Gamboa's career was once again threatened in the early 1780s, when José de Gálvez was at the peak of his power in the ministry of the Indies.

Gamboa's Spanish Exile

Gamboa and his teenage son Juan José arrived in Vigo in April 1770. He had obviously decided on the long Atlantic crossing that he was not going to humbly accept his fate as he had earlier promised. As soon as he landed in Spain, he sent a letter to Julián de Arriaga, the minister of the Indies, defending himself once again from the accusation that he had obstructed the visita. How could Gálvez have accomplished so much in so little time in New Spain, Gamboa asked, from expanding militias, establishing the tobacco monopoly, raising taxes, and leading an expedition to the north, if he faced the opposition alleged by Viceroy Croix? "There is not a minister or any individual there that has the hand or the will to frustrate anything," he told Arriaga. If there were any concrete evidence of his lack of loyalty to the king and government, he would like to see it.[3] From Vigo, Gamboa and his son traveled to the old royal city of Valladolid, where Juan José entered university, and Gamboa launched a campaign to clear his name and return as soon as possible to New Spain.

By June 1770, Gamboa had assembled a package of over forty notarized documents attesting to his loyal service to the king. They covered his success in quelling disturbances on the streets of Mexico City, his efforts in combatting the sale of illegal liquor, his protection of Native convicts confined to Mexico City's bakeries, and his willingness to mediate disputes out of court to save parties time and money. He included copies of the letters by Croix and Gálvez that commended him for resolving the labor conflict at Real del Monte. He also forwarded letters of recommendations from the Discalced Carmelites and the Augustinians, two religious orders he had represented in the 1740s and 1750s. Letters from the scribes of the audiencia described his modest lifestyle, how he kept his distance from the social whirls of Mexico City, preferring quiet study and the company of his wife and children, model behavior for a royal judge. How could he have found the time to "encourage movements and conspiracies against the government" when he devoted night and day to his duties as alcalde del crimen? He blamed his woes again on the malicious tongues of the enemies he had made as an alcalde del crimen working to expose "scandals, greed, abuses, crimes, and illegal gaming."[4]

The response from Madrid was not what he was hoping for. In August he received notice of his appointment to the Audiencia of Barcelona. This would fulfill the recommendation of the crown attorneys of Castile, Pedro Rodríguez de Campomanes and José Moñino, that he be placed in an equivalent post in Spain to what he had left in Mexico City. They had also suggested in 1768 that more creoles should come to the mother country, to study in its universities, serve in the military, and join the government. This would supposedly build a stronger feeling of Spanish unity across the Atlantic. Gamboa and his son Juan José were apparently the unwitting guinea pigs for this farfetched experiment.

Gamboa acknowledged receipt of the notice of his appointment to Barcelona but refused to budge from Valladolid. Instead, he ramped up his campaign to return to New Spain. He enlisted his wife, Maria Manuela, to write letters on his behalf. In her first letter of December 1770, she pleaded with Arriaga, "in the name of the most precious blood of Christ and the Lady of the Sorrows," to bring the plight of her family to the attention of the king, who might "allow our sad family to be reunited in this city, and if that is not possible, then that the pity of our charitable sovereign provide for our travel expenses, so that we can follow my husband, even at the risk of our own lives."[5] A year later, in November 1771 she confessed to Arriaga that she was on the verge of having to beg "from door to door to support the family."[6] This wording, nearly identical to what Gamboa had used in his official résumé to describe the hardships of his childhood, suggests that he might have been secretly drafting his wife's letters from afar.

The End of the Visita

Meanwhile, in New Spain, the visita of Gálvez was coming to an anticlimactic close. In 1768 he had presented his intendancy plan, which immediately raised bureaucratic resistance in Madrid and Mexico City. He then set off on his great American adventure, an expedition to the far northwest of New Spain. Fancying himself a modern-day conquistador, Gálvez oversaw an ambitious campaign of exploration, conquest, and settlement.[7] In Baja California he handed over the old Jesuit missions to the Franciscans, led by Junípero Serra. He coordinated land and sea missions up the Pacific coast as far north as San Francisco Bay. His young nephew Bernardo de Gálvez, who later became the governor of Louisiana and viceroy of New Spain, accompanied him. Gálvez's main task was to create a new administrative unit under military control, a captaincy general, to govern the territory encompassing Alta and Baja California, Sonora, Sinaloa, and much of Chihuahua. Only a military government, it was believed, could secure Spanish sovereignty in lands still contested fiercely by Apaches and Comanches.

In the summer of 1769, while Gálvez and his nephew were waging war against the Apache in Sonora, the strain of the past few years caught up with him. He suffered what appeared to be a serious nervous breakdown. From July 1769 to the spring of 1770, he lay incapacitated. At one point, delirious, he raved that he was the king of Prussia and would bring an army of apes from Guatemala to subdue the Indians of northern New Spain. He claimed St. Francis of Assisi—of all people—gave him military advice. When he recovered his wits, he took vengeance on anyone who dared to speak of his mental illness, including his private secretary, Juan Manuel de Viniegra, and a young military officer and future viceroy of New Spain, Miguel José Azanza. Both were imprisoned without charge and expelled from New Spain.[8]

Back in the capital, Gálvez accomplished little of note in the final year of the visita. He backed the creation of a bakers guild, the very thing Gamboa had stopped five years earlier with his order to release Natives confined to bakeries under the collera. Gálvez, however, saw the value of guilds: through them the crown could reward favored subjects while simultaneously curtailing the jurisdiction of older, more autonomous institutions, like the audiencias. In November 1770 he issued a set of detailed regulations for the bread market. It proposed that anyone not inscribed in the new bakers' guild who attempted to sell flour or bread to the public would be subject to imprisonment, a 200 peso fine, or banishment for up to five years. The plan would also reduce the number of licensed bakeries in Mexico City, another measure to limit competition. To show their gratitude for these privileges, the bakers were expected to contribute 6,000 pesos annually to the upkeep of the hospital for the poor.[9] Naturally, Croix, the deferential collaborator of Gálvez throughout the visita, endorsed the plan. Everyone else thought it was dangerous in the extreme. The audiencia, Archbishop Lorenzana, and the Mexico City council all sent protests to Madrid pointing out the harm that would befall consumers in Mexico City if a self-serving cartel was put in charge of the bread supply. On the street, a popular verse accused Gálvez of acting like a Persian tyrant, resorting to the ultimate evil, taking bread away from the people.[10] The crown wisely rejected the plan.

In September 1771 Antonio María de Bucareli, a former naval officer from Seville and captain general of Cuba since 1766, arrived in Mexico City to replace Croix as viceroy.[11] Bucareli was a particularly honest and dedicated administrator. In Cuba he had ably managed the crown's tobacco monopoly, which supplied the raw material for the Seville cigar factory. He had kept a wary eye on developments in New Spain, unimpressed by Croix and disdainful of Gálvez's heavy-handed approach to reform.[12] Once in office, he met regularly with Gálvez as the visitor general worked on his final report. Bucareli confessed to Arriaga that Gálvez was proposing things, like the intendancy system, not at all suited to American conditions. "Not everything that looks possible on paper can be put into practice."[13]

With the exit first of Croix and then of Gálvez in early 1772, the coast was clear for the return of Gamboa. Before leaving New Spain, Croix had assured Gamboa's wife that he would not stand in the way of her husband's return.[14] In Madrid, Campomanes and Moñino, the crown attorneys of Castile, again reviewed the case. They acknowledged that legal charges had never been leveled against Gamboa; his offense was strictly political, speaking up too frankly against the visita. With Gálvez's mission wrapped up, they felt it was safe if Gamboa returned to his old seat on the Sala de Crimen. They were confident that "the measure taken against Gamboa and the time that has transpired since he left Mexico should make him more cautious and moderate in the future, not just in regard to his free talk but also to his peculiar handling as an alcalde del crimen, which has made him despised among the public of that capital." In approving his return to the Sala de Crimen, they warned Gamboa that in the future "he should abstain from interfering and speaking openly about matters of government, restricting his actions to those pertinent to his judicial position."[15]

Gamboa got the good news in August 1772. He wrote to Arriaga to thank him for approving the transfer but also to let him know how much the ordeal had cost; he claimed to have spent 26,000 pesos, more than six times his annual salary as an audiencia magistrate, for travel and living expenses. Whatever fortune he had accumulated as a private lawyer, before he had joined the audiencia, was gone. On December 11, 1772, Gamboa set sail from Cadiz, accompanied by Juan Manuel de Perón, who had been acting as his private secretary in Spain, and one domestic servant, Francisco Cobian.[16] His son Juan José remained behind in Valladolid to finish university. Four

Figure 9. Viceroy Antonio María de Bucareli, the veteran official who brought calm to New Spain after the visita of José de Gálvez. Photograph by Leonardo Hernández; reproduced by permission of the Instituto Nacional de Antropología e Historia.

months later Gamboa arrived home. He met his new daughter for the first time, born shortly after his 1769 departure. If in 1764 he had returned to New Spain full of confidence, this time he knew he should keep his head down and watch his back.

The Administrative Duties of an Oidor

One year after returning to Mexico City, on March 16, 1774, Gamboa received a promotion to the Sala de lo Civil of the Real Audiencia of Mexico. The Spanish crown usually forgave the transgressions of competent officials. In fact, even when he faced sanction from the crown for his opposition to the visita, he received votes from some members of the Council of the Indies for a vacant seat on the civil bench.[17] To serve as an oidor on the Real Audiencia of Mexico represented for most judges the pinnacle of their careers. Until the creation of the office of regent in 1776, the only rung higher than the civil division of the Real Audiencia of Mexico was the Council of the Indies itself. The eight oidores of the audiencia were powerful figures.[18] They reviewed decisions by lower level judges, advised the viceroy sitting in the Acuerdo, and carried out numerous administrative functions. They had the power to challenge viceregal decisions they considered contrary to the best interests of justice. They saw themselves as akin to Roman senators, the guardians of the constitutional order.

A thorn in the side of Viceroy Croix, as oidor Gamboa became a trusted collaborator of Bucareli. The viceroy handed him several important administrative tasks, such as supervising Temporalidades, the office in charge of administering ex-Jesuit properties. His first action was to investigate accusations of fraud and embezzlement against Alejandro Paleani, the manager of the large hacienda of Xalpa, located in the municipality of Huehuetoca north of Mexico City. Its annual profits of over 20,000 pesos had supported Jesuit schools, in particular the nearby Seminary of Tepotzotlán. Gamboa audited the books and found sufficient evidence to charge Paleani on both civil and criminal grounds. Paleani died in custody and in 1776 none other than Pedro Romero Terreros, now ennobled as the Conde de Regla, purchased the Xalpa property from the government.[19] The savvy Terreros took advantage of the Jesuit expulsion to accumulate a portfolio of the order's former estates. By the 1770s he was not only producing silver but also pulque, another lucrative novohispano commodity.[20]

Gamboa also assumed responsibility over two former Jesuit schools for Native children, the Colegio de San Gregorio for boys and the Colegio de Indias Doncellas de Nuestra Señora de Guadalupe for girls. When Gamboa first examined the books of San Gregorio in 1774, he discovered the boys' school only had about 6,000 pesos in assets. Fortunately, the college could still draw upon the income of the hacienda of San José de Oculmán, left by a Basque benefactor, Juan de Echeverría. After restoring San Gregorio's finances, Gamboa approved some 13,000 pesos worth of repairs. He also ordered the return to the college's chapel of an image of Nuestra Señora de Loreto, which had been installed in the Convento de Nuestra Señora de la Encarnación for safekeeping. The nuns of Encarnación put up a fight to keep the sacred image but in the end it was returned to San Gregorio.[21] By the early 1780s, San Gregorio was once again solvent, with an endowment of 35,000 pesos and a student body of about fifty.[22]

Gamboa found particular satisfaction in his work to save the Colegio de

Indias Doncellas de Nuestra Señora de Guadalupe. This unique school for indigenous girls had been founded in 1753 by the Jesuit priest Modesto Martínez Herdoñana. At Guadalupe, Native girls learned to read and write in Spanish, studied the catechism, and honed useful skills for poor women, such as sewing and cooking. When Gamboa took charge of the school in March 1774, it was insolvent. After taking care of immediate needs, in 1777 he launched an ambitious fundraising campaign. He wrote to his acquaintances among the miners, merchants and landowners of New Spain. He reminded them that the school of Guadalupe was "almost the only refuge for the honest maidens of this miserable nation."[23] Gamboa's compadre Miguel de Berrio pledged 8,000 pesos. The students raised funds themselves by taking in sewing and selling sweets. The campaign succeeded in raising over 20,000 pesos. Under Gamboa's direction, the school purchased land for new classrooms, a garden, and a chicken coop. By 1781, after the work was complete, the school could accommodate twenty-six boarders and sixty-four day students.[24] It was a modest establishment compared to the Vizcaínas, which Gamboa had helped to establish almost thirty years earlier, but it might have brought him even more satisfaction. He remained involved in the school for the rest of his life.[25]

Bucareli also assigned Gamboa the task of supervising New Spain's first state lottery, founded in 1769 by Francisco Xavier de Sarría, a Spanish immigrant close to Gálvez. As judge-conservator Gamboa oversaw the weekly draws and his name was printed on the lottery tickets. The operation had succeeded in raising over 450,000 pesos from 1774, when Gamboa assumed oversight, to 1780. But in August 1779, he discovered a shortfall of almost 26,000 pesos in the books. He laid criminal charges against the director, Sarría, the chief accountant, Pedro Noble, the collector general, Antonio Vertiz, and the assistant accountant, Santiago Vander Eynden. To cover the loss, he ordered the seizure of Sarría's hacienda in Chalco.[26] Sarría complained bitterly to Gálvez, by then the minister of the Indies, of Gamboa's "cruel and despotic spirit."[27] Gálvez sided with Sarría and forced Gamboa to drop the case. From this distance it is impossible to know whether Gamboa's case against Sarría was substantiated. Gálvez might have seen it as a deliberate attack by Gamboa on a member of his old circle in New Spain. Sarría later turned up in northern New Spain in search of mining opportunities and even wrote a book on metallurgy, published in Mexico City in 1784.[28]

Mercury and the Gremio de los Mineros

Gálvez arrived in New Spain in 1765 with the directive to pay "particular attention to the equipment and working of the mines, their condition, the care taken in the collection of the royal fifths, and whether the supplies of mercury are furnished to mines as they are necessary, and by what means the production of precious metals may be made more copious."[29] The supply of mercury, used in the amalgamation process to refine silver, was a crucial issue. Miners and refiners had been demanding a reduction in the official price for decades. In 1743, José Antonio Fabry, an official at the Mexican mint, calculated that if the crown cut the price by 50 percent, silver production would rise so substantially that increases in other revenue lines would more than compensate for the decline in mercury profits. Manuel Aldaco, Gamboa's early patron and New Spain's principal silver banker, contributed a laudatory preface to Fabry's book.[30] José Antonio de Villaseñor, the head of New Spain's mercury monopoly, managed to stop the price reduction at the time, but advocates of cheaper mercury continued to press their case.

Gálvez was convinced of the merits of lower mercury prices. He mentioned in his 1759 policy paper that the crown sold mercury in New Spain at four times cost.[31] In his first mining initiative as visitor general, he endorsed a March 1767 petition by Joaquín Velázquez de León, Juan Lucas de Lassaga, and José de la Borda to lower the official price by 50 percent from eighty to forty pesos per hundredweight. They also asked the crown to relax its prohibition on mercury mining in New Spain, something Gamboa had recommended in the *Comentarios a las Ordenanzas de Minas.* While their demands were hardly novel, how the petitioners identified themselves certainly raised eyebrows. The three signatories, Velázquez de León, Lassaga, and Borda, called themselves the spokesmen for the *gremio de los mineros.* This was presumptuous on two counts. First, no *gremio,* or formal organization for miners, even existed. Second, what right did they, especially the first two, have to represent miners as a body? Velázquez de León, although from a mining family, was a lawyer mostly interested in astronomy. Lassaga was a recent immigrant from Spain. Only Borda, whom Gamboa had described as "the first miner in the world for his vast knowledge and great enterprises," could honestly hold himself up as a spokesman for the industry.[32] He was likely asked to sign the petition for this very reason. Also noteworthy was the encomium at the end of the petition, which praised the zeal and dedication of Gálvez.[33] Already, it seemed, a plan was being hatched by Velázquez de León, Lassaga, and Gálvez to create a corporate body for the mining industry.

In Madrid, the request to lower prices and relax the mercury monopoly reached the desk of Tomás Ortiz de Landázuri, the contador general of the Council of the Indies. Landázuri was a veteran official, who had spent twenty years in New Spain. He knew silver mining and conditions in the viceroyalty extremely well. From 1747 to 1749 he served as corregidor of Zacatecas, with responsibility for the adjudication of mining cases. He participated in the opening up of Bolaños, the site of a major bonanza in the 1740s and early 1750s. His last stop in New Spain was Guadalajara, Gamboa's hometown, where he spent most of the 1750s as a member of its city council. He married a *tapatía*, Josefa de Sierra, and developed a lasting concern for the city's welfare.[34] Recalled to Spain in the early 1760s, the crown chose him to serve on the select committee considering changes to imperial trade policies.[35] He drafted the 1764 report that recommended opening up the ports of the Caribbean to direct trade with Spanish ports.[36] In 1765 the crown named him to the Council of the Indies. He brought a wealth of first-hand knowledge of America to a body that had, up until then, mostly served as a stepping-stone for ambitious Spaniards on their way to the Council of Castile.[37]

Landázuri and Gamboa had much in common, beginning with their Basque heritage. Upon his return to Spain in the early 1760s, Landázuri joined the Congregación de San Ignacio de Loyola, the confraternity in Madrid formally linked to Nuestra Señora de Aránzazu in Mexico City. In 1766, he was elected prefect, a key position for Basques in Madrid. If the two men did not already know each other in New Spain, they certainly met in Madrid. In 1761 Gamboa wrote a short treatise on pearls, in which he mentioned seeing a beautiful string of black pearls and several pearl bracelets brought to Spain by "Don Thomas de Landázuri, regidor of Guadalajara, capital of the kingdom of New Galicia."[38] He probably wrote this paper at the behest of Landázuri. Both men knew that Guadalajara, as a center of commerce in western New Spain, would benefit from the development of the pearl fishery in the Gulf of California.

Besides their common Basque heritage and loyalty to Guadalajara, Landázuri and Gamboa shared similar ideas about silver mining. In 1764 Landázuri submitted to the crown his own report on the industry in New Spain.[39] It echoed many of the points Gamboa made earlier in the *Comentarios a las Ordenanzas de Minas*. Landázuri took the same jaundiced view of miners, accusing them of ignoring the law and engaging in frivolous lawsuits. Although not a lawyer himself, Landázuri strongly believed, like Gamboa, that mining should remain in the hands of the judges of ordinary jurisdiction. He criticized how the former viceroy, the Conde de Revillagigedo, had seized jurisdiction over the boomtown of Bolaños from the Audiencia of Guadalajara. He suggested that Revillagigedo profited personally from this maneuver. While Landázuri's paper was more descriptive than prescriptive, he did include the recommendation that the crown lower the price of mercury.

Like Gamboa, Landázuri saw no need for radical reform in America.[40] He represented many veteran officials in Madrid and throughout Spanish America skeptical of Gálvez and his approach to imperial renovation. Landázuri valued empirical knowledge, acquired from personal experience, and understood that the distinct conditions in America meant that a one-size-fits-all legal and administrative approach would never work in the Spanish Empire. Landázuri's attitude was neatly encapsulated in an opinion he wrote against a May 1767 measure supported by Croix and Gálvez to prohibit the use of raw or unminted silver in commercial transactions in New Spain.

> It frequently occurs that a general provision, sound and just in its origin, is not appropriate for certain provinces and countries, for the diversity of uses and practices in their economy and in the arrangement of things that necessity introduced and authorized. This obliges a tempering of things in prudent proportion to the constitution, state and nature of such places. In this way, what in some places is opportune, useful and proper, in others is impractical, prejudicial and ruinous, as happens every day with new measures that do not proceed from a mature examination and consultation with wise and expert people who know through experience the quality and situation of the countries and their inhabitants.[41]

This statement can be taken as an indictment of the whole Galvesian reform project. Landázuri followed Solórzano's line that Spanish law had to accommodate the diversity of America and this required experience to know the peculiarities of each place.[42] In the case of the proposed ban on the use of unminted silver in transactions, Croix and Gálvez were making the classic mistake of trying to impose a law that looked good in theory but would wreak havoc in practice. People in northern New Spain, Landázuri explained, used raw metal in transactions not to cheat the government but because they had no choice. There just was not sufficient legal tender in circulation. This was the reason both Landázuri and Gamboa recommended the establishment of a second mint in Guadalajara, to supply silver coins to the mining and agricultural communities in northern New Spain. In the meantime, the crown should simply tolerate the practice. Dissimulation, whereby the crown agreed to overlook a violation of its laws, as Landázuri understood, was sometimes the best strategy.[43] Most of the raw silver eventually made its way back into official channels anyways, where it was assayed, taxed, and minted into peso coins.

Landázuri did agree with Gálvez on the benefits of lowering mercury prices. He knew this was the simplest and most direct way to boost silver output. But he mocked the pretension of the petitioners for portraying themselves as the representatives of the gremio de los mineros. Like Gamboa, he knew from experience the lack of associative behavior by miners. As for the request to allow mercury mining in New Spain and end the monopoly the Spanish mine of Almadén controlled, Landázuri rejected it on colonialist grounds. "Prudence and politics dictate that as long as there remains an abundance of the material in Almadén, it should be provided from here, to maintain the dependence of those dominions to its Head." As a top official at the Council of the Indies, Landázuri was not willing to severe one of the most vital links binding New Spain to the mother country: the mercury supply.[44]

The crown was only prepared to reduce the official price by 25 percent, even though recent cost savings at Almadén would have made a bigger reduction feasible.[45] Miners in New Spain still felt the benefit. In 1776, after Gálvez became minister of the Indies, he managed to put through another price cut, which brought the official price down to forty pesos per hundredweight, what was originally sought in 1767. By then the evidence was clear that lowering mercury prices, as experts had been predicting for decades, boosted production and thus raised overall crown revenue. The whole point of the mercury monopoly, after all, was not to serve as a profit center in itself but as a mechanism to distribute the material quickly and equitably to New Spain's miners. The crown's decision to reduce mercury prices was likely the most consequential reason for the health of the industry until the end of Spanish rule. This was Gálvez's great contribution to the industry, not the creation of the Mining Tribunal.[46]

Real del Monte and the Birth of the Mining Tribunal

To understand the origins of the Mining Tribunal we have to return to Real del Monte, the site of so many pivotal events in the history of Mexican mining, from the invention of the patio method of mercury amalgamation by Bartolomé de Medina in the 1550s to the first significant public-private rehabilitation scheme headed by José Alejandro de Bustamante in the 1740s. The story begins with the strike of 1766, when the workers of Pedro Romero Terreros went on a violent rampage because of his attempt to end the partido. It was Gamboa who attempted to restore peace to the district. His settlement, documented in a new labor code, recognized, on the one hand, the legality of the partido and, on the other, the need for tougher penalties against worker theft. Terreros refused to accept Gamboa's resolution. For the next five years or so, he turned his back on his mining operations and concentrated on his agricultural estates. One way the crown tried to coax him back to active management was by fast-tracking his application for noble status. The former shopkeeper from Andalusia became the Conde de Regla. Yet he continued to insist that he would not return to Real del Monte until the government outlawed the partido. By 1770 he had managed to convince both Croix and Gálvez. Gálvez recommended to the crown in February 1771 that the partido should be prohibited throughout New Spain. Gálvez's protégé, Juan Antonio de Areche, a crown attorney on the Real Audiencia of Mexico and the future visitor general of Peru, blamed Gamboa—then exiled in Valladolid—for all the trouble. Gamboa should have crushed the rebellious workers at Real del Monte with military force when he had the chance, just like Gálvez did without compunction a year later against the rebels who rose up in the Bajío.[47] Encouraged by this show of support in New Spain, Regla submitted a formal request to Madrid in September 1771 to abolish the partido and revoke Gamboa's labor regulations for Real del Monte. He also took the opportunity to demand that the government provide him with additional Native draft labor and mercury at cost before he resumed full operations at Real del Monte.[48]

Bucareli, who had replaced Croix as viceroy just when Regla submitted his petition, was outraged by Regla's extravagant demands. In a blistering letter to the crown at the end of December 1771, the new viceroy strongly endorsed the partido: "While it is true that mine workers have no legal right to partidos, it is what custom dictates and there is no law or ordinance prohibiting them."[49] In the absence of Gamboa, Bucareli probably consulted with

Domingo Valcárcel, the senior oidor, long-time administrator of the mercury monopoly in New Spain, and close ally of Gamboa. Valcárcel might have explained to the viceroy how the partido benefited small miner owners, who lacked cash to pay wages, and the independent refiners, who bought ore from the workers. This made for a more stable and diversified industry. Bucareli predicted that if the crown moved to outlaw the partido, as Regla requested with Gálvez's backing, the mining districts of New Spain would rise up in rebellion, repeating on a massive scale the uprising that had taken place in Real del Monte in August 1766. Bucareli ended his letter by suggesting the need for miners to gather in Mexico City to discuss labor and other issues of mutual concern.[50]

In Madrid Landázuri, the accountant general of the Council of the Indies, agreed wholeheartedly with Bucareli. He too was shocked by the brazen request to outlaw the partido. "There is nothing more useful and reasonable in practice, for being the only effective way to stimulate poor people to undertake the hard and risky work" of mining.[51] Landázuri and Bucareli, if they knew it or not, were echoing what Gamboa had written ten years earlier in the *Comentarios a las Ordenanzas de Minas*. The prosperity of silver mining in New Spain depended on the willingness of mine owners to share their ore with their workers. This minimized cash outlays and incentivized the back-breaking work of underground labor. Landázuri reckoned that the real problem at Real del Monte was not the partido but the fact that Croix had failed to enforce the arrest warrants Gamboa had issued back in 1766 against the ringleaders of the violence. With the leaders of the revolt still at large, no wonder Regla refused to return to Real del Monte. Landázuri also agreed with Bucareli that it would be a good idea to convene miners in Mexico City to discuss labor and other issues of mutual interest. In July 1773 the invitation went out to miners across New Spain.[52]

The Mining Tribunal Proposal

Joaquín Velázquez de León and Juan Lucas de Lassaga seized upon this opportunity to pitch their plan for a formal organization for miners. The time had come to make their dream of a miners' guild, suggested in their 1767 submission on mercury, a reality. Velázquez de León, born in the mining town of Sultepec in 1732, had studied law at the University of Mexico. No one in New Spain, in the opinion of José Antonio de Alzate, the priest best known

Figure 10. Joaquín Velázquez de León, the founder of the Mining Tribunal. Reproduced by permission of the Instituto Nacional de Antropología e Historia.

El Sr. D. Joaquin Velasquez de Leon.

for his journalism and interest in science, better combined the theory and practice of mining than Velázquez de León.[53] Gálvez had taken Velázquez de León on his expedition to the northern New Spain. There he investigated potential mineral deposits in Sinaloa and Sonora and observed the 1769 transit of Venus across the sun.[54] Velázquez de León may have convinced Gálvez of the merits of a miners' guild patterned on the merchants' consulado.

In February 1774 Velázquez de León and Lassaga submitted their formal proposal to the crown, presumably written by Velázquez de León alone.[55] The fact that the plan was published by Felipe Zúñiga y Ontiveros, one of the viceroyalty's leading printers, showed that the government acknowledged its importance. The proposal opened by painting the typically bleak picture of mining conditions in New Spain. Just as Gamboa had written in 1761, Velázquez de León asserted that too many good mines had been abandoned due to flooding. There was little capital for rehabilitation, especially since the death of Aldaco in 1770, the last of the private silver bankers. But whereas Gamboa suggested reforms that could fit under the existing legislation, Velázquez de León thought the ordinances of 1584 were obsolete. He took a gratuitous swipe at Gamboa. "A few years ago," he wrote, "we received a Commentary, erudite and extensive, of our Ordinances. But the author was unable to supply what was missing in them or erase what was superfluous or enter into that high realm of interpretation reserved to the legislator." [56] Velázquez de León boldly called for the repeal of the 1584 statute and its replacement by a new code that he would happily write himself. These new mining ordinances, besides updating the substantive rules governing the industry, would authorize a self-governing corporate body for miners, with control over its own bank, its own adjudicative tribunal, and its own technical college. Miners deserved these expansive powers because only they could truly understand the intricacies of the industry. "The science of mining is too vast, obscure, and complicated to acquire easily. It demands an untiring study, experience, and thus a lifetime's dedication." [57] The logic of this argument was that because judges of the ordinary jurisdiction had never descended into the pit of a mine, they lacked the requisite knowledge to administer justice for miners. In the same way, because merchants did not know how to refine silver through mercury amalgamation, they had no right to be involved in mine finance.

The new organization would consist of a board of directors based in Mexico City and local deputies elected by miners in each district in New Spain. The deputies would handle the adjudication of disputes at first instance, with streamlined procedures that would do away with the need for meddlesome lawyers. Appeals of local decisions would go to the board in Mexico City, which would consist of an administrator general and two deputy generals, assisted by a legal advisor and scribe. Velázquez de León and Lassaga graciously offered to serve on this board for life. They would also manage the mining bank and technical college. Funding for the tribunal would come from seignorage, the fee collected at the mint. It had been doubled in the 1740s to meet wartime expenses and had remained at the same rate after hostilities ceased. Velázquez de León proposed that the tribunal receive the half still allotted to the military. They estimated this would bring in 200,000 pesos annually, enough to cover operating expenses and provide sufficient income from the start to pay investors 5 percent interest. They estimated the new body would be able to raise at least two million pesos in share capital from outside investors.

The only part of their proposal with genuine Enlightenment inspiration was the technical college. At the time, the only school of this sort was the mining college of Freiberg in Saxony, founded in 1765. The proposed mining school in Mexico City would teach young men geology, chemistry, physics, mathematics, and other useful subjects, including French. In the summers students would venture out into the field to serve practicums in mining districts. The hope was that the college would not only help to modernize novohispano mining practices but encourage the sons of miners to follow in their fathers' footsteps rather that seek safe careers as lawyers or priests.

The Case against the Mining Tribunal

The 1774 plan, so confidently presented by Velázquez de León and Lassaga, was shredded to pieces by top officials in Mexico City and Madrid. They saw it as impractical, grandiose, and manifestly contrary to the public interest. Gamboa, back in Mexico and promoted to oidor in March 1774, kept his head down at first but could not avoid becoming the intellectual author of the case against the tribunal. He had anticipated it in his 1761 book on mining. The Acuerdo, made up of the oidores of the Real Audiencia of Mexico sitting in their capacity as political advisors to the viceroy, thought it was ridiculous, as Gamboa had in the *Comentarios*, to equate miners with the merchants of the consulado. Merchants lived in Mexico City and had a long history of collaboration on important projects, such as the Mexico City drainage project.[58] Miners, in contrast, lived isolated throughout New Spain, with no history of association. The oidores attacked the banking plan for failing to provide any oversight, an invitation for fraud and self-dealing. They were understandably outraged by the proposed adjudicative system, which would strip them of any role in mining cases. At the local level, they said, it would be nearly impossible to find a mining deputy without some economic interest in the disputes he was supposed to adjudicate. They would be in effect both judges and parties in disputes. At least alcaldes mayores, for all their faults, were supposed to be impartial and their mistakes could be corrected by the audiencias of Mexico and Guadalajara. The Acuerdo concluded it would be best to leave things as they were.[59]

Valcárcel, the décano of the audiencia as its most senior oidor, the director of the mercury monopoly, and Gamboa's friend, submitted his own scathing review of the tribunal plan. He pronounced it "so unlawful and confused that it could only be enforced with a total upheaval of the laws." Valcárcel defended Gamboa from Velázquez de León's veiled attack, declaring that "only one ignorant of what is the Royal Audiencia and its mode of government and operation could proffer propositions so contrary to those expressed by the Author of the *Comentarios*, a subject who defended in the Royal Audiencia of Mexico many arduous and intricate cases of Mining law." [60] According to the veteran magistrate, outsiders would be reluctant to invest in the industry under a scheme that gave miners exclusive authority over adjudication. There would be no appeal to the audiencias in the event of bad local decisions. As for the bank, the proposal reminded Valcárcel—who was old enough to remember—of the rejected plan of 1743 by Domingo Reborato, the enterprising but penniless immigrant from Genoa. Who would trust miners, a group notorious for their reckless and extravagant spending, to manage their money? Valcárcel even deemed the mining school a waste of money. All one had to do, he said, was read Gamboa's *Comentarios*; it contained all the technical information miners needed.

Viceroy Bucareli, in an opinion that Lassaga later claimed had in fact been written by Gamboa, agreed with the oidores of the audiencia that the Mining Tribunal plan was both impractical and contrary to the public interest.[61] He recommended that the crown have another look at Gamboa's plan to create a mining bank under the auspices of the consulado.[62] Gamboa's thinking also shaped the opinion of the Council of the Indies in Madrid. Did it make sense, the council asked, to "create a guild for subjects so dispersed and scattered in the vast extension of the whole kingdom and who are judged essentially unsocial, or if it would be more opportune that the merchants of the Consulado, who generally finance mining and the rehabilitation of old mines," be put in charge of a bank?[63] Landázuri, the council's contador general, who shared most of Gamboa's ideas about mining, also thought the tribunal was completely unnecessary. Lowering mercury prices, he wrote, was "the most just, natural, and gentle way of all those imaginable to encourage that crucial body of vassals and to increase the royal treasury." [64]

Besides the practical objections raised by the officials in Mexico City and Madrid, there was another problem with the proposed Mining Tribunal: it violated the principles of economic liberalism then gaining traction in Spain and the rest of Europe. Liberals considered privileged artisans' guild, like the proposed tribunal, as dangerous constraints on individual economic liberty and competitive markets. In 1774, the same year as the tribunal proposal, Campomanes, the foremost economic liberal among the advisors of Charles III, wrote in his *Discurso sobre el fomento de la industria popular* that "nothing is more contrary to popular industry than the erection of guilds and privileged jurisdictions, which divide people into small societies often exempt from ordinary justice."[65] Campomanes did not advocate the outright abolition of guilds, as Adam Smith did in 1776, but he did oppose their exemptions from ordinary jurisdiction. If guilds were to survive, their members should be subject to the same laws and justice system as everyone else.[66]

As the crown attorney of Castile, Campomanes was not called upon to review proposed legislation for the Indies. But we can guess what his opinion of the tribunal would be from his 1762 critique of Gamboa's *Comentarios a las Ordenanzas de Minas*. In rejecting Gamboa's idea of a consulado mining bank, Campomanes declared that any government help for silver mining was unnecessary: "When a branch of industry produces with liberty, it is a fundamental maxim of government not to interfere, especially if it is destructive of liberty."[67] Campomanes pointed to the example of England as a country wealthy due to its productive population rather than precious metal mines. Adam Smith in *The Wealth of Nations* stated it plainly that state aid for silver and gold mines was economically counterproductive:

> Of all those expensive and uncertain projects, however, which bring bankruptcy upon the greater part of the people who engage in them, there is none perhaps more perfectly ruinous than the search for new silver and gold mines. . . . They are the projects, therefore, to which of all others a prudent law-giver, who desired to increase the capital of his nation, would least choose to give any extraordinary encouragement, or to turn towards them a greater share of that capital than what would go to them of its own accord.[68]

Although *The Wealth of Nations* did not appear in Spanish until the early 1790s, many of the ideas it articulated were already taking hold in Spain. Campomanes pushed them at the highest level of the Spanish government. He had no say, however, in the deliberations over the Mining Tribunal.

But perhaps the biggest problem with the Mining Tribunal was that it was based on a false premise. Mining was not in crisis in New Spain. It was flourishing, although that might have been difficult for contemporaries to see. Bad news about flooded miners captured more attention than incremental increases in production. But since the late seventeenth century, production had increased steadily decade after decade, from 1.3 million kilograms in the 1670s to 2.9 million in the 1750s, a 223 percent increase. The drivers of this growth were a revival in demand in China and general population growth on both sides of the Atlantic. There was indeed a slump in production in the 1760s—when Gamboa wrote the *Comentarios*—but the industry quickly recovered in the 1770s, up 34 percent from the previous decade and 21 percent from the 1750s.[69] Economic historian Richard Garner estimated that silver production increased an average of 1.4 percent per year over the course of the eighteenth century, somewhat faster than overall economic growth.[70] A more recent estimate put the average annual growth rate of 1.8 percent. For every flooded or abandoned mine, entrepreneurs discovered new deposits, such as at Bolaños, or dug deeper at existing operations, like in Zacatecas. The rise in production of Guanajuato, where the gargantuan Valenciana mine became a must-see attraction for visitors to New Spain, was probably the primary reason for the prosperity of the industry.

So if the viceroy of New Spain, the Real Audiencia of Mexico, and the Council of the Indies, including the respected Landázuri, all opposed the Mining Tribunal, how did it receive royal approval on July 1, 1776? It always had one very ardent supporter, José de Gálvez. He had backed the idea of a gremio de los mineros since at least 1767. In his final report as visitor general in December 1771, he had recommended that all the miners of Spanish America be organized into "privileged bodies, like the consulados of commerce." Only then would miners overcome:

The prejudicial discredit in which they find themselves as a profession, the affronts and extortions they suffer from the ordinary judges and their subalterns in legal matters they pursue before them, the losses they continually live exposed to from the ignorance, disorder and thievery of mine workers, and, above all, the fatality of the best mines being suddenly abandoned for the lack of capital.[71]

Gálvez could see that a formal organization of miners would not only protect them from arrogant judges, thieving miners, and skinflint merchants but also serve other important purposes: it would trim the sails of the audiencias, which would lose jurisdiction over mining cases; it would lessen the merchants' dominance of financing; and, perhaps most significantly, it would provide the crown a new mechanism to tap the silver wealth of New Spain. On February 19, 1776, Charles III named Gálvez to succeed Julián de Arriaga as the secretary of state for the Indies. Gálvez could count on the strong support of José Moñino, Conde de Floridablanca, formerly Campomanes' partner as crown attorney of Castile and now the king's chief minister. Gálvez thus had amassed the power by 1776 to override the well-founded concerns of the opponents of the tribunal and get the king's signature on a cédula authorizing it. Velázquez de León and Lassaga immediately showed their gratitude to the crown: in early 1777, even before the tribunal's first general meeting, they arranged a 300,000 peso loan, secured by the tribunal's income from the seignorage fee, to build a naval shipyard in Coatzacoalcos. They later approved a 4,000 peso annual payment to Gálvez and his heirs in perpetuity. The tribunal's bank immediately showed its effectiveness, not in supplying badly needed capital to its constituents, the miners of New Spain, but in funding the government and its ministers.

Gamboa Returns to the Fight

Although relieved to operate behind the scenes at first, in early 1778 Gamboa made his feelings about the Mining Tribunal abundantly clear. He took advantage of a lawsuit before the Real Audiencia of Mexico. At the time, before the new law code promised by Velázquez de León could be enacted, the old 1584 ordinances and old adjudicative system remained in effect. The dispute involved Tomás de Liceaga, the tribunal's deputy in Guanajuato and a member of its board of directors in Mexico City. In order to retain title to a mine in Guanajuato, which had been revived by another operator, José Muñoz Castelblanque, after Liceaga and his partner Vicente Maldonado had abandoned it, Liceaga and Maldonado argued that the *buscones*, or scavengers, who had invaded the property after they had abandoned it but before Muñoz Castelblanque could register the claim, were in fact their employees. According to ordinance thirty-seven of the 1584 statute, titleholders had to keep at least four workers active on site to maintain title.[72] By claiming the scavengers were their employees, Liceaga and Maldonado would be able to retain title to the now valuable mine and oust Muñoz Castelblanque. They won their case at first instance in Guanajuato. Muñoz Castelblanque then appealed the decision to the Real Audiencia of Mexico, which found in his favor.

Gamboa wrote a letter to the Council of the Indies, the highest authority for judicial matters in America, excoriating the behavior of Liceaga and his partner. What hope could there be for the administration of justice under the tribunal if "the first Deputy of the most famous and opulent mining district in the kingdom approves as legal and consistent with the ordinances the fraud of claiming scavengers as proper workers?" He then broadened his attack to the tribunal's board. Its two senior directors, Velázquez de León and Lassaga, were self-appointed and not even active miners. Of board members, only Liceaga and Marcelo de Anza operated mines, and that latter was too infirm, according to Gamboa, to be able to sign his own name. What made the situation even more outrageous was that Liceaga, as an ordinary director of the tribunal, received an exorbitant salary of 13,000 pesos annually, far more than that earned even by the regent of the Real Audiencia of Mexico. The mining industry of New Spain, Gamboa predicted, would be ruined if "illiterates, without judgment, discretion, or experience" were put in charge. He asked the crown to stop the transfer of jurisdiction from the audiencias for "the extremely grave difficulties that would result not just in the opulent mining district of Guanajuato but in all the rest if jurisdiction were conceded over mining cases to the Administrator-general, Director, and Deputies." [73]

Gamboa's attack on the tribunal did not go unnoticed. Lassaga wrote to Gálvez to warn him that Gamboa was up to his old tricks. "In spite of the well-known protection that the mining profession owes Your Excellency," Lassaga wrote in June 1778, "a few judges of the Audiencia attack us through various means. In the last post, they sent a representation to the Council, promoted and dictated by the oidor Don Francisco Xavier de Gamboa (signed as well by señor Don Domingo Valcárcel, who in these matters will never be retired). They add nothing new this time, but if Your Excellency does not see fit to show them your displeasure, they will continue in their conduct and thwart whatever provisions Your Excellency may take to benefit this body." [74]

Gamboa was safe as long as Bucareli remained viceroy of New Spain. But on April 9, 1779, the sixty-two-year-old Bucareli died after a short illness. Gálvez had been planning to put his brother Matías de Gálvez on the viceregal throne. But Bucareli's sudden death upended this plan. According to the terms of Bucareli's appointment, he would be replaced—if his successor had not yet been officially named—by Martín de Mayoraga Ferrer, the captain general of Guatemala.[75] Gálvez had no choice but to accept Mayoraga but he did place a trusted confidante, Pedro Antonio de Cossío, in the viceregal palace. Cossío sent Gálvez a steady stream of acerbic letters about the politics and personalities of the government of New Spain.[76] He particularly targeted

Gamboa. Cossío claimed that the oidor used his knowledge of the levers of powers to thwart Gálvez's reforms. For instance, he "carried the banner" for all those opposed to the government's plan to consolidate the cash accounts of the church and government in the Mexico City mint. This plan would have made it easier for the crown to obtain capital in the event of a crisis but at the cost, as Gamboa recognized, of running roughshod over the established jurisdictions of New Spain.[77] Gamboa had also resisted Madrid's attempt to allow treasury officials to audit estates, with the goal of increasing tax revenue, on the grounds that audience magistrates exercised primary jurisdiction over the matter.[78]

Gamboa stood firm in defending the old ways and jurisdiction of the audiencias, even if it made it harder for the crown to access the wealth of New Spain. In 1780, when Cossío was reporting to Gálvez on Gamboa's maneuverings, Spain needed cash from New Spain more than ever. It was supporting North American rebels fighting against the British crown while simultaneously trying to suppress Andean rebels fighting against the Spanish crown in Peru. In the end, the crown managed to collect over four million pesos from New Spain to fund the independence of the United States. Meanwhile, trade between New Spain and South America, especially the cacao trade from Ecuador to Acapulco, helped to prop up the Peruvian economy and prevent imperial collapse in the Andes.[79] At the end Spain did meet both challenges but that was far from certain in 1780, when Gamboa's jurisdictional preoccupations seemingly made it more difficult for the Spanish crown to draw upon the wealth of New Spain in the case of emergency.

Gálvez finally delivered his strike against Gamboa at the end of 1780. He appointed him as regent, or chief justice, of the Audiencia of Santo Domingo, the oldest but least prestigious high court in America.[80] Santo Domingo was a colonial backwater by the eighteenth century, its stagnant economy of cattle ranching and contraband in stark contrast to the wealth of its French neighbor, the sugar dynamo of Saint Domingue. Plagued by malaria, yellow fever, and hurricanes, the island of Hispaniola understandably repelled people of European descent. Gamboa saw the transfer as a death sentence. At sixty-three years old, he claimed he was "more ready for the tomb than voyages by sea and land."[81] Dr. José Ignacio Bartolache, New Spain's most celebrated physician, certified that Gamboa looked ten years older than his true age. Worse off were his wife, María Manuela, who suffered from chronic digestive problems, and his three adult daughters, Gertrudis, Josefa, and Francisca, all still unmarried, living at home, and enduring an assortment of afflictions, including *"vapor histérico."*[82] Gamboa sought permission to retire from the bench rather than report to duty in Santo Domingo. Viceroy Mayorga supported his request.[83] Even Cossío recommended that Gamboa be allowed to retire honorably.[84] But Gálvez was adamant. He wanted Gamboa out of New Spain for good. The minister of the Indies still had a lot of unfinished business in the viceroyalty, such as the consolidation of the Mining Tribunal and the implementation of the intendancy system. He rightfully considered Gamboa a formidable obstacle to the realization of these plans.

For more than two years Gamboa resisted the appointment to Santo Domingo. He claimed only a personal order from the king would change his mind. In the meantime, he had legal matters to take care of in Mexico City, none more complicated than the disposition of the estate of his old compadre, Miguel de Berrio y Zaldívar, Marqués de Jaral del Berrio and Conde de San Mateo Valparaíso, who had died on November 23, 1779.[85] Presumably following the advice of Gamboa, Berrio had set up a *mayorazgo*, or entailed estate. This allowed him to designate his grandchildren as his primary heirs instead of his two sons and daughter. The main reason for skipping a generation was Berrio's intense dislike for Pedro de Moncada y Branciforte, the husband of his daughter Mariana. The Moncadas blamed Gamboa for the loss of their expected inheritance. Mariana wrote to Gálvez, with allegations that even the minister of the Indies must have found ridiculous: "Señor Gamboa enriches himself, lives leisurely, with abundance, with splendor, with ostentation, receiving the praise of everyone, for taking what is properly mine. He laughs, and I cry; he dresses up elegantly, I wear mourning clothes; he has his fill, I go hungry." As long as he remained in Mexico City, she told Gálvez, he would continue to "plant discord in the heart of my gullible mother, as he did for my father."[86]

It took Gamboa until the end of 1782 to finish his work as executor of the Berrio estate. As he explained in a letter to Gálvez, it was hugely complicated. Berrio left a vast collection of urban and rural properties, including assets in Spain and Cuba. Gamboa had to go through more than a century of documentation to produce an inventory. Meanwhile, Mariana and her mother were receiving generous annual allowances of 11,000 pesos; the daughter, he said, had nothing to complain about.[87] In December 1782 he reported to Viceroy Mayoraga that his work on the estate was done. He hoped Gálvez would show his appreciation by relieving him of the obligation to serve in Santo Domingo.[88]

Gálvez was implacable. He did make one concession, however, to help the Gamboa family: he approved the appointment of Gamboa's son Juan José to the cathedral chapter of Mexico City.[89] After an absence of more than thirteen years in Spain, where he finished university and entered the priesthood, Juan José arrived home in May 1783. The condition of his parents and sisters shocked him. He reported to Gálvez: "All are transformed: my father old, ruined, almost dead; my mother and sisters finished, so full of ailments I don't know how they survive. . . . I see the destruction of my household if the mercy of our lord the king does not exonerate my father from the Regency of Santo Domingo."[90] But the door had already shut. Gálvez had finally placed his brother Matías as the new viceroy of New Spain. The time had come to push through the last items on his old reform agenda in New Spain. In October 1783 Gamboa, now almost sixty-six years old, finally accepted his fate and set off for Santo Domingo.

The Failures of the Mining Tribunal

It is hard to understate the failure of the Mining Tribunal in its first decade of operations. The trouble began at the top with the leadership of Velázquez de León. Cossío, always dependable for a caustic comment on a fellow official, told Gálvez in 1781 that the "apathy and neglect" of Velázquez de León was providing fuel for the enemies of the tribunal, especially the oidores of the audiencia.[91] Pedro María de Monterde, the first independent auditor to examine the Tribunal's books, said Velázquez de León "seemed to work with greater effort to ruin mining than to establish and adorn its Tribunal."[92] Velázquez de León's untethered self-regard was on full display in a dispute in 1784 with José Antonio de Alzate, the scientifically minded priest who once held Velázquez de León in high regard. Alzate had proposed several commonsense modifications in the design of the malacate, the mechanical winch used in New Spain to haul water and ore from mines. The main wheel, for instance, should be circular instead of octagonal. Velázquez de León rebutted all of Alzate's suggestions, for no other reason, it would seem, than to assert his standing as New Spain's leading mining expert.[93]

The management of the mining bank was particularly lax. By lending to favored insiders instead of miners with sound projects, the bank managed to lose 800,000 pesos by 1786.[94] The directors also spent lavishly on salaries for themselves, commemorative medals, bullfights, and other frivolities, seemingly to prove Gamboa correct in his view that miners were irredeemable spendthrifts. They also made large loans to the crown without consultation with their members. In 1782 leading figures in the mining industry, including the Fagoaga brothers, the son of José de la Borda, and Miguel Pacheco Solís, complained to the viceroy of the directors' financial management. For instance, Velázquez de León and Lassaga first approved a one-million-peso loan to the government for war expenses without seeking approval from members of the tribunal and then unilaterally imposed a new charge on miners delivering metal to treasury offices. The senior miners contrasted the tribunal's management to that of the consulado, which consulted its members before approving loans to the crown and then found the least onerous ways to fund them.[95]

Velázquez de León and Lassaga died within one month of each other in 1786, which allowed the government to rethink the whole Mining Tribunal concept. Many officials thought the best solution to the financial catastrophe was to return to Gamboa's original plan of twenty-five years earlier: give the merchants of the consulado responsibility for running the mining bank. Ramón de Posada, the respected crown attorney for treasury matters in New Spain, thought Gamboa's idea made the most sense in the circumstances.[96] The crown did appoint in 1786 a prominent consulado merchant, Antonio Bassoco, a Basque close to Gamboa, to the board of directors of the Mining Tribunal. In 1790, the viceroy of New Spain, Juan Vicente de Güemes, Conde de Revillagigedo, the son of the first Revillagigedo who had served as viceroy in the 1750s, proposed a joint venture between the consulado and tribunal. By then, as we will see, Gamboa was back on the Real Audiencia of Mexico and a member of the committee considering whether the tribunal should survive or not. In his opinion, he said he stuck to "my old thinking, modified for the present state of things and situation of mining."[97] Only the consulado, he insisted, could provide the expert and responsible management to operate a mining bank. He admitted, however, that he had little hope the crown even then would follow his advice.

While not as clear a failure as the mining bank, the new adjudicative system of the tribunal did not bring any appreciable benefits to miners. In 1785, when the new system finally went into operation, the local deputies of the tribunal did hear cases at first instance, but regional panels consisting of two miners and an experienced civil judge heard appeals. For the Guadalajara and Mexico City regions, these appeal judges remained audiencia magistrates. Thus while mining was no longer in the ordinary jurisdiction, magistrates of the audiencias continued to play a role. But there was still no right to appeal local mining decisions to the full panel of the audiencias, a significant loss considering the quality of justice at the local level. Gamboa did not hold back in his 1790 opinion on the reorganization of the tribunal. He wrote "it causes me sadness and pain to see the rights of vassals of His Majesty sacrificed to a bunch of ignoramuses, not to say idiots, which without a doubt describe the deputies."[98] Even Fausto de Elhuyar, the distinguished Basque mining expert who took over as the director of the tribunal in 1787 admitted that the local deputies were next to useless.[99] They were often failed miners, more interested in collecting their salaries than serving the interests of other miners. While the intention had been to speed up litigation by excluding lawyers and reducing formality, miners in disputes still felt compelled to hire lawyers. This caused new problems, Gamboa argued, since lawyers advising miners in secret could not be held accountable for their actions. It is hard not to conclude that it would have been better for everyone, especially the miners, if the old system of adjudication within the ordinary jurisdiction had survived.

Velázquez de León had managed to draft a new mining code before his death, promulgated in 1783, to replace the 1584 ordinances. However, according to Audiencia of Mexico magistrate Balthazar Ladrón de Guevara, all Velázquez de León did was follow "the light of the erudite and learned commentary, the only one on the subject, of Señor Don Francisco Gamboa."[100] Indeed, the new code drew heavily from the *Comentarios a las Ordenanzas de Minas*, no matter how much Velázquez de León had belittled its importance in 1774. As a creole lawyer, he shared Gamboa's appreciation of the importance of local customs. When he submitted his draft in 1778, Velázquez de León wrote that "many [customs] are healthy, useful and well prescribed and we judge that they should be authorized and secured."[101] One such custom enshrined in the new code was the partido. The draft legislation received extensive revisions in Madrid at the hand of Antonio Porlier, a former audiencia magistrate in Peru and later the successor to Gálvez as the minister of the Indies.[102] By 1790 Gamboa himself conceded the 1783 code was superior to the old 1584 ordinances. He nevertheless had his criticisms. For example, he saw no reason for the prohibition on priests operating mines, especially considering their distinguished history in the industry.[103] He also disapproved of the new crown monopoly over salt, a crucial element in the mercury-amalgamation process. This measure hurt both the muleteers who shipped the salt and the native communities who produced it. He had defended the old ordinances in his *Comentarios* because they created a framework that encouraged entrepreneurialism; he feared the new code was overly restrictive in this regard.

Perhaps the most surprising failure of the tribunal was in technical matters. The experts it brought to New Spain from Europe to enlighten the benighted American miners quickly discovered that novohispano methods were in many cases equal or even better than their own. Frederick Sonneschmidt led the team that arrived in 1788 to introduce the Born technique of refining silver, developed with great acclaim in Vienna by Baron Ignaz von Born. But he realized that miners in New Spain already knew the basic technique, which they called *beneficio por cazo*, or the cauldron method of beneficiation. In fact, it had been described by Barba in 1640 in *El arte de los metales* and by Gamboa himself in the *Comentarios*. Sonneschmidt, who settled in New Spain, later wrote a book about the patio method of mercury amalgamation, so he could "do justice to this outstanding method that Europeans had treated with great disdain."[104] Alzate, who in the 1760s and 1770s had assumed like everyone else the laggardness of mining in New Spain, acknowledged in the late 1780s that the artisanal knowledge produced in America was in many cases superior to the formal science of Europe.[105] "Those known as scavengers here for their practice of digging in outcroppings and scouring hills from top to bottom," he wrote, "could be professors at the College of Freiberg."[106]

Fausto de Elhuyar, who had studied at Freiberg, finally established the mining college in 1793. It was an expensive endeavor, requiring the importation of scientific equipment and the hiring of professors from Europe. Few of its graduates, however, wanted to get their hands dirty in actual mine work. The sons of miners who attended the college still preferred to pursue professional careers in Mexico City. Gamboa opposed the college from the start. He thought it would be far cheaper to endow a chair at the University of Mexico, at the cost of just 700 pesos a year, for the teaching of the requisite technical subjects. Mine surveyors could be trained in draftsmanship at the new Academy of San Carlos, established in 1781 to support the fine arts. After all, the tribunal was already contributing 5,000 pesos a year to support this school. Celebrating the mining college as the paradigmatic case of enlightened Bourbon reform ignores the fact that technical and scientific subjects could have been taught at much lesser cost at existing institutions. One of the most distinguished graduates of the mining college, the nineteenth-century

Figure 11. Photograph of the Palacio de Minería, where Mining Tribunal was held. One of the landmarks of downtown Mexico City, its durable grandeur obscures the failings of the organization it once housed. Photograph by Sandra Guerrero.

statesman Lucas Alamán admitted that it failed to live up to expectations: "its utility never matched its cost." [107]

The Mining Tribunal survived its late 1780s crisis. It continued to receive a share of the seignorage fee, which assured it a steady income. But even Elhuyar was ready to concede in 1813, as the rebellion that would lead to Mexican Independence gathered force, that the Mining Tribunal had done next to nothing to contribute to the prosperity of mining. "Its income," he wrote, "has served rather as a recourse for the Government than as the fund which the miners hoped would be used for their benefit." [108] The main beneficiary of the tribunal, it turned out, was the cash-strapped Spanish crown, which found it a useful intermediary to raise loans and donations. [109] Perhaps this had been its purpose all along.

Fortunately, mining prospered in New Spain in spite of the tribunal. It continued to attract entrepreneurs, including many immigrants from Spain, eager to stake claims or take over old mines. The rising population of New Spain assured that operators rarely lacked workers willing to risk life and limb for partidos and above-average daily wages. Merchants still financed mining projects. And big miners continued to receive government support without any assistance from the tribunal. In fact, in the late 1780s, agreements like that pioneered by José Alejandro Bustamante and Pedro Romero Terreros at Real del Monte became standard in the industry. Beneficiaries included the Fagoaga family at Sombrerete, Juan Francisco Echarri in Oaxaca, Juan de Sierra y Uruñuela at Bolaños, and Miguel Pacheco Solís in Real del Monte.[110] These men were all major operators, many of Basque descent, with good relationships with merchant-financiers and proven records of success. They were also among those who first criticized Velázquez de León and Lassaga back in 1782. By 1790 the crown had processed enough applications to develop a formula for these public-private arrangements. For instance, miners would receive reductions in royalties owed until the completion of a specific project, such as the excavation of a drainage adit. They received blasting powder at cost but not discounted mercury.[111] This casuistic approach was what Gamboa had recommended in the *Comentarios* of 1761; the crown should support miners on a case-by-case basis.[112] There was no need for a guild for miners, especially one with exclusive jurisdiction over legal matters. Perhaps its magnificent neoclassical headquarters, designed by Manual Tolsá and completed in 1813, known today as the Palace of Mining, has always given the false impression of the stature of the organization it once housed.

CHAPTER SEVEN

The Resilience of the Old Order

Perhaps you knew there the regent of this Audiencia, Gamboa, when he was
the deputy of the Consulado in charge of pursuing various matters before
the court and then certainly when he was ordered out of this kingdom at the
time of the Jesuit expulsion; in sum, all of his sorry history, as he has proven
to be disobedient, petulant, and not at all loyal to the interests of the king, and
therefore extremely dangerous in these kingdoms, for which he was made to
leave and should not have returned except for Porlier.

—CONDE DE REVILLAGIGEDO, VICEROY OF NEW SPAIN, 1790

✦ FRANCISCO XAVIER DE GAMBOA PROVED AS TOUGH AS THE LEGAL
order he long served. He survived five long years in Santo Domingo, separated from his family and friends in Mexico City. There he joined an ambitious if frustrated attempt to revitalize the Dominican economy. He outlasted
his nemesis José de Gálvez, who died in 1787. The following year Antonio de
Porlier, the new minister of the Indies in charge of matters of justice, named
Gamboa to the regency of the Real Audiencia of Mexico, a rather remarkable
turn of events for a judge so often at odds with the Spanish Empire's top
policy makers. His appointment, however, proved that the old juridical order
of local custom, casuistic adjudication, and judicial independence had largely
withstood the challenges of Gálvez and the Bourbon reforms.[1] In a diverse,
far-flung empire, with a state far weaker than ambitious imperial reformers
cared to admit, a flexible approach to law was simply a necessity. It was
impossible to enforce strictly written law made in Spain by ministers who
lacked practical knowledge of conditions on the other side of the ocean.
Justice and mercy, rooted in a Christian conception of human society,

149

remained values the Spanish crown could not abandon if it wanted to maintain order and sovereignty in America.[2]

Yet some things did change for the worse, especially in the eyes of jurists like Gamboa. The already complex jurisdictional matrix of Spanish America became even more bewildering, thanks to the proliferation of exemptions to ordinary jurisdiction promoted by Gálvez. In this sense, Bourbon or Galvesian reform in New Spain did more to fragment than consolidate authority. It was only natural that Gamboa and other magistrates would fight tooth and nail to defend their jurisdictional turf; after all, their power and prestige depended on it. But others without such obvious self-interest raised the same alarm. In his 1794 instructions to his successor, the viceroy of New Spain, the Conde de Revillagigedo, argued that the erosion of ordinary jurisdiction due to the proliferation of exemptions undermined public respect for the law and legal system. Litigation became even more tortuous as parties fought increasingly over questions of jurisdiction. Everyone, Revillagigedo claimed, now presumed to enjoy some waiver from ordinary civil and criminal laws. Gamboa exasperated Revillagigedo. As regent, Gamboa constantly challenged the much younger viceroy. They fought over the proper honors audiencia magistrates should receive at the viceregal palace and the quantity of barley consumed by horses in Mexico City. The viceroy thought the crown should never have let Gamboa back into New Spain, let alone to head the audiencia. But Revillagigedo did agree with Gamboa on one fundamental question of government: justice would best be guaranteed by maintaining, rather than restricting, the ordinary jurisdiction exercised by the audiencias.

Going to Santo Domingo

Santo Domingo, Spain's first American colony, founded by Christopher Columbus in 1493, was nearly forgotten by the eighteenth century. In contrast, its neighbor on the western side of the island of Hispaniola, French Saint-Domingue, was the most valuable piece of colonial real estate in the world. Its plantations, worked by African slaves, produced half of the world's sugar and coffee and a third of France's total overseas trade. By the 1780s the French were bringing to the colony over thirty thousand African slaves a year. About 90 percent of Saint-Domingue's total population of half a million were enslaved Africans.[3] Although the first place in America to employ

African slaves in sugar production, Spanish Santo Domingo never became a full-fledged sugar colony or slave society. Only about 15 percent of its population of around sixty thousand were slaves.[4] It was known more for its runaway slave communities than its plantations. Its most important economic activity was cattle ranching. The Spanish crown maintained it thanks to a 200,000 peso annual transfer from New Spain. But it remained the seat of an audiencia, the oldest in America, exercising jurisdiction over the entire Spanish Caribbean, including the more dynamic Spanish colonies of Cuba, Puerto Rico, and Venezuela.

Just as Gamboa arrived, the Spanish crown was finally turning its attention to Santo Domingo. Inspired by the success of French Saint-Domingue, Spain belatedly wanted to turn its side of the island into another sugar plantation colony, with an enslaved African work force. The effort began in the early 1780s when a Spanish entrepreneur, Juan Bautista de Oyarzabal, purchased an old sugar mill. To rehabilitate it, he sought concessions from the Spanish crown, including preferential access to African slaves. He was sufficiently connected in Madrid to spur the Council of the Indies to action. Bernardo de Iriarte, a minister *de capa y espada* of the Council (a councilor without judicial responsibilities), saw Oyarzabal's request as an opportunity to formulate a more general economic plan for Santo Domingo, similar to what the crown had implemented with success in Cuba after 1763.

Bernardo de Iriarte was the nephew of Juan de Iriarte, the classics scholar and royal librarian under Philip V, and the older brother of the poet Tomás de Iriarte, the author of *Fábulas literarias*, a Spanish best seller in the early 1780s.[5] He coincidently already knew Gamboa. In his first letter, apprising him of the project, Iriarte asked the new regent if he remembered him from Madrid.[6] Gamboa replied to Iriarte that "your image remains so fresh in my memory that I could paint it with a brush."[7] He recalled meeting the two Iriarte boys in the house of their uncle Juan, which he had frequented during his time as the deputy of the consulado in Madrid. He also told Iriarte how much he enjoyed his brother's *Fábulas literarias*, which poked fun at Spanish literary personalities. Gamboa pledged to help Iriarte in any way possible. Work on the project, he said, might help to provide "the exhilarating spirit to revive this cadaver."[8]

Gamboa included with his March 1785 reply to Iriarte his own assessment of the island and the work done so far on the project.[9] He praised the new slave code drafted by a young Basque oidor on the audiencia, Agustín de Emparán.[10] This was the centerpiece of the entire project. Gamboa, who owned domestic slaves in Mexico and surely employed them in Santo Domingo as well, judged Emparán's proposed law more humane that the famous 1685 *Code Noir* of the French Caribbean. He did propose one interesting modification: the crown attorney of the Audiencia of Santo Domingo should act as the official protector of the blacks on the island, both free and enslaved, just as crown attorneys on the mainland served as protectors of the Natives in matters before the audiencias.

Gamboa was hardly optimistic, however, about the prospect of success in making over the economy of Santo Domingo. The big problem, he said, was the large population of free blacks and escaped slaves, living entirely "outside of justice and religion" in the mountains. They would have to be forcibly resettled before a stable plantation society could be established. He thought that the people living in the coastal lowlands, whether white, black, or mulatto, were hardly more industrious than the escaped slaves in the mountains. They survived, he claimed, on bananas and cassava and the export of cattle illegally to the British and French islands. Gamboa believed it would be necessary to bring European immigrants to Santo Domingo to make its fertile but neglected river valleys and coastal plains flourish. In his disdain for the local people of Santo Domingo, Gamboa sounded a lot like one of the arrogant Spanish officials sent to New Spain at the time of the visita.

Throughout 1785, the effort to reform Santo Domingo gathered momentum. In the city of Santo Domingo, the cabildo and audiencia agreed on a plan to improve public security. It divided the city into four precincts, each headed by an audiencia magistrate and patrolled by two alcaldes de barrio. This reform had already been implemented in Madrid and Mexico City.[11] In addition, the freed blacks who lived around the city—described uncharitably by the magistrates of the audiencia as "beasts, savages, runaways, who had robbed from their inattentive masters their freedom"—would be resettled in the nearby town of San Lorenzo de las Minas.[12] Meanwhile, in Madrid in June 1785, Iriarte submitted his plan to the Council of the Indies for its consideration and sent a copy to Gamboa.[13] On April 12, 1786, the crown issued a royal cédula approving the plan. It provided for the tax-free importation of slaves and equipment for sugar mills into Santo Domingo, the enactment of Emparán's draft slave code, the rounding up and resettlement of runaway slaves, tax exemptions for planters, regulations to prevent the contraband trade of beef products, and the legalization of mahogany exports and rum production.[14]

There was just one catch. No one had bothered to consult the locals. They wanted nothing to do with the makeover of their island home. According to Gamboa, the bishop of Santo Domingo almost had a heart attack when he learned that the church would have to lower the interest rate it charged on loans from 5 to 3 percent in order to jumpstart development. The powerful cattle ranchers attacked the proposed price control on beef, which was intended to encourage domestic consumption over contraband exports. Even the local military commanders objected. They had been assigned the formidable task of capturing escaped slaves and resettling them in towns under government control. How could you reimpose slavery in a society full of people who had already escaped its shackles? Without a strong local constituency in favor of the plan, it didn't stand a chance. Gamboa sympathized more with the outside reformers than the local population. Throwing up his hands, he confessed to Iriarte "this island is utterly miserable in all its actions."[15] Of course, the failure to go forward with the plan soon proved to be a blessing. Just a few years later French Saint-Domingue, the model for the new Santo Domingo, erupted in the largest and most consequential slave rebellion in history.[16]

The Audiencia of Santo Domingo

Gamboa occupied most of his time on the island supervising the small but busy audiencia. It employed four royal magistrates and one crown attorney. In the mid-1780s, the court handled several hundred civil and criminal cases a year.[17] They ran the gamut from property disputes between heirs to contested sales of slaves to charges of illicit sexual relationships. Many were *causas de oficio*, cases originated by government officials rather than private individuals. While the court exercised first instance jurisdiction in Santo Domingo, the majority of the cases came from off island, especially from Venezuela and Cuba. In these cases, the audiencia mostly exercised its review and appeal functions, examining the writs and documents relating to cases decided by local justices or determining legal questions referred by local officials.

In 1786 the audiencia complained to Madrid that it needed help to handle its heavy caseload. The court asked for funds to hire local lawyers to assist the crown attorney.[18] Some relief came when the new Audiencia of Caracas began operations in 1787 to handle all Venezuelan cases. In 1788 the Council of the Indies did approve the hiring of one local lawyer of good reputation to assist the crown attorney.[19] But it was unwilling to spend more in Santo Domingo, such as on a new courthouse. By the end of the eighteenth century, military spending clearly took priority over the administration of justice, especially in a Caribbean colony like Santo Domingo.

Like elsewhere, the military fuero, the exemption that soldiers enjoyed from ordinary jurisdiction, caused trouble for judges in Santo Domingo. A case in early 1786 illustrated how jurisdictional exemptions complicated the administration of justice. One of the new alcaldes de barrio appointed under the 1785 municipal reform, Antonio González Cobos, arrested two fishermen, Bernardo Guzmán and Pedro de la Cruz, for failing to deliver their catch to the public market as required by local regulation. Instead, they sold their fish directly to a shopkeeper at a higher price. The interim military governor of Santo Domingo, Joaquin García, came to the men's defense, claiming they enjoyed the protection of the military fuero since Guzmán belonged to the local militia, and Cruz served as an ensign in the navy.[20] Gamboa refused to relinquish the audiencia's authority over the men or release them from jail.[21] He probably remembered his own days patrolling the streets of Mexico City as an alcalde del crimen in the 1760s; the military fuero then had blocked him from arresting soldiers who had caused a drunken ruckus in front of a pulqueria.[22] García, the military governor, complained to José de Gálvez about Gamboa's refusal to respect the military fuero. Gálvez, if he took any notice of the case, might have agreed with Gamboa for a change. The Council of the Indies as a whole did. In its opinion, it ruled that the military fuero should not protect militiamen and sailors when they broke the law in activities unrelated to their military service.[23] This decision, however, set no binding precedent in a legal system with a casuistic orientation.

Life in Santo Domingo must have been extremely lonely for Gamboa. He enjoyed the company of Emparán but missed his family in Mexico City. Letters from home would have reminded him of the poor health of his wife and daughters. Just like during his exile in Valladolid in the early 1770s, Maria Manuela wrote plaintive letters to crown officials, including Gálvez, begging for the return of her husband. In late 1785 she told the minister of the Indies that she yearned for "the sweet company of my husband, whose memory, day and night, in every moment, crucifies me in the midst of the grave sufferings of myself and those of my poor daughters."[24] In 1786 an opportunity arose to return Gamboa to New Spain when the regency of the Real Audiencia of Mexico became vacant. But Gálvez chose instead Eusebio

Sánchez Pareja, a veteran Spanish judge, as the new regent of the court.[25] This might have closed the door on any hope Gamboa entertained that he would live to see his family again.

His despair might explain but hardly justified his harsh treatment of the Labastida family. Juan Labastida, the father, was a treasury official and former lawyer on the Audiencia of Santo Domingo. His son was also lawyer while his daughter, Manuela, was married, unhappily, to the porter of the court. One night Manuela fled her abusive husband and returned to her father's house. Gamboa intervened, insisting he had authority over the matter as the regent of the audiencia, and forced the young woman to return to her husband. When she ran away again, Gamboa, accompanied by the sheriff of the court, arrested her and fined her father 200 pesos for contempt of court. He claimed the whole family was notorious for making trouble and deserved no sympathy. The Labastidas complained to the Council of the Indies. Its crown attorney criticized Gamboa but reserved judgment until additional documentation arrived from Santo Domingo.[26] From the evidence at hand, it would appear Gamboa put a young woman at risk of serious harm simply to exercise his authority as the regent of the audiencia.

On June 17, 1787, just as this disturbing matter reached the Council of the Indies, José de Gálvez died in Madrid. He had undoubtedly accomplished a lot in his government career. In New Spain as visitor general he established the lucrative crown tobacco monopoly and pushed through reductions in mercury prices, which boosted silver production. As minister of the Indies, he oversaw the creation of the Viceroyalty of Rio de la Plata in 1776 and the end of Cadiz's monopoly over imperial trade with the *libre comercio* decree of 1778.[27] He could take some credit for soaring crown revenue from the Indies, although the administrative reforms he pushed through were probably less important than general demographic and economic growth. But he did not come close to accomplishing all he set out to do. There were always too many contradictions in his approach. For instance, Gálvez might have railed against nepotistic creoles but relied on his own kin from Málaga, who proved just as determined to enrich themselves in royal service as the men they replaced.[28] It took over twenty years for the intendancy reform, presented as a priority in 1765, to finally be implemented in New Spain and South America in diluted form. The jurists he convened in Madrid to rewrite the 1680 *Recopilación de las leyes de Indias*, which he thought would be a simple job, made scant progress in turning it into a decisive law code for America.[29] The visita to Peru he authorized, headed by José Antonio de

Areche, who had served in the Sala de Crimen with Gamboa in the 1760s, triggered a cascade of indigenous rebellions in the Andes, the biggest threat to Spanish rule in colonial history.[30] In New Spain, Gálvez's attempt to tighten his personal control failed when both his brother Matías and then nephew Bernardo died shortly after taking office as viceroy.[31]

The death of Gálvez upturned Gamboa's fortunes. Gálvez was succeeded by Antonio de Porlier in a reorganized ministry of the Indies, exercising authority over matters of justice and grace. Porlier had served for almost twenty years in the audiencias of Charcas and Lima. He was another of the veteran Spanish officials, like Tomás Ortiz de Landázuri and Antonio María de Bucareli, who saw little reason to renovate the legal regime of Spanish America. When an opportunity to return Gamboa to New Spain unexpectedly arose, with the retirement of Eusebio Sánchez Pareja after just one year as regent of the Real Audiencia of Mexico, Porlier named Gamboa to the position.[32] Gamboa was overjoyed. He called Porlier "my redeemer," who had silenced "the clamors of my family anguished by my absence."[33] After a stop in Havana, where more misfortune struck—a servant absconded with over 2,000 pesos, set aside for travel expenses and the *media anata* tax he owed upon assuming the regency—Gamboa made it back to Mexico City in April 1788.[34] In forty years of marriage, Gamboa had lived apart from his wife María Manuela for eighteen of them. He was at least with her at the end; she died in 1789 at the age of fifty-nine.[35]

The Regency of Mexico

Gamboa took the oath of office as the regent of the Real Audiencia of Mexico on April 29, 1788. It was an astonishing comeback for a judge twice exiled from New Spain due to his differences with the government. All the same, even though he had reached the top of the judicial hierarchy, he still feared, he confessed to Porlier, the "pens of the Indies." His enemies had attacked him in the past with scurrilous charges and they were likely do so again. He mentioned two likely adversaries, Pedro de Moncada y Branciforte, the estranged husband of Mariana de Berrio, the daughter of Gamboa's close friend Miguel de Berrio. Moncada was still furious that Gamboa had helped Berrio set up the entailed estate that denied him and his former wife the family's fortune.[36] More dangerous still was the archbishop of Mexico, Alonso Núñez de Haro y Peralta. He had nothing personally against Gamboa, but the imperious cleric, who briefly served as viceroy after the sudden death of Bernardo de Gálvez in 1786, still demanded to be treated with the full honors of the office. According to Gamboa, all audiencia magistrates kept their heads down and votes secret when dealing with the irascible Núñez de Haro.[37]

The crown introduced the position of regent in 1776 to improve the internal administration of the high courts.[38] The regent handled work formerly done by the president, which in the case of the Real Audiencia of Mexico was the viceroy himself, and the senior oidor, or *décano*. Since Madrid appointed the regent while the décano gained his position through seniority, the reform promised the crown greater royal control over the audiencias. But it did not work out quite this way. Most regents defended their institutions against any measures, including reform initiatives, they thought might compromise their jurisdiction and power.

Before Gamboa, the most notable occupant of the regency of Mexico was Vicente de Herrera, who served from 1782 to 1786. Herrera, born in Santander in northern Spain, had quickly risen up the judicial ladder, starting off in 1764 as the crown attorney in the Audiencia of Santo Domingo. He then served in the Real Audiencia of Mexico, first in its criminal chamber and then, from 1774 to 1776, beside Gamboa in the civil chamber. In 1776 the crown named him the first regent of the Audiencia of Guatemala. Before assuming the same position in Mexico in 1782, Herrera sent Gálvez a long memorandum on the administration of justice in Spanish America.[39] Gamboa would have agreed with almost all of it.

The worst problem for Herrera was the continual shrinkage in the jurisdiction of the audiencias. Echoing Solórzano, who had called them "the stone fortresses of the Indies," Herrera described the high courts as "bulwarks of justice, which are as necessary for the survival of the Republic as is the heart for man and the sun for the day."[40] Yet the crown had created numerous exceptions to their authority that hampered their effectiveness in delivering justice. In Herrera's opinion, the diminution of the jurisdiction of the audiencias was "the surest beginning for the disorder and ruin of a Republic."[41]

Herrera pleaded for more support from the Spanish crown for the court system of northern Spanish America. In New Spain, he recommended the creation of two new high courts, one in Sonora to handle the northern provinces of the viceroyalty and another in Oaxaca in the south, where Native farming villages had long handled their own matters of justice with little involvement by royal judges. Herrera thought these new audiencias should have separate civil and criminal chambers like the Real Audiencia of Mexico. To relieve the burden of the Audiencia of Santo Domingo, he called for new courts in Caracas (which was done in 1787) and Havana. He also suggested an audiencia in Nicaragua, which was then under the Audiencia of Guatemala. There is little doubt that the expansion of the audiencia system would have made the delivery of justice faster and more effective. After all, the vast swath of territory from California to Venezuela, despite dramatic demographic and economic expansion, still had the same judicial infrastructure as two hundred years earlier. But cost remained the issue. The crown had to prioritize military spending at a time of increasing imperial competition in the Atlantic world.

Herrera also proposed an intriguing reform for local justice administered by the alcaldes mayores. Since the late sixteenth century, no one had a kind word to say about these officials, entrusted with hearing cases in first instance as well as general administrative duties, such as the collection of tribute. In 1641 Juan de Palafox, the bishop of Puebla and scourge of the Jesuits, complained to the king that "in the high courts some justice is done, but the alcaldes mayores do little justice or none at all. . . . [They] are the ruin of these provinces and the least necessary magistrates."[42] Many of these local judges supplemented their incomes by acting as agents of city merchants, providing credit and goods to people in their districts, a practice known as the *reparto* or *repartimiento de mercancías*.[43] To combat their veniality and motivate them to administer justice more conscientiously, Herrera proposed not just paying them better salaries (hardly a novel suggestion) but creating a new promotion ladder.[44] Just as the hope of rising up the ranks in the audiencia hierarchy helped to keep alcaldes de crimen and oidores in line, the same would presumably work for local judges. They would be more likely to administer justice diligently in the provinces if they knew their reward would be a promotion to a more attractive place in time. Such a reform, incidentally, would also make the proposed intendancy system unnecessary; no audiencia magistrate contemplated that reform with equanimity.

Herrera made one especially curious recommendation in his report to Gálvez. The crown should positively encourage audiencia magistrates to marry into families in their districts. Since the sixteenth century, the crown had tried, mostly in vain, to keep judges detached from local society to protect their impartiality. Audiencia judges and even their children needed royal permission to marry within district. Yet even Gálvez admitted in his final report as visitor general in 1771 that the fear behind this rule was overblown; magistrates recused themselves in any cases in which their personal or family interests were at stake.[45] Herrera argued that marriages between Spanish audiencia magistrates and American women served a political purpose: they united families across the ocean and thus promoted greater imperial cohesion. This turned out to be a rather self-serving argument. Once Herrera arrived in New Spain from Guatemala, he met a young woman, none other than the daughter of Pedro Romero Terreros. Although she was apparently reluctant to marry the much older Spanish judge, Herrera received the crown's permission, the couple married, and he immediately became a very rich man.[46]

Herrera's report represented the view of most legal professionals in New Spain, especially those in higher judicial positions. It was a warning to the crown not to take the administration of justice for granted. Rather than seeing the power of the audiencias as a problem that impeded economic and administrative reforms, Herrera held to the older idea that the delivery of justice, handled by strong and autonomous institutions, was the best way for Spain to govern its American dominions.

The Intendancy Reform

There was little prospect of Madrid acting on Herrera's proposals as long as Gálvez remained minister of the Indies. He would not give up on the intendancy system. The idea of appointing royal intendants, who would report directly to Madrid rather than the viceroy or audiencias, was first raised in the early 1740s in the *Nuevo sistema de gobierno económico para América* attributed to José Campillo.[47] The plan entailed dividing New Spain up into twelve or so departments, each one under an intendant. These officials would exercise broad jurisdiction over judicial, economic, and military affairs. They would appoint subdelegates to handle the tasks formerly assigned to alcaldes mayores, such as first instance adjudication and the collection of Indian tribute. The system, based on the French system of provincial administration, was implemented in Spain in 1749 and in Cuba in 1764. In January 1768, when he first presented the plan for New Spain, Gálvez sold it as a way to restore order to colonial administration. He proclaimed that those opposed to it "were only interested in anarchy and disorder, and others who did not take the trouble of examining the abuses, but rather venerated them in the name of the old system."[48]

Intendants would wield immense power in their districts with little over-sight. According to Gálvez's original plan, a person would not be able to appeal a decision by an intendant to the audiencia, even though one could still appeal a viceregal decision to the audiencia. This reform would deci-sively shift power away from the judiciary in New Spain to executive-style administrators accountable only to the minister of the Indies. Most veteran officials condemned the plan. According to Juan Pizarro de Aragón, the president of the Council of the Indies in 1768, the scheme would "change a method of government observed since the conquest, sanctioned by numer-ous laws, ordinances, and royal cédulas issued by ministers endowed with the greatest intelligence and prudence." Pizarro wrote there was no need to standardize administration across the empire since "the diversity of nations calls for differences in government and the remedies appropriate for the head do not always benefits the other parts of the body." [49] This might have come straight from the pen of Solórzano, who had urged the Spanish monarchy to celebrate the variety of its American domains. [50]

Viceroy Bucareli of New Spain helped to keep it off the table throughout the 1770s. He counted on the firm support of the Real Audiencia of Mexico. The Basque oidor Francisco Leandro de Viana, who arrived in New Spain in 1768 after a stint in Manila, wrote a particularly scathing critique of the intendancy plan, focusing on its fiscal implications. [51] There was simply no need, he said, to make radical changes in tax collection; revenue was flowing better than ever. Viana, married to a rich pulque heiress, knew that the crown was reaping higher profits every year from taxes on New Spain's most popular alcoholic beverage. [52] According to Viana, the intendancy system would cost more money than it would bring in. As for the much-derided repartimiento de mercancía, by which alcaldes mayores profited from the sale of goods, Viana defended the practice. He said it served the essential function of drawing Natives into the cash economy. If the crown really wanted to stop abuses against the poor Natives, the solution was not to deny them goods and credit from local officials but to give them more land, as the original plan of Campillo had proposed. [53]

Another notable critic of the intendancy plan was Antonio de Ulloa, the main author of the *Noticias secretas*, which had exposed the corruption of government in Peru in the 1740s. [54] As a young naval officer accompanying the French geodesic mission to South America, Ulloa shared the assump-tion among enlightened thinkers in Madrid that the system of government in the Indies needed urgent repair. But after a long career as an imperial administrator, which included controversial stints as the administrator of the Huancavelica mercury mine in Peru and as the first Spanish governor of Louisiana, Ulloa had come to appreciate the old system. However improvisationally, it managed to balance the differing interests of the crown and local subjects. While in New Spain in 1778 as the commander of the last fleet dispatched from Cadiz, Ulloa confided to his friend Bucareli that he failed "to understand what improvement [the Intendancy] will bring the King. In order to support the loyalty of the subjects here, we must respect their distinct liberties."[55] He predicted that intendants and their subdelegates would enrich themselves, just like the alcaldes mayores they would replace, but with even more tools at their disposal. This would surely alienate the local population and destroy New Spain's two greatest assets, its silver mines and its Native population.[56]

Why did the crown finally approve the intendancy system in New Spain and South America if so many respected and veteran officials rallied against it? Just as with the Mining Tribunal, the answer seems to be simply that Gálvez had the power as minister of the Indies to push it through. To be sure, in most matters he had the backing of José Moñino, Conde de Floridablanca, the chief minister of Charles III since 1777. For Gálvez, the intendants offered him another way to control New Spain after the deaths in quick succession of his brother and nephew as viceroys. He handpicked all of the new officials, who arrived in New Spain 1786 and 1787.

Just like the Mining Tribunal, the intendancy reform failed to live up to the expectations of its backers.[57] To begin with, the crown failed to fund it properly. The local subdelegates who answered to the intendants and handled local matters received as salary just 5 percent of the Native tribute they collected. This varied greatly across districts and was rarely enough to deter them from engaging in the same practices as alcaldes mayores: they signed up as agents for city merchants to distribute goods and credit to the people in their local districts.[58] After the death of Gálvez in 1787, the crown heeded the advice of critics like Porlier and created in New Spain a supervisory board to oversee the intendants, made up of the viceroy, the regent of the audiencia, the crown attorney for Hacienda, and other senior treasury officials.[59] In the end, as David Brading pointed out, the old Habsburg institutions of viceroy and audiencia managed to remain on top.[60]

Gamboa thus found himself as regent exercising significant influence over the new officials he considered totally unnecessary. It is hard to think of better revenge against the legacy of his long-time nemesis Gálvez. Gamboa resisted every push by the intendants to exercise their authority at the expense of the high courts. For example, he opposed their attempt to take over the administration of intestate estates, a job long handled by audiencia magistrates.[61] Gamboa also insisted that an audiencia magistrate, not an intendant, should continue to serve, as he had in the 1770s, as supervisor of New Spain's state lottery.[62] He pushed back on efforts by intendants to assert themselves as superior in rank to ordinary audiencia members. He demanded that in public ceremonies intendants accord magistrates the traditional honors they received as representatives of the king in matters of justice. He was appalled by the presumption of the intendant in Mexico City to demand notification of resolutions taken by the audiencia.[63]

Gamboa's intransigence especially exasperated Manuel de Flon, the intendant of Puebla and brother-in-law of Gálvez's nephew Bernardo de Gálvez. In a letter to Diego de Gardoqui, the minister of finance in Madrid, Flon asked, "what will we say about America, whose inhabitants have the misfortune of living so far from the Sovereign and can not count on any other protection than the exact and punctual compliance with the written royal will?" He then attacked Gamboa:

> This man, who as a native of this kingdom and for his advanced age, should not command in it, let alone lead it, is the decisive vote in many deliberations. Because of his character, fertile in machinations, he easily attracts others to his side and uses them for whatever mischief he finds convenient. This evil would not be so bad if this minister conducted himself in all things with a loyal and sincere desire to carry out the great responsibilities with which the king has entrusted him. Disgracefully, however, he instead commonly favors the worst interest.[64]

Fortunately for Gamboa, Spain was far more concerned at the time with revolution in France than bickering among its officials in America.

Revillagigedo the Younger, the Last of the Bourbon Reformers

Gamboa's tenure as chief justice of the Real Audiencia of Mexico coincided with the government of Juan Vicente de Güemes, the second Conde de Revillagigedo, the son of the first, viceroy of New Spain from 1746 to 1755. If his father can be considered the first of the Bourbon reformers in New Spain—an

Figure 12. Juan Vicente de Güemes, the second Conde de Revillagigedo, viceroy from 1789 to 1794. If his father was the first, he might be considered the last of the Bourbon reformers in New Spain. Photograph by Leonardo Hernández; reproduced by permission of the Instituto Nacional de Antropología e Historia.

assertive army general who oversaw tax reform (ending the consulado's collection of the alcabala), promoted Spanish economic interests (allowing Cadiz merchants to establish themselves in Mexico City), and challenged the authority of the audiencias (inviting the Acordada to patrol Mexico City and stripping the Audiencia of Guadalajara of jurisdiction over Bolaños)—his son can fairly be seen as the last of the breed. But if they lacked reverence for the established customs and institutions of America, both understood, unlike Gálvez, the necessity of good relations with creoles. In the opinion of the second Revillagigedo, Gálvez had "completely exasperated the hearts of people born in America." [65] He heard through Thomas Jefferson, the envoy of the United States government in Paris at the time, that Britain was waiting to pounce on New Spain at the first sign of disaffection with Spanish rule. Revillagigedo's two governing maxims as viceroy were to restrict all contact between New Spain and Britain's remaining Caribbean colonies and to foster genuine love for the Spanish crown among its American subjects. [66]

Despite his avowed concern to keep Americans happy, his relationship with Gamboa, the most senior creole official in New Spain's government, got off to an inauspicious start. Soon after taking power on October 17, 1789, Revillagigedo notified Gamboa and Archbishop Núñez de Haro that the palace guards would no longer do them the honor of performing a military salute when they arrived for ceremonial occasions.[67] The raising of guns and beating of drums were reserved, he said, for the viceroy alone in his capacity as captain general of New Spain. He cited written law, the military ordinances of 1728 and 1768, in support of this position.[68]

Gamboa immediately protested to the king. The military salute accorded to all audiencia magistrates by the palace guards was an ancient custom that recognized the dignity and power of the high court. The high court, in his reckoning, was not just independent of the viceroy but even superior. "This audiencia is the supreme tribunal of the kingdom and does not recognize any superior other than your Sovereign, whom it directly represents and, in matters of justice, it hears appeals from the decisions of the viceroy."[69] Denying magistrates the same honor as the viceroy would diminish the high court in the eyes of the public. Revillagigedo replied to this in the typical style of a Bourbon reformer: it did not matter if "customs were immemorial, as long as they are contrary to royal determinations."[70] Archbishop Núñez de Haro also complained that people would lose respect for him and his ecclesiastical office if the military salute ceased.[71] The Council of the Indies decided that, in this case, local custom should prevail over royal statute. It urged Revillagigedo to restore the honorary salute.[72]

Revillagigedo seemed to learn a lesson from this initial fracas with Gamboa: it was better to consult the cranky old regent before taking any action that might incur his wrath. Over the next few years, the viceroy asked Gamboa's opinion, often obsequiously, on a plethora of questions. Handled properly, the regent could be an invaluable resource. For instance, in October 1789, the viceroy asked Gamboa to look over a new manuscript on the history of New Spain written by Diego Panes, a military officer. Perhaps making a tongue in cheek reference to Gamboa's age, Revillagigedo praised Gamboa's "high character and the Enlightenment that you famously possess on the antiquities and events of this New Spain before and after the conquest."[73] In his discussions with Gamboa over urban reform Revillagigedo said "I am persuaded that your talent, application, and practical knowledge of this city and experience in this government must have provided you with the wisdom that is not easy to acquire."[74] When Revillagigedo asked him to comment on proposed revisions to the legislation regulating pulquerías, Gamboa could reply "I was there at their formation," and could recite from memory what the viceroy's father had done forty years earlier.[75] The two men ended up communicating with each other almost daily, even if their relationship was frosty to say the least.

Cleaning Up Mexico City

Like almost all people not born and raised in New Spain, Revillagigedo was appalled by the conditions he found in Mexico City. The magnificence of its palaces, churches, and convents clashed with the ramshackle poverty of many of its inhabitants. It was a city of wealthy merchants and filthy beggars. The main square was packed with makeshift market stalls, a single fountain used by poor women to clean the diapers of their babies, and a public lavatory that gave off an unbearable stench. One corner was used by thieves to sell pilfered merchandise and another by the Sala del Crimen to punish criminals.[76] The streets radiating out from the square were littered with household waste and dead animals. Summer downpours flooded the canals that intersected the city, washing raw sewage back into the streets. Even the viceregal palace was little more than "a fancy tenement," according to the chronicler Francisco Sedano. Night and day people gathered within its patios to eat, drink, gamble, and draw graffiti on its walls.[77]

In the fall of 1789 Revillagigedo initiated an ambitious program of urban renewal, beginning with the refurbishment of the main square, now known as the Zócalo.[78] After clearing out all the market stalls and other structures, work crews lowered the level of the plaza by more than a meter. In so doing they unearthed a massive stone disc, now known as the Piedra del Sol, or Aztec calendar stone, as well as a statute of Coatlicue, the Aztec earth goddess.[79] They then installed a drainage system, erected ornate fountains at each corner of the square, and covered the vast expanse with new paving stones. The market was relocated to the nearby Volador plaza. Revillagigedo also ordered repairs to the city's aqueducts and the construction of new neighborhood fountains. He instituted the first regular garbage collection for the city.[80] Thirty years after Madrid was cleaned up in the early years of the reign of Charles III, Mexico City received the same treatment. Gamboa, incidentally, was present for both.

The problem was how to pay for these desirable civic improvements. The municipal government complained that the viceroy had left it with the bill for the resurfacing of the plaza, which they estimated cost five or six times the 23,000 pesos claimed by the viceroy. In the summer of 1790 Revillagigedo sought Gamboa's advice on how to raise revenue to pay for street paving and illumination. The viceroy proposed a new tax on barley, the main feed for horses, since these animals caused the most damage to the streets. To pay for streetlights, he suggested a surcharge on rents. Gamboa disagreed vehemently with both ideas. "Believe me, your Excellency, a tax on barley is a despicable measure, not to say an act of robbery."[81] He said it would hurt the poor Natives who brought it into the city and the *tocineros*, or pork butchers, who needed barley to fatten their pigs before slaughter. According to Gamboa's informant on the matter, Antonio Bassoco, the prominent Basque merchant and a main provisioner of meat for the city, butchers in Mexico City purchased over ten thousand bushels of barley a year to feed their pigs.[82] As for the viceroy's proposed surcharge on rents, Gamboa claimed that it would hurt poor residents the most. It would be better to raise the existing property tax, already authorized by law, to pay for both street paving and lights. For several weeks the viceroy and regent exchanged almost daily letters on such topics as pigs, barley, and street cleaning. Despite their disagreements, Revillagigedo reassured Gamboa that "I have read with pleasure your thinking and have seen with satisfaction that it manifests the desires to alleviate the burden on the public, which is the only thing I desire."[83]

At the same time Revillagigedo was flattering Gamboa, he was denouncing him to José Moñino, Conde de Floridablanca:

> Perhaps you knew there the regent of this Audiencia, Gamboa, when he was the deputy of the Consulado in charge of pursuing various matters before the court and then certainly when he was ordered out of this kingdom at the time of the Jesuit expulsion; in sum, all of his sorry history, as he has proven to be disobedient, petulant, and not at all loyal to the interests of the king, and therefore extremely dangerous in these kingdoms, for which he was made to leave and should not have returned except for Porlier.[84]

Floridablanca would certainly have remembered Gamboa. In 1768 he and Campomanes, then crown attorneys on the Council of Castile, had recommended that Gamboa be removed from New Spain because of his hostility to the government. In 1772 they allowed his return but warned him to keep his mouth shut in the future and stick to his judicial duties. Somehow this troublesome figure was now the top judicial official in Spain's most important American viceroyalty. In a subsequent letter to Floridablanca, Revillagigedo confessed "I will never have confidence in the regent because, as you know and as I have presented to you, he has been and still is a disobedient spirit, full of pride . . . and it is almost impossible to correct these defects now at his advanced age."[85] Gamboa was protected by his position at the top of the audiencia, which endowed him with independence, as well as the support of Porlier. All Revillagigedo and Gamboa's other enemies could hope for was that death would soon remove him from the field of battle.

Viceroy and regent went at it again in the spring of 1791. This time the issue was jurisdiction over the theater in Mexico City, which Revillagigedo wanted to refurbish after decades of neglect. The problem, however, was that the theater, known as the Coliseo Nuevo, inaugurated in 1753 under Revillagigedo's father, operated as a commercial arm of the Real Hospital de Indios, which was under the jurisdiction of the audiencia.[86] Revillagigedo argued that as viceroy he should exercise authority over the theater. After all, just a few years earlier, in 1786, Viceroy Bernardo de Gálvez had issued new regulations for theatrical productions, in an attempt to improve decency, decorum, and order. Gamboa rejected Revillagigedo's position and compared him unfavorably to his father, who always respected the jurisdiction of the audiencia over both the hospital and the theater. Gamboa admitted that he himself had little interest in the theater and never used the seats reserved for him as regent.[87]

Gamboa's refusal to consider any compromise to the audiencia's jurisdiction, which thus frustrated the viceroy's plan to remodel the theater, infuriated the touchy Revillagigedo. This time he complained to Porlier about Gamboa's "disrespectful tone, his lack of obedience to my commands, and the bad example of insubordination of a minister who should be the first to show his respect and submission to the superior head of the kingdom." [88] The theater needed repairs but Gamboa refused to allow them as long as his authority was not recognized. For Gamboa, it was more important to protect the audiencia than to fix up the theater. The Council of the Indies had to resolve the dispute. The Council recommended that the audiencia continue to exercise jurisdiction but only so that oidores could monitor theatrical productions, as their counterparts already did in Madrid.[89]

Revillagigedo's Reflections on the Justice System

In early 1794 Revillagigedo began to write the report that viceroys left their successors. It turned out to be the most extensive ever written by an outgoing viceroy. It covered every aspect of his government and gave frank opinions on what deserved the most attention in the future. Although his experience with Gamboa had evidently soured him on the office of regent—"I do not understand the need or utility of such magistrates"—he did share with Gamboa a deep preoccupation with the future of the administration of justice in New Spain. He echoed Herrera from a decade earlier in stating that the increase in jurisdictional exemptions constituted "a great nuisance and obstacle for the administration of justice, creating much delay with the frequent motions to deny a court's jurisdiction made by parties, more to gain time than to pursue justice in the action." [90] Besides the ecclesiastical exemption and the military fuero, whose beneficiaries had multiplied many times since the 1760s, Revillagigedo mentioned the specialized tribunals for Hacienda, the Tribunal de Cuentas, the Casa de la Moneda, and even the gunpowder and playing cards monopolies. Even the heirs of Hernán Cortés still enjoyed jurisdictional privileges. He criticized the adjudicative system of the Mining Tribunal, declaring that the local deputies had proven incapable of handling the responsibility. Revillagigedo told the crown that in his opinion the profusion of privileges and specialized tribunals had sapped public confidence in the law.

Revillagigedo also shared Gamboa's old concerns for the state of criminal justice in New Spain. Although like all viceroys before him, especially his father, Revillagigedo appreciated the effectiveness of the Acordada in fighting crime, he felt it needed judicial supervision. He praised the creation in 1787 of the panel to review its death sentences.[91] He also objected to the frequency of forced labor at the presidios as punishment. These were nothing better than "schools of criminality." [92] Thirty years earlier the viceroy of New Spain, the Marqués de Croix, had ordered the Sala de Crimen and the other criminal courts to send all their prisoners to the fortresses of Veracruz, Havana, and Manila; now the viceroy of New Spain was saying that Madrid should invest for the first time in the construction of prisons to house dangerous criminals. Coming from a military man, Revillagigedo's grim assessment of the justice system lends credence to what Gamboa, Herrera, and others had been saying for decades.

Revillagigedo was also critical of the intendancy system. Gálvez had botched the reform, he said, first by dividing the viceroyalty into too few districts. Rather than twelve intendancies, the crown should have created at least twenty. Secondly, Gálvez had selected men whose highest qualification was their loyalty to him. He should have "chosen persons knowledgeable about these kingdoms and the character of their inhabitants, and even experience in government matters."[93] Here in the words of the last dedicated reformer to occupy the viceregal palace in New Spain was one of the main weaknesses of the Galvesian style of imperial reform. Gálvez lacked confidence in local experts, especially creoles like Gamboa, because he thought they were just defending a system that served their own interests above those of Spain and the monarchy. So he had to rely on relatives, fellow *malagueños* and other Spanish outsiders, few of whom took the trouble of studying the place they were entrusted to administer. As for the intendancy system, Revillagigedo believed it had made no improvement at all at the local level. The new subdelegates under the intendants were no better than the old alcaldes mayores, unschooled in the law and focused primarily on self-enrichment.

The Death of the Regent

Gamboa's health had been in decline for years. By the evidence of his increasingly shaky handwriting, he suffered from tremors, perhaps even Parkinson's disease. The forced sojourn in Santo Domingo must have taken a heavy toll. Life tenure for audiencia magistrates had its obvious advantages but it also meant they had difficulty getting permission to retire at the end. Gamboa likely did not have the savings that would have allowed a comfortable retirement. His fortune, built up painstakingly in the 1740s and 1750s, had been drained by the crushing expenses incurred in his transfers to Spain in the early 1770s and Santo Domingo in the 1780s. His library, once one of the best in New Spain and a great source of personal pride, had been sold off piece by piece to pay his bills. He was still supporting his sick and unmarried daughters.

On June 4, 1794, Gamboa passed away at the age of seventy-six. Nuestra Señora de Aránzazu, the Basque lay brotherhood he joined as a young lawyer fifty years earlier, celebrated a funeral mass for him on June 17, in the chapel of the Vizcaínas, the residential school for girls whose charter he had written forty years earlier. He left behind at least four children but no grandchildren. His oldest daughters Gertrudis, Josepha, and Francisca, born in 1749, 1750, and 1753 respectively, had all suffered from poor health that prevented both marriage and convent life. Two of them might have predeceased their father. His oldest son Juan José, born in 1751, educated in Spain, enjoyed a long career as a canon in the cathedral chapter of Mexico City. In 1816 he sponsored the return, almost fifty years after they had been expelled, of the Jesuit order to New Spain.[94] Another son apparently died shortly after birth in 1754 and a third, Manuel, born in 1765, would marry Mariana Sandoval de la Vega in 1796. The couple would baptize eleven children between 1800 and 1824.[95] Gamboa's youngest child, Maria Dolores, was born in 1770. His son Manuel and two unmarried daughters applied for financial assistance as survivors from the Junta de Montepíos de ministros, the retirement fund established in 1770 for audiencia magistrates.[96]

José Antonio de Alzate published an obituary of Gamboa in his *Gacetas de México*.[97] Alzate had little to work with because "the Señor Regente always had a life full of work and other occupations, he never had time to organize the innumerable and valuable papers of his office." [98] Due to the lack of written sources, Alzate could only provide the broad-brush strokes of Gamboa's life and career. He noted that Gamboa, a brilliant student of jurisprudence, "dedicated himself to all sciences with equal ardor and looked in them for new lights to illuminate his understanding." [99] Gamboa's love of geometry, according to Alzate, sharpened his analytical thinking, his ability "to deduce from a single factor many consequences." [100] His immersion in philosophy, poetry, and history accounted for his eloquence as a jurisconsult. Drawing from the 1757 official curriculum, Alzate reviewed Gamboa's legal career, including his early courtroom triumph after the death of his mentor Méndez (whom Alzate mistakenly identified as Martínez); the various commissions he carried out for top viceregal authorities, including the Real Audiencia of Mexico and cathedral of Mexico City; and his published defense of Manuel de Rivas-Cacho. "It should not be surprising," he said, "that everyone saw him as the first lawyer of the kingdom." [101] Alzate especially paid homage to Gamboa's *Comentarios a las Ordenanzas de Minas*. He described it as "a volume of medium size that contains a library where one can find all the useful information spread out in a multitude of Spanish and foreign books."

As for Gamboa's three decades on the audiencias of Mexico and Santo Domingo, Alzate knew or revealed little. He did mention Gamboa's dedication to fighting crime in Mexico City as an alcalde del crimen, his compassion for poor convicts enslaved by owners of obrajes (he mistakenly attributed the abolition of the collera to his representations), and his mediation of the labor strife at Real del Monte. Alzate said nothing about Gamboa's expulsion from New Spain in 1769. As for his years as an oidor in the 1770s, Alzate only highlighted his work saving the former Jesuit schools of San Gregorio and Guadalupe from financial distress. His opposition to the Mining Tribunal was not mentioned. Alzate wrote, rather vaguely, that in Santo Domingo Gamboa created "new regulations for the government of that royal audiencia." As for his final years as regent of the Real Audiencia of Mexico, Alzate wrote there was no reason to get into details because "everyone knows his integrity in the administration of justice, his zeal for the public good, and his care in handling all matters, in spite of the unavoidable ailments of his advanced age."[102] With his death, the public could be consoled, Alzate wrote, that all of the remaining magistrates on the audiencia were capable of "administering justice with all the rectitude and integrity that the laws provide."[103]

Conclusion

꧂

✦ I HAVE WRITTEN THIS BIOGRAPHY OF FRANCISCO XAVIER DE GAMBOA
primarily as a way to understand the legal culture of eighteenth-century New
Spain. I have portrayed the jurist as an exemplary product of this culture and
its most articulate defender. It should be emphasized again how different this
world of law was compared to today's. First, it fit into a larger Christian normative system. The laws made by state and society, whether royal legislation
or unwritten custom, were always subject to this higher constitution of
divine creation. No matter how absolute the power of the king might appear
as earthly ruler, he was ultimately accountable to the higher norms of justice
and fairness emanating from God. The Christian foundation of the legal
order makes its pluralism easier to understand. Legislation issued formally
by public institutions made up just one strand of a rich juridical tapestry.
Lawyers still used the ius commune, the European common law derived
from Roman jurisprudence, although less for specific rules than general
principles of interpretation. The customs of the people, whether the uses and
practices of indigenous villages or protocol formulated for public institutions, often overrode the prescriptions of royal law. And beneath it all was
natural law, the universal principles inscribed in nature by God (according
to Catholic doctrine) and discernible through human reason.

Legal pluralism then begat jurisdictional complexity. Various bodies,
from the Catholic Church to the Consulado of Mexico, exercised jurisdiction, the power to make rules and adjudicate disputes. The boundaries
between these public or quasi-public bodies were always subject to challenge.
But what could seem like pointless skirmishes for jurisdictional turf, when
aggregated, served to check and balance power. As Montesquieu recognized
in *The Spirit of the Laws* of 1748, competition among institutions, a hallmark
of early modern monarchies, protected against despotism. Finally, since the
king was conceived as the supreme judge, the legal order was oriented

towards justice (*derecho*), not law enforcement (*ley*). The king had extended his sovereignty to America by promising his new vassals the services of justice, to assure that each received what they were owed and that the weak were protected from the powerful. Law enforcement was just a means to this end, not an end in itself, and thus could be softened if justice required. In addition, since every vassal was promised justice, each needed access to legal processes, such as the right to send petitions to royal officials or bring suit before a judge. Subjects of the Spanish king in America should also enjoy the right to appeal unfavorable decisions to the audiencias, the high courts of royal justice. As Woodrow Borah put it, in his pioneering study of the General Indian Court, "for the Spanish . . . the idea of appeal and accountability was part of the very fabric of the state. . . . It was unthinkable to the crown bureaucracy that a civilized and Christian state should deny the right of appeal to any subject."[1] This legal order offered the flexibility needed to govern a sprawling, diverse empire in the absence of a state with much coercive power. Law provided the vocabulary, practices, and forums for the continual negotiations required to maintain Spanish rule from New Mexico to the Río de la Plata.

When attacking black legends there is always the danger of conjuring up white ones in their place. I am not arguing that the legal system of Spanish America somehow redeemed Spanish colonialism. It did not prevent small elites of white people from dominating people of indigenous, African, and mixed descent. Colonial oppression was real, and law greased its wheels from the beginning. People with money and influence got their way no matter what fine principles of justice the high courts invoked. Audiencia magistrates, typically Spaniards posted in alien lands, often shirked their responsibilities and put more effort into improving their social and economic standing than rendering justice fairly and impartially. But, again, by what standard do we judge the colonial justice system? Even the most sophisticated systems of justice today fail to live up to their ideals. For the early modern age, the legal order of Spanish America measured up surprisingly well to others in Europe and North America, especially considering the vast distances and social diversity of the Spanish Empire. Ordinary people, including the Native population, well aware of its limitations, still made abundant use of its instruments to improve their lives.[2]

Yet as the story of Gamboa reveals, this legal order came under unprecedented stress during the era of the Bourbon reforms. Rationalist jurists complained of its indeterminacy; regalist ministers found it a poor vehicle for the assertion of royal power. I have argued that José de Gálvez, as visitor general of New Spain and later minister of the Indies for Charles III, personified this challenge. In an era of increasing imperial competition in the Atlantic, it was his mission to strengthen Spanish control over the Indies in order to boost tax revenue and reinforce defenses. He can thus be seen as a principal agent for the attempted construction, for the first time, of a strong state for colonial government. This entailed a shift in authority from the judiciary to executive officials and military officers, whom the crown could more easily manage. It required the stricter enforcement of royal law over norms contained in the ius commune and local custom. But it did not necessarily mean centralization; one of the hallmarks of Galvesian reform was the fragmentation of jurisdiction, as the crown promoted exemptions from the ordinary jurisdiction to favor certain groups, such as police captains (the Acordada) and silver miners (the Mining Tribunal).

Gamboa, who understood the ins and outs of the old system as well as anyone, strongly resisted these changes. He defended the authority of the audiencias against the Acordada, the Mining Tribunal, the intendants, and a series of assertive viceroys. He argued that local custom continued to deserve a prominent place in the legal order, as it represented the needs and desires of people on the ground better than royal laws drafted in Madrid. To be sure, he was driven by self-interest; as an audiencia magistrate he stood to lose power with the erosion of the audiencias' jurisdiction. But there was more to it than that. Gamboa was a loyal servant of the crown. He sincerely believed that the Spanish Empire was best served by retaining the old juridical order, with its multiple ways to accommodate the diverse interests of its subject communities. Without disruptive administrative changes, New Spain would continue to thrive economically and provide the Spanish crown with all the tax revenue it needed to compete with Britain. Many veteran officials with experience in America, notably Tomás Ortiz de Landázuri, Antonio María de Bucareli, and Antonio de Ulloa, agreed with Gamboa. They could appreciate better than reformers in Spain the real limitations of state power in America. They saw no need to test the loyalty of Spanish Americans by restricting their liberties. The old system did survive, even if many ilustrados considered it archaic and inefficient. There was simply no alternative to the old practices of consultation, negotiation, and conciliation it followed. Nevertheless, the fraying of ordinary jurisdiction was real and worrisome. It may have caused a deterioration in the quality of the administration of justice in the final decades of Spanish rule.

Gamboa's career, as we have seen, was shaped by more than law. This study has also sought to untangle the complex nature of identity in the Spanish world. Gamboa was a Spaniard born in America, what we would now call a *criollo*, or creole. It might seem remarkable that the Spanish-born, or *peninsular*, merchants on the Consulado of Mexico would send a creole lawyer to represent them before the king in Madrid. But this is strange only if we assume the reality of a meaningful difference between creoles and *peninsulares*. They were all white Spaniards united by common privileges in a racially stratified, colonial society. In any case, Gamboa's appointment as consulado deputy in 1755 might be better understood within the Basque context. Old ethnic and regional identities of Spain took root in America and could subsume whatever differences existed between European and American Spaniards. Within the Basque community in eighteenth-century New Spain, whether one was born in Guadalajara or Gipuzkoa hardly mattered. Gamboa, admittedly, was somewhat exceptional as a creole. He won an audiencia seat in 1764, in part due to his influential Basque connections, when the crown had essentially stopped appointing creoles to their local benches.[3] In fact, in the famous 1771 representation by the city of Mexico complaining about the lack of opportunities for creole professionals, Gamboa was held up as an example—a creole official loyally serving the crown—to show why the discriminatory policy was unjust.

I have argued that there was more than common ethnicity and shared privileges uniting creoles and peninsulares in New Spain; they both wanted to retain as much as possible the viceroyalty's economic autonomy within the empire. It was obviously in the best interests of the Spanish-born merchants of the Consulado of Mexico to maximize their economic opportunities in their new homeland. Although as a lawyer Gamboa was skilled at crafting arguments that might not accord with his own beliefs, in the case of his representation of the consulado in Madrid, he could in good conscience defend the old fleet system of imperial trade and pitch a consulado-led mining bank. Both would insulate the novohispano economy and promote domestic investment, not just in mining but also agriculture and manufacturing. But the Spanish crown believed that tightening its control over the American economy would best serve its interests; Gamboa argued throughout his career that looser ties, which would encourage the autonomous economic development of New Spain, would ultimately serve Spain and the monarchy as much as America.

Silver mining, as the anchor of New Spain's economy, was central to Gamboa's career as a lawyer, author, and judge. The *Comentarios a las Ordenanzas de Minas* allows us to see the industry from a perspective that challenges several conventional historiographical notions. He did accept the widely held assumption at the time, which has survived to this day, that American mining lagged European mining in technical matters. He had little positive to say about the silver miners of New Spain. He took pride in his role of diffusing through the *Comentarios* the latest ideas about mining and metallurgy from Saxony and France. But he also gave ample evidence to the contrary; he filled a whole chapter of the *Comentarios* with descriptions of the numerous innovations that enterprising individuals in New Spain and Peru had devised since the sixteenth century to improve smelting and refining. It was only in the 1780s, when European experts arrived to educate the ignorant miners of New Spain, Peru and New Granada, that the truth came out. American techniques beat out European techniques, especially taking into account the more difficult geographic conditions faced by miners and refiners in America. The artisanal production of knowledge proved superior to what formal science could come up with. A scavenger in New Spain might not have made it as a professor at the College of Freiberg, as Alzate cheekily suggested, but we should not disdain the knowledge accumulated by humble and even illiterate practitioners in colonial Spanish America.[4]

The *Comentarios* also allows us to see the weakness of the claim made by many economic historians and social scientists that Spanish law impeded the economic development of America.[5] Gamboa set out clearly how the ordinances of 1584 encouraged individuals of all social ranks to pursue opportunities in mining. The statute and the customs that developed around it protected private property rights while laying out a supportive role for the government. There were clear procedures for anyone wanting to stake a claim and a variety of incentives to maximize production. Meanwhile, the state lowered transaction costs through an efficient distribution of mercury and blasting powder and kept fiscal charges moderate. At least in the case of eighteenth-century New Spain, the infamous Laffer curve actually worked: by lowering the royalty rate from 20 to 10 percent and then cutting the official price of mercury, the Spanish government reaped higher fiscal revenue overall because of the stimulus lower taxes had on production. It is clear from what Gamboa wrote about the regulation of silver mining in the 1760s that the Spanish crown did not need lessons from Adam Smith on the finer points of liberal economics. Even the Mining Tribunal, which complicated adjudication and diverted capital from the mines to the crown, was unable to brake the dynamic mining sector in the decades before 1808.

Finally, does this history of the most prominent jurist in eighteenth-century New Spain hold any lessons for Mexico today? The country may be more open and democratic than ever, thanks to the economic and political reforms of the past few decades, but its administration of justice remains deeply troubled. The state can neither contain the violent drug cartels operating on its territory nor provide reliable justice to the victims of everyday crimes. The rich and well-connected continue to flout laws with impunity. No one has been found guilty for such atrocities as the femicides of Ciudad Juárez or the disappearance of forty-three students in Ayotzinapa. On the other hand, innocent people are convicted on the basis of falsified evidence.

Gamboa's World illustrates that a healthy system of justice requires, first of all, robust and independent legal institutions. Mexico had a higher degree of judicial independence in the eighteenth century than it does today. The audiencias represented the king in matters of justice, a huge grant of power. Audiencia magistrates, as we have seen, could initiate action on their own, as Gamboa did in freeing the Native prisoners of Mexico City bakeries, and challenge viceregal decisions, as Gamboa did throughout his long judicial career. He and his colleagues on the bench were intensely aware, however, of the fragility of this independence. It rested on the broad but contested jurisdiction, defined as much by custom as written law, that the high courts exercised over ordinary civil and criminal matters. Executive-style officials, whether the viceroy or the minister of the Indies, were always trying to trim this jurisdiction, usually for considerations of cost and efficiency. The Acordada, for example, which might be considered Mexico's first national police force, was favored over the police captains appointed by the Sala de Crimen because it was cheap to operate, answered directly to the viceroy, and dealt with criminals expeditiously by ignoring procedural rights. The erosion of ordinary jurisdiction, especially through the proliferation of exemptions, did not just curtail the power of the audiencias, it also arguably exacerbated inequality under the law. As the second Revillagigedo noted in 1794, more and more people in New Spain brandished special privileges to escape the force of the general laws. While he often came across as stubborn and arrogant, Gamboa's defense of the jurisdiction, power, and prerogatives of audiencia magistrates should be viewed in a positive light. He did not think that the administration of justice should be sacrificed for the sake of administrative efficiency, economic reform or tighter colonial control.

As Mexico knows today, once the rule of law is broken, it is excruciatingly hard to rebuild. A basic problem is that people wielding power, such as elected officials, cabinet ministers, bureaucrats, and the rich, never want to surrender it, especially not to prosecutors and judges who could hold them to account. There is also limited public support for the long-term policies needed to fix Mexico's much maligned police forces, such as increased spending on salaries and training. Yet reforming the administration of justice is not impossible. It will require, first of all, the recognition by Mexican leaders that economic reform, whether neoliberal or populist, is never enough to make a happy and secure society if the system of justice is neglected. Making the promise of justice a reality again will require long-term investment and steady pressure from a wide range of civic actors. It will require international cooperation, especially from the United States, whose insatiable appetite for illegal drugs and uncontrolled gun industry makes corruption and violence in Mexico next to inevitable. And it will require lawyers and judges in Mexico willing to fight—as ruthlessly as Gamboa did, if necessary—to restore the autonomy and honor of legal institutions.

Notes

⤞

Introduction

Note to Epigraph: Otero, "Apuntes para una biografía," 336. All translations from Spanish are mine unless otherwise noted. The original: "Si un día se escribe la historia literaria y social de México, este personaje, que nacido en principios del siglo XVIII, murió en su fin (4 de Junio de 1794) viendo cuanto en él pasó, hará un gran papel, porque es una grande época la suya, y porque él fue tambien grande en ella."

1. Gamboa, *Comentarios*.
2. I have chosen to use the eighteenth-century spelling and style of Gamboa's name. It is now usually written Francisco Javier Gamboa. The first account of his life appeared shortly after his death, written by the scientist-priest-journalist José Antonio de Alzate and published in the *Gacetas de literatura* on December 22, 1794. One hundred years after Otero's sketch, the legal scholar Toribio Esquivel Obregón studied Gamboa's legal thinking in Obregón, *Biografía de Don Francisco Javier Gamboa*. More recently, the Mexican historian of science, Elías Trabulse, published a short biography that highlighted the Enlightenment's influence on Gamboa's thinking: see Trabulse, *Francisco Xavier Gamboa*.
3. Castañeda, *Mañana Forever?*, 186.
4. For example, according to Alan Knight, "Royal officials took refuge in the famous motto of colonial government: *obedezco pero no cumplo* ('I obey but do not carry out'). . . . A display of formal obedience could mask a multitude of sins, and the gulf between administrative theory and practice often gaped, in colonial as in modern Mexico." See Knight, *Mexico: The Colonial Era*, 61.
5. Hanke, "A Modest Proposal," 117. The debate in the *Hispanic American Historical Review* between Hanke and Benjamin Keen on the Black Legend and law remains pertinent. See Keen, "The Black Legend Revisited"; Keen, "The White Legend Revisited."
6. On popular legal culture see Cutter, *The Legal Culture of Northern New Spain*, 31–43. On popular participation in criminal proceedings, see Herzog, *Upholding Justice*. On native engagement with Spanish justice, see Borah, *Justice by*

Insurance; Owensby, *Empire of Law*; Novoa, *The Protectors of Indians*; Susan Kellogg, *Law and the Transformation of Aztec Culture*; Yannakakis, *The Art of Being In-between*; Taylor, *Drinking, Homicide, and Rebellion*. On how slaves used the legal system, see McKinley, *Fractional Freedoms*. On late colonial litigation, including that initiated by women against their social superiors, see Premo, *The Enlightenment on Trial*.

7. This is the position most associated with the new institutional economics pioneered by economic historian Douglass North. See North, *Institutions*. For a recent ambitious work from this school, see Acemoglu and Robinson, *Why Nations Fail*.

8. Coatsworth, "Inequality, Institutions and Economic Growth," 557.

9. On New Spain's silver capitalism in general, see Tutino, *Making a New World*. For a convincing rebuttal of the institutional assumption that Spanish law and regulation held back economic growth see Dobado and Marrero, "The Role of the Spanish Imperial State."

10. Tau Anzoátegui, *Nuevos horizontes*. See also Duve and Pihlajamaki, *New Horizons in Spanish Colonial Law*.

11. On the historiography reconsidering ancien régime politics and law, see Garriga, "Orden jurídico y poder político en el Antiguo Régime." Historians reexamining colonial empires generally assume the relative weakness of colonizing powers and thus the necessity to negotiate terms of sovereignty with colonial subjects. On negotiated empires see especially Greene, "Negotiated Authorities." On the relationship between law and colonialism, see Benton, *Law and Colonial Cultures*. For a convenient summary of new, mainly English-language studies on law and governance in the Spanish empire see Tutino, *Mexico City, 1808*, 110–17.

12. For a recent summary of recent Spanish legal historiography, see Garriga, "¿De qué hablamos los historiadores del derecho?"

13. I want to thank Alejandro Agüero, a fellow participant in Bernard Bailyn's last International Seminar on the History of the Atlantic World, held at Harvard in 2010, for clarifying this idea for me. He summarizes his account of the Spanish juridical order in Agüero, "Las categorías básicas de la cultura jurisdiccional," 19–58.

14. Quoted by Tau Anzoátegui, *La ley en América hispana*, 434–35.

15. On the *ius commune* see Bellomo, *The Common Legal Past of Europe*; Stein, *Roman Law in European History*; Merryman, *The Civil Law Tradition*.

16. Tau Anzoátegui, *La ley en América hispana*, 18.

17. See especially Tau Anzoátegui, *El poder de la costumbre*.

18. Borah, *Justice by Insurance*, 51–55. On the judicial duties of the viceroy, see Cañeque, *The King's Living Image*; Sembolini Capitani, *La construcción de la autoridad*; Lira, "La actividad jurisdiccional del virrey."

19. Quoted in Garriga, "Los límites del reformismo borbónico," 789.

20. On petitioning and legal communication see Ross, "Legal Communications and Imperial Governance"; Masters, "A Thousand Invisible Architects."

21. See especially Tau Anzoátegui, *Casuismo y sistema.*

22. The first Mexican audiencia failed when its president, Nuño Beltrán de Gúzman, proved even more destructive than the man he came to subdue, Hernán Cortés. The court was reorganized in 1530.

23. Sembolini Capitani, *La construcción de la autoridad*, 145.

24. Solórzano Pereyra, *Política Indiana*, book 5, chapter 3, paragraph 7. In 1971 historian Lewis Hanke remarked that the audiencia was "the most important and interesting institution in the government of the Spanish Indies." Hanke, "A Modest Proposal," 124. Studies of the audiencias include J. H. Parry, *The Audiencia of New Galicia*; Sanciñena Asurmendi, *La audiencia en México*; Martiré, *Las audiencias y la administración de justicia en las Indias*; Burkholder and Chandler, *From Impotence to Authority*; Gayol, *Laberintos de justicia.*

25. On connections between high court judges and oligarchic families in the eighteenth century, see Tutino, *Mexico City, 1808*, 43–46.

26. On the legal culture of Castile at the time of American colonization, see Kagan, *Lawsuits and Litigants in Castile*. See also Pagden, "Law, Colonization, Legitimation, and the European Background." 1–31.

27. Owensby puts the importance of negotiations between the crown and the Natives of New Spain nicely: "Spanish rule over Mexico's Indians did not rest mainly on strict obedience. Everything from royal to viceregal orders to requests by a local corregidor could be subject to discussion and negotiation.... Power could only be exercised by admitting that the Indians would contest and negotiate it at every step." Owensby, *Empire of Law*, 39.

28. Recent studies include Kuethe and Andrien, *The Spanish Atlantic World in the Eighteenth Century*; Stein and Stein, *Apogee of Empire*; Paquette, *Enlightenment, Governance, and Reform*. See also Guimerá, *El reformismo borbónico*; Tandeter and Hidalgo Lehuedé, *Procesos americanos hacia la redefinición colonial*; Garriga, "Los límites del reformismo borbónico."

29. On Gálvez and his family see Folguera et al., *Los Gálvez de Marcharaviaya.*

30. Brading, *Miners and Merchants in Bourbon Mexico.*

31. Brading, *Miners and Merchants in Bourbon Mexico*, 162. Stanley and Barbara Stein made a similar judgment on Gamboa: "Ostensibly, the *Comentarios* were a manual on silver-mining technology in New Spain, but Gamboa's hidden agenda (on instructions from the Mexico City Consulado) was to enhance the image of Mexico City's merchant magnates and promote the continued insulation of their economic space from the *flotistas* of the *comercio de España* at Jalapa, both during and after the ferias." Stein and Stein, *Apogee of Empire*, 229. Recently Vera Candiani, in her exceptional environmental history of colonial Mexico City, repeats this reductive view of Gamboa, calling him "a relentless ally and consultant for the merchant guild" who "in 1761 presented a vast program that would

have allowed Mexican merchant capital to control mining." Candiani, *Dreaming of Dry Land*, 214–15.

32. Solórzano Pereyra, *Política Indiana*, book 5, chapter 3, paragraph 48. On Solórzano's understanding of the role of custom in the legal order see Tau Anzoátegui, *El poder de la costumbre*, 311–40.

33. On the mining tribunal generally, see Howe, *The Mining Guild of New Spain*; Flores Clair, *El Banco de avío minero novohispano*.

Chapter One

Note to Epigraph: Relación de méritos, 1757, Archivo General de Indias, Indiferente General 157. Gamboa submitted his official curriculum vita to the crown in 1757 and again in 1759, part of his effort to win an audiencia posting.

1. On eighteenth-century Guadalajara see Van Young, *Hacienda and Market in Eighteenth-Century Mexico*.

2. Originally located in Compostela near the Pacific coast, it was moved to Guadalajara in 1560.

3. Parry, *The Audiencia of New Galicia in the Sixteenth Century*, 3.

4. Otero claimed that the executors of his estate may have embezzled or squandered his fortune. Otero, "Apuntes para una biografía," 304.

5. Relación de méritos, 1757, AGI, Ind Gen, 157.

6. Relación de méritos, 1757, AGI, Ind Gen, 157.

7. Gamboa probably started his education, like most young boys at the time, with his parish priest.

8. Van Young, *Hacienda and Market in Eighteenth-Century Mexico*, 216–19.

9. Luque Alcaide, *La educación en Nueva España en el siglo XVIII*, 146.

10. See Navarro, "Tradition and Scientific Change in Early Modern Spain," 331–87.

11. On the Colegio Imperial see also Simon-Díaz, *Historia del Colegio Imperial de Madrid*.

12. Navarro, "Tradition and Scientific Change in Early Modern Spain," 355–58.

13. Otero, "Apuntes para una biografía," 322–23.

14. See Crawford, *The Andean Wonder Drug*.

15. Ramos Lara, *Difusión e institucionalización de la mecánica newtoniana*, 48–53; Sánchez-Blanco, *Europa y el pensamiento español del siglo XVIII*, 40–41.

16. Chiaramonte, *Pensamiento de la ilustracion*, xv–xvi.

17. Feingold, "Preface," ii–xi. See also Sánchez-Blanco, *Europa y el pensamiento español del siglo XVIII*, 108–14; Navarro, "Tradition and Scientific Change in Early Modern Spain," 354–57.

18. Burkholder and Chandler, *Biographical Dictionary of Audiencia Ministers*, 212.

19. See Garciadueñas, *El antiguo Colegio de San Ildefonso*, 13–15.

20. Brading, "Government and Elite in Late Colonial Mexico," 405.
21. Osores, *Historia de todos los colegios de la ciudad de México desde la conquista hasta 1780*, 59; Gonzalbo, *Historia de la educacion en la epoca colonial*, 223–25.
22. Osores, *Noticias bio-bibliograficas de alumnos distinguidos del Colegio de San Pedro, San Pablo y San Ildefonso de Mexico*, 199.
23. Osores, *Historia de todos los colegios*, 76.
24. Gonzalbo, *Historia de la educacion en la epoca colonial*, 106–23.
25. Acevedo, *El discreto estudiante*. The Jesuit priest Acevedo wrote the book in the early seventeenth century and the college reprinted it after a student disturbance at the college in 1719.
26. Acevedo, *El discrete estudiante*.
27. Acevedo, *El discreto estudiante*.
28. Molina del Villar, *Por voluntad divina*, 37–40.
29. Molina del Villar, *Por voluntad divina*, 68.
30. Molina del Villar, *Por voluntad divina*, 64.
31. Brading, *Mexican Phoenix, Our Lady of Guadalupe*, 124.
32. Molina del Villar, *Por voluntad divina*, 106–7.
33. On the rise of Our Lady of Guadalupe as the main figure in Mexican religion in the eighteenth century, see Taylor, *Magistrates of the Sacred*, 277–87.
34. Like Gamboa, Eguiara was of Basque descent. Their paths likely crossed during Gamboa's days as a student at San Ildefonso and certainly in the 1740s when both were active members of the Basque confraternity of Nuestra Señora de Aránzazu.
35. Gamboa and Berrio shared a love of books and science, with the later possessing one of the best collections of scientific instruments in New Spain. See Reyna, "La biblioteca de José Miguel Calixto de Berrio y Zaldívar, segundo conde de San Mateo de Valparaíso y primer marqués del Jaral de Berrio."
36. Osores, *Noticias bio-bibliograficas*, 1:101–2.
37. Osores, *Noticias bio-bibliograficas*, 1:104–6.
38. While in Madrid representing the Consulado of Mexico, Gamboa forwarded their petition to establish the college. Gamboa to the crown, 1760, AGI, Mexico 1702. See Mayagoitia, "Los rectores del Ilustre y Real Colegio de Abogados de México," 101–6.
39. Osores, *Noticias bio-bibliograficas*, 1:129.
40. Maneiro and Fabri, *Vidas de mexicanos ilustres del siglo XVIII*, 3–48.
41. On the riot, which took place in the main square, see Cope, *The Limits of Racial Domination*, 125–80.
42. In November 1773, when Gamboa was an alcalde del crimen, he ordered the arrest of thieves on university property. The church complained he violated their jurisdiction by doing so. He filed a long letter explaining the origin of the mixed jurisdiction of the university and said there was no doubt the audiencia had the right to arrest ordinary criminals on university property. Biblioteca Nacional de España (BNE), Papeles referentes a Hacienda, MSS.3535, no. 11.

43. The popularity of law may have declined in the 1720s and 1730s after Francisco de Garzarón, the visitor general to New Spain in the 1710s, removed all the locally born magistrates from the Real Audiencia of Mexico for alleged corruption. See Salvador, *El mérito y la estratégia*, 79–80.

44. Bellomo, *The Common Legal Past of Europe*, 38; Stein, *Roman Law in European History*, 44.

45. Stein, *Roman Law in European History*, 33–35.

46. For a recent English edition see Burns, ed., *Las Siete Partidas*.

47. Barrientos Grandón, *La Cultura Jurídica en la Nueva España*, 31.

48. Stein, *Roman Law in European History*, 61.

49. Tau Anzoátegui, *Casuismo y sistema*, 78–79.

50. Stein, *Roman Law in European History*, 64.

51. Merryman, *The Civil Law Tradition*, 6.

52. Stein, *Roman Law in European History*, 71–74.

53. On the role of juridical opinion in Spanish America, see particularly Luque Talaván, *Un universo de opiniones*.

54. Peter Stein offers a nice description of the main difference between civil, or Roman, law and canon law: "The civil law was concerned with the common good of man on earth and the canon law with keeping him from sin and ensuring the salvation of his immortal soul." Stein, *Roman Law in European History*, 51.

55. Sánchez-Arcilla Bernal, *Manual de Historia del Derecho*, 497.

56. Berní Catalá, *El abogado instruído en la práctica civil de España (1738)*, 32.

57. Quoted in Tomás y Valiente, *Manual de Historia del Derecho Español*, 37–39; Sánchez-Blanco, *El absolutismo y las luces en el reinado de Carlos III*, 113–19.

58. The jurist and government minister Gaspar Melchor de Jovellanos expressed this attitude clearly in his speech upon entering the Real Academia de Historia. See Jovellanos, "Discurso académico en su recepción a la Real Academia de la Historia (1780)." 71–102.

59. Tau Anzoátegui, *El Jurista en el Nuevo Mundo*, 8–14; Pérez-Perdomo, *Latin American Lawyers*, 27; Kagan, *Lawsuits and Litigants*, 147.

60. Esquivel Obregón, *Biografía de Don Francisco Javier Gamboa*, 44–45.

61. On the life of Solórzano see García Hernán, *Consejero de ambos mundos*.

62. Tau Anzoátegui, "Entre leyes, glosas y comentos," 147–66.

63. On his position regarding imperialism and creole rights, see Brading, *The First America*, 213–27.

64. Quoted in Tau Anzoátegui, "La variedad indiana, una clave de la concepción jurídica de Juan de Solórzano," 208.

65. Osores, *Historia de todos los colegios*, 138.

66. The sources on this event are muddled. The *Mercurio de Mexico*, an early newspaper, reported that the ceremonies took place in March 1740 but did not mention either Gamboa or Torres. Gamboa did not mention his participation in his résumé. On the other hand, the nineteenth-century historian Manuel Orozco y

Berra, drawing upon an unpublished Jesuit manuscript, mentioned it in his entry on Mexico City in the 1854 *Diccionario Universal de Historia y de Geografia*. He gave the date as December 1739. Despite the uncertainty, especially due to Gamboa's failure to mention it, I think it likely took place as described in the *Mercurio de Mexico* in 1740 and later in the manuscript cited by Orozco y Berra. On Torres, who became a prebend at the Mexico City cathedral, see Sainz, "Un retrato olvidado del salón General de Actos del Colegio de San Ildefonso," 48–57.

67. Burkholder and Chandler, *Biographical Dictionary of Audiencia Ministers*, 212.

68. Mesía won a first-place prize in the college's 1748 poetry contest, in which Gamboa also participated, for his Latin epigrams. *Certamen Poetico, con que la humilde lealtad y reconocida gratitud del Real, y mas antiguo Colegio de S. Ildefonso de México, Seminario de la Compañia de Jesus, celebró el dia 23 de enero del año de 1748 la exaltacion al Solio de su Augustissimo Protector.*

Chapter Two

Note to Epigraph: Gamboa received as a prize in a 1748 poetry contest held at San Ildefonso a set of polished silver buckles. The inscription read: "Gamboa, Estrados, y Parnasso / Para ti lo mismo juzgo; Aqui Papinio pareces; Allá Papiniano culto. De las hevillas que llevas / Para ceñir tu cothurno, No temas el aguijón, Que es tu ingenio mas agudo." Papinius was a first-century Roman poet and Papinian a celebrated Roman jurist of the second century.

1. Relación de méritos, 1757, Archivo General de Indias (AGI), Indiferente General, 157.

2. Quoted in Tau Anzoátegui, *Nuevos horizontes*, 71.

3. Castro, *Discursos críticos sobre las leyes y sus interpretes*, 1.

4. On legal professionals in Castile see Kagan, *Lawsuits and Litigants*, 52–61.

5. Premo, *Enlightenment on Trial*, 36.

6. Osores, *Historia de todos los colegios*, 23.

7. Sahagún de Arévalo Ladrón de Guevara et al., *Gacetas de Mexico*, vol. 3, 230.

8. Relación de méritos, 1757, AGI, Ind Gen, 157.

9. Relación de méritos, 1757, AGI, Ind Gen, 157.

10. The case is discussed in Esquivel Obregón, *Biografía de Don Francisco Javier Gamboa*, 103–17.

11. Esquivel Obregón, *Biografía de Don Francisco Javier Gamboa*, 118–19.

12. *Representación del Lic. D. Francisco Xavier de Gamboa al Virrey Primero Conde de Revillagigedo, en defensa de Fr. Joseph Torrubia, Custodio de la Provincia de Filipinas, preso en el castillo del Morro de la Habana a pedimento del Vice-comisario General Fr. Gregorio López, Año 1749.* Biblioteca Nacional de México. Fondo Reservado, Colección Archivo Franciscano.

13. On Torrubia see Sequeiros, "*El Aparato para la Historia Natural Española* del franciscano granadino fray José Torrubia (1698–1761)," 59–127.

14. For a popular account of late eighteenth-century geological knowledge in Britain, see Winchester, *The Map that Changed the World*.

15. Tutino, *Making a New World*, 36. On the importance of Chinese demand for Mexican silver, see Schell, "Silver Symbiosis," 89–133.

16. The surviving record of the case, Gamboa's brief to the legal advisor of the viceroy, dates from shortly after Méndez's death. *Representación jurídica que haze Don Antonio de Arrieta en el pleito que trahe con Don Manuel San Juan Santa Cruz . . . sobre restitucion de sus minas en el Real de Santa Eulalia* (1743), BANC MSS M-M 529, The Bancroft Library, University of California, Berkeley.

17. Conquista lasted just one year in office, succumbing to dysentery on August 22, 1741.

18. *Representación jurídica que haze Don Antonio de Arrieta en el pleito que trahe con Don Manuel San Juan Santa Cruz*, BANC MSS M-M 529, The Bancroft Library, University of California, Berkeley.

19. Solórzano Pereyra, *Política Indiana*, book 5, chapter 3, paragraphs 29–30.

20. *Representación jurídica que haze Don Antonio de Arrieta en el pleito que trahe con Don Manuel San Juan Santa Cruz*, BANC MSS M-M 529, The Bancroft Library, University of California, Berkeley.

21. *Representación jurídica que haze Don Antonio de Arrieta en el pleito que trahe con Don Manuel San Juan Santa Cruz*, BANC MSS M-M 529, The Bancroft Library, University of California, Berkeley.

22. On Romero Terreros see Couturier, *The Silver King*; Canterla and Tovar, *Vida y obra del primer conde de Regla*.

23. Couturier, *The Silver King*.

24. Gamboa, *Comentarios*, 320–21.

25. Gamboa, *Comentarios*, 327.

26. Couturier, *The Silver King*, 64–65.

27. Brading, *Mexican Phoenix*, 135.

28. On the secularization of the doctrinas, see O'Hara, *A Flock Divided*, 55–64; Taylor, *Magistrates of the Sacred*, 83–86. In practice, the impact of secularization was softened. The regular orders were allowed to maintain a couple of parishes in each province for revenue purposes and to maintain their larger convents. Transfers of parishes were often delayed until the deaths of their pastors. On church-state politics in eighteenth-century New Spain see also Brading, "Tridentine Catholicism and Enlightened Despotism in Bourbon Mexico," 1–22.

29. *Reconocimiento debido a las supremas regalías de el rey nuestro señor en la fundación de la Real Insigne Colegiata de la Santísima Virgen María Nuestra Señora de Guadalupe, extramuros de México*, Genaro García Collection (G283), Nettie Lee Benson Latin American Collection, University of Texas Libraries, The University of Texas at Austin.

30. Brading, *The First America*, 347.

31. *Reconocimiento debido a las supremas regalías de el rey nuestro señor en la fundación de la Real Insigne Colegiata de la Santísima Virgen María Nuestra Señora de Guadalupe, extramuros de México*, Genaro García Collection (G283), Nettie Lee Benson Latin American Collection, University of Texas Libraries, The University of Texas at Austin.

32. Gamboa, *Por el coronel D. Manuel de Rivas-Cacho*.

33. Gamboa, *Por el coronel D. Manuel de Rivas-Cacho*, 93.

34. Gamboa, *Por el coronel D. Manuel de Rivas-Cacho*.

35. Gamboa, *Por el coronel D. Manuel de Rivas-Cacho*, 116.

36. Gamboa, *Por el coronel D. Manuel de Rivas-Cacho*, 97.

37. Gamboa, *Por el coronel D. Manuel de Rivas-Cacho*, 48.

38. Rivas Cacho got into trouble a few years later. In 1759 he was briefly jailed on the order of the viceroy, the Marqués de Amarillas, after he challenged the viceroy's right to name new officers for the consulado's militia, of which Rivas Cacho was the presiding colonel. Once again he suffered a blow to his reputation. He received vindication, however, when Madrid sent Amarillas a reprimand for taking such arbitrary action against the elderly merchant. Letters on Militia nominations, October 1759–August 1760, AGI, Mexico 2502.

Chapter Three

Note to Epigraph: Cadalso, *Cartas marruecas*, letter 26, 107.

1. On the importance of trust in overseas trading in the Spanish world, see Lamikiz, *Trade and Trust in the Eighteenth-Century Atlantic World*; and Baskes, *Staying Afloat*.

2. For an excellent study of this network in action, see Pescador, *The New World inside a Basque Village*.

3. On the fueros see Fernández Pardo, *La independencia vasca*; and Heiberg, *The Making of the Basque Nation*.

4. Baltasar de Echave, *Discursos de la antiguedad de la lengua cántabra bascongada*. Echave's book was republished repeatedly in Spain and Mexico for the next two hundred years. Zaballa Beascoechea, "Mentalidad e identidad de los vascos en México, siglo XVIII," 157–69.

5. Azcona Pastor, *Possible Paradises*, 2; Ruiz de Azúa y Martínez de Ezquerecocha, *Vascongadas y América*, 23–25.

6. Caro Baroja, *La hora navarra*, 60–65, 293; Stein and Stein, *Silver, Trade, and War*, 165.

7. Callahan, *Honor, Commerce, and Industry in Eighteenth-century Spain*; Caro Baroja, *La hora navarra*, 110–19.

8. See Caro Baroja, *Los vascos*, 195; Pescador, *New World inside a Basque Village*, xxi–xxii; Caro Baroja, *La hora navarra*, 20–25.

9. On the basis of their correspondence, Basques in America spoke Spanish even among themselves. Zaballa Beascoechea, "Cartas de vascos en México: vida privada y relaciones de paisanaje," 98–99. In promoting a Basque dictionary in the early 1770s the RSBAP reminded its members: "Even though the peculiar language of the country is Basque, that of the Nation is Castilian, and therefore the native tongue of all the Spaniards." *Extractos de las juntas generales celebradas por la Real Sociedad Bascongada de los Amigos del País (1771–1773)*, 91–101.

10. *Extractos de las juntas generales celebradas por la Real Sociedad Bascongada de los Amigos del País (1774–1776)*, 122

11. The minutes of the RSBAP are full of tributes to the social virtues of commerce. The Basque economic writer, Victor Forondo, wrote a defense of merchants in 1778, *Sobre lo honroso que es la profesión del comercio*. See Sánchez-Blanco, *El absolutismo y las luces*, 285.

12. Lamikiz, *Trade and Trust*, 30–34.

13. Jeremy Baskes, in his study of Spanish transatlantic commerce, provides the example of the far-flung Marticorena y Laurnaga clan of Navarre. One brother resided in Cadiz, another in Lima, a third in Guatemala, and the youngest in Veracruz. Meanwhile cousins involved in the business lived in Mexico City, Caracas, Veracruz, and Cadiz. Baskes, *Staying Afloat*, 18. For a comprehensive study of one important Basque family network, see Torales Pacheco, ed., *La compañía de comercio de Francisco Ignacio de Yraeta*.

14. Lamikiz, *Trade and Trust*, 9–14.

15. Luque Alcaide, "Asociacionismo vasco en Nueva España, 68–70.

16. Luzuriaga, *Paranympho celeste*.

17. Luque Alcaide, *La Cofradía de Aránzazu*, 40–41.

18. Luque Alcaide, "Asociacionismo vasco en Nueva España," 71.

19. Luque Alcaide, *La Cofradía de Aránzazu*, 61–69.

20. Kicza, *Colonial Entrepreneurs*, 59.

21. García, "Sociedad, crédito y cofradía," 54–64.

22. Aránzazu Book of Elections, Archivo Histórico del Colegio Vizcaínas (AHCV), 006-111-015.

23. Aránzazu Book of Elections, AHCV, 006-111-015.

24. Pescador, *New World inside a Basque Village*, 84–91; Brading, *Miners and Merchants*, 76–79.

25. The fact that his father was not ordained at the time of his birth saved him from the stigma of being considered a *sacrilegio*. In 1746 he was able to petition successfully for legitimization.

26. Gazeta de Mexico, no. 80, 1734, AHCV, 005-V-007.

27. Echeveste specialized in trade with Asia through Acapulco. He served as rector, the chief officer of Aránzazu, in 1740. Ruiz de Azúa y Martínez de Ezquerecocha, *Vascongadas y América*, 222.

28. Muriel, "El Real Colegio de San Ignacio de Loyola (1734-1863)," 26.

29. Constitution, 1753, AHCV, 005-V-007.

30. On Basque religiosity see Caro Baroja, *La hora navarra*, 47.

31. Rubio to Aldaco, September 20, 1751, AHCV, 005-V-007; Porras Muñoz, "La situación jurídica del Colegio de las Vizcaínas," 115-24.

32. Quoted in Olavarría y Ferrari, *El Real colegio de San Ignacio de Loyola*, 30.

33. Decree, November 6, 1729, AHCV, 006-IV-006. See Angulo Morales, "La Real Congregación de San Ignacio de Loyola de los naturales y originarios de las tres provincias vascas en la corte de Madrid (1713-1896)," 15-34; *Noticia del origen, fundación, objeto y constituciones de la Real Congregación de naturales y originarios de las tres provincias vascongadas establecida bajo la advocación del glorioso San Ignacio de Loyola*. Mariluz Urquijo, "El indiano en la corte, 17-18.

34. Stein and Stein, *Silver, Trade, and War*, 236-37, 319.

35. On Ordeñena, a native of Bilbao in Biscay, see González Caizán, "La Biblioteca de Agustín Pablo de Ordeñana," 227-67.

36. In the late 1740s Echavarri ran afoul of the Viceroy Revillagigedo, who orchestrated his recall to Spain. The board of Aránzazu wrote to San Ignacio in May 1749 to vouch for Echavarri and ask for assistance in securing him a high judicial position in Spain. Echavarri, perhaps through the good offices of the Madrid congregation, returned to New Spain in 1752, his name cleared, and served on the Real Audiencia of Mexico until 1769, when the crown appointed him to the Council of the Indies. Aránzazu to San Ignacio, May 14, 1749, AHCV, 005-V-006. Burkholder, *Biographical Dictionary of Councillors of the Indies*, 36-37.

37. Aldaco to San Ignacio, June 15, 1752, AHCV, 005-V-007.

38. San Ignacio to Aldaco, January 24, 1753, AHCV, 005-V-007.

39. Ruiz de Azúa y Martínez de Ezquerecocha, *Vascongadas y América*, 234.

40. Ensenada to Rubio, September 1, 1753, AHCV, 005-V-007.

41. Lamikiz, *Trade and Trust*, 88-94.

42. The consulado sent petitions to the crown on at least three occasions, in 1744, 1747, and 1750. See instructions to the deputies, 1755, Archivo General de la Nación, (AGN), Archivo Histórico de Hacienda (AHH), 635-8.

43. On the exaggerated impact of the 1778 decree, see also Baskes, *Staying Afloat*, 7, 69-109.

44. The regulations on commerce in Jalapa had been issued in 1729 by Viceroy Casafuerte. They required that all merchandise landed in Veracruz to be sold at Jalapa to members of the Mexican consulado. The goods wouldn't be moved upcountry to Mexico City until the fleet set sail from Veracruz, usually six or seven months after arrival. The crown's main interest was the expeditious shipment of silver

from New Spain to Spain. Mexican merchants also bought goods from nonmatriculated merchants in Cadiz, another violation of the rules shut down by the crown in 1729. See Stein and Stein, *Apogee of Empire*, 128–29.

45. All of the consulado's concerns were enumerated in the instructions they provided their Madrid deputies on June 8, 1755, found in AGN, AHH, 635-38.

46. See Salvucci, "Costumbres viejas, 'hombres nuevos,'" 228–33.

47. A committee struck in 1750 to discuss trade, after the end of the War of Jenkins' Ear, had decided to resume the fleet system to Mexico. Ferdinand's chief minister Ensenada was unsure, thinking registros sueltos were preferable but not wanting to alienate the Consulado of Cadiz. Only after his ouster did the crown finally authorize the first fleet since the late 1730s. Llombart Rosa, *Campomanes*, 125.

48. Power of attorney to deputies, May 31, 1755, Archivo General de Indias (AGI), Mexico 2502.

49. Valle Pavón, "Los excedentes del ramo Alcabalas," 985–86.

50. Quoted in Olavarría y Ferrari, *El Real colegio de San Ignacio de Loyola*, 64.

51. Travel Authorization, August 8, 1764, AGI, Contratación, 5507, N. 1, R. 8; Domínguez Ortiz, *Carlos III y la España de la Ilustración*, 207.

52. On the confraternity of Guadalupe see Mariluz Urquijo, "El indiano en la Corte," 10–38.

53. Weisser, "Crime and Punishment in Early Modern Spain," 91–93.

54. Francisco Sánchez-Blanco argues that Spain in the first half of the eighteenth century was more intellectually open and dynamic than during the era of Charles III, usually seen as the high-water mark of the Enlightenment in Spain. See Sánchez-Blanco, *Europa y el pensamiento español del siglo XVIII*, 12–13.

55. For recent reevaluations of the Enlightenment, see Ferrone, *The Enlightenment*; Hamnett, *The Enlightenment in Iberia and Ibero-America*.

56. On Feijóo see Sánchez-Blanco, *Europa y el pensamiento español del siglo XVIII*, 43–56; López, "Aspectos específicos de la Ilustración española," 23–39; Hamnett, *The Enlightenment in Iberia and Ibero-America*, 29–30.

57. Sánchez-Blanco, *El absolutismo y las luces*, 37.

58. Gamboa, *Comentarios*, 83.

59. François López, "El libro y su mundo," 73–78.

60. Sánchez-Blanco, *El absolutismo y las luces*, 181.

61. Llombart Rosa, "Introducción: El pensamiento económico de la Ilustración en España (1730–1812)," 16.

62. Robert Sidney Smith, "*The Wealth of Nations* in Spain and Hispanic America, 1780–1830," 104.

63. Sánchez-Blanco, *El absolutismo y las luces*, 24–28.

64. See Torales Pacheco, *Ilustrados en la Nueva España*.

65. See Llombart Rosa, "Introducción," 69–70.

66. Gamboa to Bernardo de Iriarte, March 25, 1785, British Library, Egerton Manuscripts 517, pp. 162–64.

67. Tortella, "La España discreta," 147.

68. Avaria to Arriaga, April 27, 1756, AGI, Mexico 2980. Valle Pavón suggests that Gamboa and Cotera may have greased some palms at the Council of the Indies and the Casa de Contratación. See Valle Pavón, "Los excedentes del ramo alcabalas," 991.

69. Memorial of March 21, 1756, AGI, Mexico 2980.

70. Antonio de Ulloa, the commander of the last fleet to Veracruz in 1776, made the same argument. In a letter to Viceroy Antonio María de Bucareli, his friend and ally, he wrote, "what Spain should consider is that silver and gold needs to circulate first in America, for up to five years, before it can be shipped abroad. These vassals are those processing the metal and putting it into circulation until it ships out. And even before metal is mined, it is contributing to the king's coffers: from the alcabalas paid by the mines, from mercury, from the royal fifth or tenth, from revenue at the mint, to the tributes of Indians and even to the papal bulls sold indiscriminately to even those too ignorant to understand the nature of the religious feasts." Quoted in Solano, *Antonio de Ulloa y la Nueva España*, 151–52.

71. Güemes y Horcasitas, "Relación de Don Francisco de Güemes y Horcasitas a Agustín de Ahumada y Villalón (1755)," 811.

72. Güemes y Horcasitas, "Relación de Don Francisco de Güemes y Horcasitas a Agustín de Ahumada y Villalón (1755)," 820.

73. Güemes y Horcasitas, "Relación de Don Francisco de Güemes y Horcasitas a Agustín de Ahumada y Villalón (1755)," 825.

74. Valle Pavón, "Los excedentes del ramo alcabalas," 975.

75. Gamboa, *Comentarios*, 168.

76. Valle Pavón, "Los excedentes del ramo alcabalas," 998.

77. Gamboa, *Comentarios*, 168–71.

78. Brading, *Miners and Merchants*, 162.

79. Stein and Stein, *Apogee of Empire*, 229.

80. Güemes y Horcasitas, "Relación de Don Francisco de Güemes y Horcasitas a Agustín de Ahumada y Villalón (1755)," 811.

81. Campomanes, "Del beneficio de las minas," 435. On Campomanes's opposition to Gamboa's plan, see Stein and Stein, *Apogee of Empire*, 231–32.

82. Campomanes, "Del beneficio de las minas," 441.

83. Campomanes, "Del beneficio de las minas," 443.

84. Campomanes, "Del beneficio de las minas."

Chapter Four

Note to Epigraph: Saint Isidore, considered perhaps the last great scholar of the ancient world, was the bishop of Seville from ca. 600 to 636. He compiled an encyclopedia of universal knowledge, known as the *Etymologiae*. He is the patron saint of computers. Quoted by Tau Anzoátegui, *La ley en América hispana*, 434–35.

1. Gamboa, *Comentarios*, prologue.
2. The Colegio Imperial included the Seminary of Nobles, an exclusive school within the college dedicated to the education of aristocratic youth. See Simon-Díaz, *Historia del Colegio Imperial de Madrid*.
3. Navarro, "Tradition and Scientific Change in Early Modern Spain," 346–48. Gamboa would also have met Andrés Marcos Burriel, who in the 1750s led the effort to reorder church archives in Spain, and Esteban de Terreros, a philologist and paleographer who later wrote a quadrilingual dictionary of scientific terms in Castilian, French, Italian, and Latin. Sánchez-Blanco, *El absolutismo y las luces*, 68.
4. Pérez Melero, *Minerometalurgia de la plata en México*, 59.
5. Legal historian Bernardino Bravo Lira called Gamboa the last of the Baroque jurists of Spanish America. See Bravo Lira, "La Literatura Jurídica Indiana en el Barroco," 229.
6. Gamboa, *Comentarios*, 73.
7. On Matienzo see Tau Anzoátegui, "El *Gobierno del Perú* de Juan de Matienzo." Gamboa must have known Matienzo's work in manuscript form since it was not published in full until the twentieth century.
8. Gamboa, *Comentarios*, 84.
9. Trabulse, "Francisco Xavier de Gamboa y sus Comentarios a las Ordenanzas de Minas de 1761," 27–28.
10. Solórzano Pereyra, *Política Indiana*, book 2, chapter 6, paragraph 23. On how diversity was reflected in law see Tau Anzoátegui, "La variedad indiana, una clave de la concepción jurídica de Juan de Solórzano"; Solórzano Pereyra, *Política Indiana*, book 2, chapter 6, paragraph 23.
11. Gamboa, *Comentarios*, 467.
12. Sembolini Capitani, *La construcción de la autoridad virreinal en Nueva España*, 143.
13. Gamboa, *Comentarios*, 468–72.
14. Gamboa, *Comentarios*, 467–68.
15. On the administration of justice in Mexican mining see also Gómez Mendoza, "Las nociones normativas de justicia y gobierno en la minería mexicana del siglo XVIII al XIX," 109–26.
16. Gamboa, *Comentarios*, 187.
17. See Hirschman, *The Passions and the Interests*.
18. Tutino, *Making a New World*, 8–14; Dobado and Marrero, "The Role of the Spanish Imperial State in the Mining-Led Growth of Bourbon Mexico's Economy," 860–61.
19. Dobado and Marrero, "The Role of the Spanish Imperial State in the Mining-led Growth of Bourbon Mexico's Economy," 862.

20. Gamboa, *Comentarios*, 7–8.

21. Gamboa, *Comentarios*, 108.

22. Gamboa, *Comentarios*, 230.

23. Gamboa, *Comentarios*, 373.

24. Gamboa, *Comentarios*, 83–90.

25. Gamboa, *Comentarios*, 95.

26. On the use of mercury to refine silver, see Guerrero, *Silver by Fire, Silver by Mercury.*

27. Motten, *Mexican Silver and the Enlightenment*, 26–27.

28. Gamboa, *Comentarios*, 413.

29. On this culture of state secrecy, see Cañizares-Esguerra, "Introduction," 1–6.

30. Gamboa, *Comentarios*, 166.

31. Gamboa, *Comentarios*, 61.

32. Gamboa, *Comentarios*, 166.

33. Gamboa, *Comentarios*, 379.

34. Gamboa, *Comentarios*, 229–30.

35. Motten, *Mexican Silver and the Enlightenment*, 18.

36. Gamboa, *Comentarios*, 284.

37. Gamboa, *Comentarios*, 132.

38. Gamboa, *Comentarios*, 381.

39. Gamboa, *Comentarios*, 160.

40. Gamboa, *Comentarios*, 338.

41. Gamboa, *Comentarios*, 461.

42. Gamboa, *Comentarios*, 403.

43. Gamboa, *Comentarios*, 462.

44. José Saenz de Escobar, *Geometria práctica y mecánica, divida en tres tratados,* 1706, Biblioteca Nacional de España (BNE), MSS. 7645.

45. Gamboa, *Comentarios*, prologue, unpaginated.

46. Gamboa, *Comentarios*, 236.

47. For an overview of metallurgy in colonial Spanish America, see Pérez Melero, *Minerometalurgia de la plata en México*, 69–109.

48. Gamboa, *Comentarios*, 407.

49. Torre Barrio y Lima, *Arte del nuevo beneficio de la plata en todo genero de metales frios, y calientes.*

50. Feijóo, *Cartas eruditas y curiosas*, vol. 2, letter 19.

51. Gamboa, *Comentarios*, 353.

52. On this fascinating attempt at technology transfer, see Sempat Assadourian, "La bomba de fuego de Newcomen y otros artificios de desague," 385–57. See also Pérez Melero, *Minerometalurgia de la plata en México*, 56–57.

53. Gamboa, *Comentarios*, 359–60.

54. Gamboa, *Comentarios*, 360.

55. *Medidas de minas y beneficio be los metales según Gamboa y otros para el uso de su dueño año de 1789,* John Carter Brown Library, Brown University, Codex Sp 139.

56. Alzate y Ramírez, "Elogio Histórico del Señor D. Francisco Xavier de Gamboa," 449.

57. Gamboa, *Comentarios*, 80.

58. Quoted in Gamboa, *Comentarios*, 78–79, note 39.

59. Gamboa, *Comentarios*, 78–79n39. In the same footnote, Gamboa quoted the arbitrista Martín González de Cellorigo, who in 1600 had already identified the bullionist fallacy. "Our Spain has its eyes so fixed on trade with the Indies, from which it gets its gold and silver, that it has given up trading with its neighbors; and if all the gold and silver that the natives of the New World have found, and go on finding, were to come to it, they would not make it as rich or powerful as it would be without them."

60. Gamboa, *Comentarios*, 79.

61. Gamboa, *Comentarios*, 168–81.

62. Gamboa, *Comentarios*, 168.

63. Brading, *Miners and Merchants*, 162; Stein and Stein, *Apogee of Empire*, 229.

64. Gamboa, *Comentarios*, 33.

65. Aldaco provided a foreword to a book by José Antonio Fabry, a mint official, who explained mathematically why lowering the mercury price would increase tax revenue from other sources. Fabry, *Compendios a demostracion de los crecidos adelantamientos que pudiera lograr la Real Hacienda de Su Magestad mediante la rebaja en el precio de azogue.*

66. Gamboa, *Comentarios*, 422.

67. Landázuri mentioned his early advocacy in a later opinion as *contador-general* of the Council of the Indies. Opinion of Landázuri, July 20, 1767, AGI, Mexico 1266.

68. Ibarra was considered one of the finest printers in all of Europe, for the quality of his paper and ink. See López, "El libro y su mundo," 113.

69. Sánchez-Blanco, *El absolutismo y las luces*, 41–42; Domínguez Ortiz, *Carlos III y la España de la Ilustración*, 54–56.

70. Appointment to Sala de Crimen, April 11, 1764, Archivo General de Simancas (AGS), Dirección General del Tesoro, 24–184–58.

71. Burkholder and Chandler, *From Impotence to Authority*, 167.

72. Travel Authorization, August 8, 1764, AGI, Contratación, 5507, N. 1, R. 8. Both of the Perón brothers would thrive in Mexico. After serving as Gamboa's personal secretary, Manuel began a long career as a government accountant, first in the gunpowder office and then in the Mexico City mint. His brother Antonio became a mine and estate owner in Durango and served as a deputy on the Mining Tribunal. Ayarzagoitia followed his uncle into commerce and served as the executor of his estate in 1781. All three men became respected members of the Basque community in New Spain, charter members of the Mexican branch of the Real Sociedad Bascongada de los Amigos del País. Torales Pacheco, *Ilustrados en la Nueva España*, 64, 226, 399.

73. A few months later eighty boxes of books arrived from Madrid. The Inquisition gave its approval, as was routine for the private importation of books. Unfortunately, the record does not include an inventory though it does include Gamboa's license to read prohibited books, issued in Madrid on March 12, 1761. Permission, July 23, 1765, AGN, Inquisition, 1094, 163.

Chapter Five

Note to Epigraph: "Representación Vindicatoria," 97–98. The probable author of this manifesto for creole rights was the oidor Antonio Joaquín de Rivadeneira, an alumnus of San Ildefonso.

1. On the obrajes in the economy of colonial Mexico, see Salvucci, *Textiles and Capitalism in Mexico.*

2. Residencia de Cruillas, Archivo Histórico Nacional (AHN), Consejos 20716.

3. Burkholder and Chandler, *Biographical Dictionary of Audiencia Ministers,* 298–99.

4. His appointment was made more in recognition of the long service of his father, Luís Manuel Fernández de Madrid, a former audiencia magistrate in Guatemala and Mexico, than his own merits as a jurist. Burkholder and Chandler, *Biographical Dictionary of Audiencia Ministers,* 116.

5. Burkholder and Chandler, *Biographical Dictionary of Audiencia Ministers,* 298.

6. Croix to Arriaga, February 27, 1767, Archivo General de Indias (AGI), Mexico 1126.

7. See MacLachlan, *Criminal Justice in Eighteenth Century Mexico,* 22.

8. The other jails were managed by the municipal government, the archdiocese, the Inquisition, the royal mint, and the Acordada. The jail of the Acordada, the biggest and most feared, was the only purpose-built one. Haslip-Viera, *Crime and Punishment in Late Colonial Mexico City,* 88.

9. Hevia Bolaños, *Curia Philipica.* See also Bravo Lira, "Literatura Jurídica Indiana," 231.

10. In Oaxaca, and perhaps in most regions some distance from the capital, even the most serious criminal cases were handled at the village level, without involvement by crown officials. Only murder, aggravated assault, and sedition had to be reported to colonial courts. See Taylor, *Drinking, Homicide, and Rebellion,* 74. On the informality of frontier justice see Cutter, *Legal Culture of Northern New Spain,* 105–24.

11. On the importance of the support staff of the audiencia, see Herzog, *Upholding Justice,* 47–53.

12. On procuradores see Gayol, *Laberintos de justicia.*

13. Haslip-Viera, *Crime and Punishment in Late Colonial Mexico City,* 83.

14. Besides the agents directly appointed by the Sala de Crimen, the municipal government of Mexico City also commissioned constables and night watchmen (*guardas de pito*), who assisted the alcaldes ordinarios, the city judges. Soldiers and militia members also were called upon to police the city on occasion.

15. On criminal justice in eighteenth-century England, see the classic if controversial article Hay, "Property, Authority and the Common Law," 17–64.

16. Scardaville, "Alcohol Abuse and Tavern Reform in Late Colonial Mexico City," 645.

17. Valle-Arizpe, *Historia de la Ciudad de México segun los relatos de sus cronistas*, 423.

18. Güemes y Horcasitas, "Relación de Don Francisco de Güemes y Horcasitas a Agustín de Ahumada y Villalón (1755)," 814.

19. Gamboa to Cruillas, May 31, 1765, AGI, Mexico 1130.

20. Appointment to Sala de Crimen, April 11, 1764, Archivo General de Simancas (AGS), Dirección General del Tesoro, 24–184–58. See also Solórzano Pereyra, *Política Indiana*, book 5, chapter 3, paragraph 17.

21. Alencastre Noraña y Silva, "Relación dada por el Excmo. Señor Duque de Linares," 773.

22. Gamboa to Cruillas, May 31, 1765, AGI, Mexico 1130.

23. José de Gálvez later championed the *Gremio de Panaderos de Mexico*, approving regulations that would have given bakers huge control over the market, at the expense of wheat farmers, millers, and independent market vendors. Gálvez on Panaderos, November 12, 1770, Real Biblioteca (RB), MS Ayala LVI/2829. The crown did not approve this very unpopular initiative.

24. Campillo y Cossío, *Nuevo sistema de gobierno ecónomico para América*. On whether Campillo wrote the paper attributed to him see Navarro García, "Campillo y el Nuevo sistema: Una atribución dudosa," 22–29. See also Kuethe and Andrien, *The Spanish Atlantic World in the Eighteenth Century*, 136–38; Owensby, "Between Justice and Economics," 143–69.

25. Kuethe and Andrien, *The Spanish Atlantic World in the Eighteenth Century*, 248.

26. Gálvez, *Discurso y reflexiones de un vasallo sobre la decadencia de Nuestras Indias*, RB, MS Ayala II/2816. See also Navarro García, *La política americana de José de Gálvez según su "discurso y reflexiones de un vasallo."*

27. The *Discurso y reflexiones de un vasallo* was a typical product of eighteenth-century *proyectismo*. According to Kuethe and Andrien, "*Proyectistas* were usually self-promoters, often seeking appointments as the result of their Panglossian expositions. Most pieces contained little that was truly original or even innovative." Kuethe and Andrien, *The Spanish Atlantic World in the Eighteenth Century*, 204.

28. Juan and Ulloa, *Discourse and Political Reflections on the Kingdoms of Peru*.

29. MacLachlan, *Spain's Empire in the New World*, 76–77.

30. Gálvez, *Discurso y reflexiones de un vasallo*, RB, MS Ayala II/2816.

31. Gálvez, *Discurso y reflexiones de un vasallo*, RB, MS Ayala II/2816. To his credit, Gálvez admitted in his 1771 final report as visitor general that the magistrates of the audiencia, even the creoles he instinctively mistrusted, fulfilled their duties loyally. "I have not seen verified the inconveniences that I feared from their relationships and alliances with the major families of this city." Gálvez, *Informe del marqués de Sonora al virrey don Antonio Bucarely y Ursúa*.

32. Gálvez to the crown, November 20, 1765, AGI, Mexico 1701.

33. Cruillas to Arriaga, March 20, 1766, AGI, Mexico 1265.

34. To be sure, Cruillas might have had something to hide. There were rumors that his secretaries demanded "gratifications" before dispatching routine work and Madrid was already contemplating charges against him. Audiencia to Cruillas, February 8, 1763, Residencia de Cruillas, AHN, Consejos 20716. See also Gálvez, *Informe del marqués de Sonora al virrey don Antonio Bucarely y Ursúa*, xxxii.

35. Gálvez to Arriaga, March 20, 1766, AGI, Mexico 1703.

36. The bloodshed might have been much worse if the former viceroy of New Spain, the Conde de Revillagigedo, now captain general of the army, had not refused to order his troops to fire on the crowd. Domínguez Ortiz, *Carlos III y la España de la Ilustración*, 104–05. Revillagigedo served as an advisor to Charles and Esquilache on colonial affairs. See Stein and Stein, *Apogee of Empire*, 49–50.

37. On the Madrid riot see especially López García, *El Motín contra Esquilache*; Kuethe and Andrien, *The Spanish Atlantic World in the Eighteenth Century*, 256–58. Lluis Roura i Aulinas argues that the popular unrest in spring 1766 was a genuinely revolutionary moment, perhaps the first sign in Europe of the rupture of the ancien régime. See Roura i Aulinas, "Expectativas y frustración bajo el reformismo borbónico," 181.

38. The best account of the troubles of 1766 and 1767 remains Castro Gutiérrez, *Nueva ley y nuevo rey*. See also Tutino, *Making a New World*, 235–37.

39. On mine labor and the partido see Pérez Melero, *Minerometalurgia de la plata en México*, 27–30.

40. Bergamo, *Daily Life in Colonial Mexico*, 162. On the strike in Real del Monte see Ladd, *The Making of a Strike*; Danks, "The Labor Revolt of 1766 in the Mining Community of Real del Monte," 143–65; Chavez Orozco, ed., *Conflicto de trabajo con los mineros de Real del Monte, año de 1766*.

41. See Taylor, *Drinking, Homicide, and Rebellion*, 115–24.

42. While on patrol in January 1766, Gamboa put down two brawls that pitted soldiers against civilians started in pulquerias. Gamboa to the crown, May 6, 1767, AGI, Mexico 1707.

43. Documents on Real del Monte, Archivo General de la Nación (AGN), Civil 2166, exp. 2.

44. Aldaco had apparently lost a fortune trying to restore the Santa Brigida mine along the Vizcaína vein. See Valcárcel opinion on the Mining Tribunal, August 29, 1774, AGI, Mexico 2240; Gamboa, *Comentarios*, 355.

45. Gamboa, *Comentarios*, 337.

46. Quoted in Canterla and Tovar, *Vida y Obra del primer Conde de Regla*, 109.

47. Gamboa to Arriaga, February 26, 1768, AGI, Mexico 2778. Unfortunately, Terreros refused to accept Gamboa's new labor code. He continued to insist that the partido should be abolished and soon convinced Croix and Gálvez of the same. For the next few years one of the most important mining complexes in New Spain operated well below capacity as Terreros refused to return to active management unless the partido was eliminated.

48. Croix to Sala de Crimen, September 10 and 15, 1766, AGI, Mexico 1265; Sala de Crimen to Croix, September 16, 1766, AGI, Mexico 1265.

49. Vagrancy decree, February 26, 1767, AGI, Mexico 1266.

50. The memorial was included in a package of reports sent to Madrid by the viceroy. Croix to Council of the Indies, November 26, 1766, AGI, Mexico 1265.

51. Fabián y Fuero to Croix, October 4, 1766, AGI, Mexico 1265. Fabián became unpopular with the elite of Puebla when he tried to impose greater austerity in convent life. Brading, *The First America*, 495–96.

52. Palacios to Croix, September 27, 1766, AGI, Mexico 1265.

53. Book 2, title 17 of the *Recopilación de las leyes de Indias* covered the duties of the alcaldes del crimen.

54. Although all three alcaldes del crimen signed the Sala de Crimen's correspondence, Gamboa later admitted that he was the lead author. Gamboa to Arriaga, February 26, 1768, AGI, Mexico 2668.

55. Sala de Crimen to Croix, October 14, 1766, AGI, Mexico 1265.

56. Solórzano seemed to support this reading of the five-league limit. Alcaldes del crimen could only hear cases "in the places where the courts are located and within five leagues." Solórzano Pereyra, *Política Indiana*, book 5, chapter 5, paragraph 1.

57. Gamboa, *Comentarios*, 467.

58. Tau Anzoátegui, *El poder de la costumbre*, 102.

59. Cornide to Croix, November 22, 1766, AGI, Mexico 1265.

60. Cornide was despised by opponents of the visita. One pasquinade at the time, addressed to Croix, who liked to play cards, put it this way: "Llévate a tu Cornide / ese tosco gallego / que robaba a dos manos / mientras que tú jugabas a los cientos." In English, "Take Cornide out of here, that rude Galician, who robbed with both hands while you played card games." *Varias composiciones en verso contra Gálvez y el Marqués de Croix*, Biblioteca Nacional de Epaña (BNE), MSS/20258–31.

61. Castro, *Discursos críticos sobre las leyes y sus interpretes*.

62. Castro, *Discursos críticos sobre las leyes y sus interpretes* 183.

63. On Castro's critique of the legal order see Tau Anzoátegui, *El poder de la costumbre*, 105; Sánchez-Blanco, *El absolutismo y las luces*, 116–17.

64. Solórzano Pereyra, *Política Indiana*, book 5, chapter 3, paragraph 10.

65. Tau Anzoátegui, "La variedad indiana, una clave de la concepción jurídica de Juan de Solórzano."

66. On the Acordada see MacLachlan, *Criminal Justice in Eighteenth Century Mexico*; Mendoza Muñoz and D'abbadie Soto, *El capitán Miguel Velázquez Lorea y el Real Tribunal de la Acordada de la Nueva España*; Hidalgo Nuchera, *Antes de la Acordada*.

67. *Las Siete Partidas*, part 7, title 8, law 3.

68. *Las Siete Partidas*, part 7, title 14, law 8.

69. In 1755 one of the tasks assigned to Gamboa, then the consulado's deputy in Madrid, was to seek relief for the consulado from the obligation to fund the Acordada.

70. MacLachlan, *Criminal Justice in Eighteenth Century Mexico*, 33–34.

71. Espinosa de los Monteros, *Oración contua funebre*, . . . *al Theniente Coronel D. Joseph Velázquez Lorea*.

72. Taylor, *Drinking, Homicide, and Rebellion*, 98.

73. Güemes y Horcasitas, "Relación de Don Francisco de Güemes y Horcasitas a Agustín de Ahumada y Villalón (1755)," 799.

74. Provisions on Illegal Liquor, August 22, 1755, AGI, Mexico 2502. In 1772, the Acordada absorbed this jurisdiction as well.

75. In 1756 the crown ratified this decision. MacLachlan, *Criminal Justice in Eighteenth Century Mexico*, 91. Although conflict between the two forces was frequent, the Acordada tended to concentrate on property crimes, like robbery, while the Sala de Crimen handled violent offences against persons, such as murder and rape. See Haslip-Viera, *Crime and Punishment in Late Colonial Mexico City*, 54.

76. Güemes y Horcasitas, "Relación de Don Francisco de Güemes y Horcasitas a Agustín de Ahumada y Villalón (1755)," 814.

77. MacLachlan, *Criminal Justice in Eighteenth Century Mexico*, 56.

78. Sala de Crimen to Council of the Indies, November 24, 1766, AGI, Mexico 1265.

79. Sala de Crimen to Croix, November 24, 1766, AGI, Mexico 1265.

80. Council's decision, October 29, 1767, AGI, Mexico 1126. The crown attorney had recommended that the Sala de Crimen's jurisdiction be affirmed but with the requirement that the court reduce the excessive number of lieutenants in Puebla. Fiscal's opinion, October 8, 1767, AGI, Mexico 1265.

81. Fabián to Croix, 1768, AGN, Real Audiencia, Vol. 14, Correspondence, p. 445

82. Sala de Crimen to Croix, December 18, 1769, AGN, Real Audiencia, Vol. 14, Correspondence, p. 443.

83. Sala de Crimen to Croix, December 16, 1769, AGN, Real Audiencia, Vol. 14, Correspondence, p. 440.

84. MacLachlan, *Criminal Justice in Eighteenth Century Mexico*, 51.

85. MacLachlan, *Criminal Justice in Eighteenth Century Mexico*, 74.

86. MacLachlan, "Acordada," 108–16.

87. MacLachlan, "Acordada," 114–16.

88. Quoted in MacLachlan, *Criminal Justice in Eighteenth Century Mexico*, 34.

89. The whole matter is covered in Council of the Indies on Presidios, May 21, 1771, AGI, Mexico 1130. On presidio punishment see Mehl, *Forced Migration in the Spanish Pacific World*.

90. Haslip-Viera, *Crime and Punishment in Late Colonial Mexico City*, 112.

91. Sala de Crimen to the Crown, June 26, 1767, AGI, Mexico 1130.

92. On special treatment for Indians in the criminal justice system, see Uribe-Uran, "Innocent Infants or Abusive Patriarchs?" 812.

93. There was some truth to this apparently racist assumption. Sedentary Indians from the central highlands of Mexico had little exposure to the tropical diseases that flourished on the coast and were thus more likely to die. On the historical importance in America of mosquito-spread diseases like malaria and yellow fever, see McNeill, *Mosquito Empires*.

94. Haslip-Viera, *Crime and Punishment in Late Colonial Mexico City*, 112–16.

95. Sala de Crimen to the Crown, December 23, 1767, AGI, Mexico 1707.

96. Sala de Crimen to Croix, July 8, 1768, AGN, Real Audiencia, Vol. 14, p. 178.

97. Sala de Crimen to Croix, March 9, 1769, AGN, Real Audiencia, Vol. 14, p. 394.

98. Nothing was done to fix the problem until the late 1770s when the crown finally allotted a share of pulque revenue to the Sala de Crimen as well. It also agreed to restore the collera, at least in part. Courts could resume sending convicts to bakeries and pork butchers but not to the more abusive obrajes. Opinion of the Council of the Indies, May 29, 1777, AGI, Mexico 1126.

99. Stanley and Barbara Stein concluded that an array of conservative forces, but not necessarily the Jesuits, were behind the trouble. "The coup of March 1766 suggests a wide consensus among privileged groups behind the decision to abort Esquilache's reform policy. The colegiales in the Consejo de Castilla and its Sala de Alcaldes who precipitated the *motín* were reinforced by Andalusian magnates in furnishing actors, intermediaries, and advisors in the crisis. Informal and formal webs tied these groups to the secular and regular clergy, whose participation was clarified by the activity of the bishops of Cuenca and Cartagena, the Cinco Gremios Mayores, and—less visible—the Consulado de Cadiz." Stein and Stein, *Apogee of Empire*, 114. This seems a bit too conspiratorial to me and takes agency away from hungry, angry plebeians.

100. In theology the Jesuits supported the doctrine of probablism, which held that when there was a question solely of the lawfulness or unlawfulness of an action, it was permissible to follow a solidly probable opinion in favor of liberty, even if the opposing view might be more probable. This allowed the Jesuits flexibility in their worldwide missionary endeavors but in the eyes of its critics was dangerously relativistic. In philosophy the Jesuits upheld the work of Francisco Suárez, one of their own, who argued that the people had the right to rebel against tyrannical rulers. This support for notions of popular sovereignty offended regalists

and absolutists. See Sánchez-Blanco, *El absolutismo y las luces*, 86; Tau Anzoáte-gui, *Casuismo y sistema*, 57–60.

101. There were clear anti-Semitic undertones to the accusations against the Jesuits. Their enemies saw them as greedy and arrogant cosmopolitans, who pulled secret levers of power to get their way and harbored among their ranks many *conversos* (converted Jews) and crypto-Jews. See Roura i Aulinas, "Expectativas y frustración bajo el reformismo borbónico," 189–91.

102. Garcidueñas, *El antiguo Colegio de San Ildefonso*, 18.

103. Decorme, *La obra de los jesuitas mexicanos durante la epoca colonial, 1572–1767*, vol. 1 of 2, 447–48.

104. The cabildo of Mexico City complained to Madrid about the desecration of the college, seeking to maintain it as a school. Cabildo of Mexico to Arriaga, July 27, 1767, and August 27, 1768, AGI, Mexico 1126.

105. Clavijero, "Breve descripción de la Provincia de México de la Compañia de Jesús, segun el estado en que se hallaba en año de 1767," 297.

106. López de Priego, "Carta de un religioso de los extintos Jesuitas, a una hermana suya, religiosa del convento de Santa Catarina de la Puebla de los Angleles (1785)," 24–25.

107. Gálvez, *Informe sobre las rebeliones populares de 1767 y otros documentos inéditos*.

108. Taylor, *Drinking, Homicide, and Rebellion*, 122. Similarly, David Brading judged the visitor general's response "a watershed in Mexico's colonial history." Brading, *The First America*, 468.

109. *Varias composiciones en verso contra Gálvez y el Marqués de Croix*, Biblioteca Nacional de España, MS/20258-31.

110. Decree by Croix on Jesuit pamphlets, November 27, 1767, AGI, Mexico 2778.

111. Remarkably, at this precise moment, Archbishop Francisco Antonio de Lorenzana, who had supported the Jesuit expulsion, presided over the long-delayed opening of the Basque school for girls, the Vizcaínas, officially named after the founder of the Jesuit order, San Ignacio de Loyola. Aránzazu to the king, September 27, 1767, AGI, Mexico 1701.

112. Lorenzana to Arriaga, December 1, 1767, AGI, Mexico 2778.

113. According to Gamboa, when he went to speak about the dangers of exposing the Native population to the rigors of the presidios, Croix's legal advisor Cornide insulted him. Gamboa to Arriaga, February 26, 1768, AGI, Mexico 2778.

114. Croix to Arriaga, August 27, 1769, AGI, Mexico 1369.

115. Croix to Arriaga, August 27, 1769, AGI, Mexico 1369. Croix, an enthusiastic card player himself, might have just been upset that he not been invited to the visitor general's parties.

116. Lorenzana to the crown, December 1, 1767, AGI, Mexico 2778. Lopez Portillo, a generation younger than Gamboa, was also a native of Guadalajara educated at the Jesuit college of San Ildefonso. Juan José de Eguiara y Eguren, author of the

Bibliotheca mexicana (1755) mentioned Lopez Portillo as a paragon of American intellectual accomplishment. See Brading, *The First America*, 389.

117. Croix to Arriaga, August 27, 1769, AGI, Mexico 1369.

118. Quoted in Navarro García, "Destrucción de la oposición política," 3.

119. Gamboa to Arriaga, February 26, 1768, AGI, Mexico 2778.

120. Solórzano Pereyra, *Política Indiana*, book 5, chapter 10, paragraph 20.

121. Gamboa to Arriaga, February 26, 1768.

122. Opinion of Campomanes and Moñino, March 5, 1768, AGI, Mexico 2778.

123. They refer specifically to "criollos" in their report.

124. On the new Spanish tax collectors who arrived with Gálvez, who sought opportunities to enrich themselves as enthusiastically as those whom they replaced, see Salvucci, "Costumbres viejas, 'hombres nuevos.'"

125. When Gamboa was writing the *Comentarios* in Madrid, Campomanes was writing a tract urging radical reforms to colonial trade, including the abolition of the Cadiz monopoly. Rodríguez de Campomanes, *Reflexiones sobre el comercio español a Indias (1762)*. See Stein and Stein, *Apogee of Empire*, 61.

126. "Representación Vindicatoria (1771)," 86.

127. "Representación Vindicatoria (1771)," 97–98.

128. David Brading has called the representation the "last grand statement of the traditional themes of creole patriotism in New Spain before the debates of 1808." Brading, *The First America*, 483. See also Tutino, *Mexico City, 1808*, 122–26.

129. Lorenzana to Croix, July 19, 1768 and Croix to Arriaga, July 26, 1768, AGI, Mexico 2778.

130. Opinion of the Council of Castile, January 6, 1769, AGI, Mexico 2778.

131. At the same time he was preparing to leave Mexico by order of the king, he was also being considered by the Council of the Indies for a promotion in Mexico. In October 1769 he received one first-place vote in the election to replace Francisco Echevarri as oidor in the Sala de lo Civil. The position went to his Spanish-born colleague Francisco Leandro de Viana. Consultation of Cámara de Indias, October 6, 1769, AGI, Mexico 1641.

132. Gamboa to Arriaga, August 29, 1769, AGI, Mexico 2778.

133. Gamboa to Arriaga, August 29, 1769, AGI, Mexico 2778.

134. Notarized transfer between Gamboa and Meave, AGI, Mexico 2778.

135. Gamboa reported to Croix that he had to pay 2,000 pesos for a single cabin for himself and son, plus another 2,000 pesos in costs. Gamboa to Croix, November 4, 1769, AGN, Real Audiencia, Vol. 14, Correspondence 1767–68, p. 459.

136. Might Gamboa and his son have crossed the Atlantic on the premier ship of the Spanish navy, built in Havana and launched in March 1769? Or was this a humbler ship with the same name, *Santisima Trinidad*?

Chapter Six

Note to Epigraph: Gálvez, *Informe*, 1771, quoted in Howe, *The Mining Guild of New Spain*, 1.

1. Gálvez, "Abril 20 de 1765, Inventorio de los bienes, créditos y alhajas pertenecientes al Señor Don Joseph de Gálvez Gallardo," 7–58.

2. A representative opinion attributing the increase to the Mining Tribunal is offered by TePaske and Brown, *A New World of Gold and Silver*, 77.

3. Gamboa to Arriaga, April 13, 1770, Archivo General de Indias (AGI), Mexico 2778.

4. Representation, June 13, 1770, AGI, Mexico 1876. This package was included in a 1781 submission, when he was fighting his transfer to the Audiencia of Santo Domingo.

5. Urrutia to Arriaga, December 1, 1770, AGI, Mexico 2778.

6. Urrutia to Arriaga, November 27, 1771, AGI, Mexico 2778.

7. Priestley, *José de Gálvez*, 245–66.

8. Priestley, *José de Gálvez*, 278–81.

9. Reglamiento del Gremio de Panaderos de Mexico, November 12, 1770. Real Biblioteca (RB), MS Ayala LVI/2869.

10. *Varias composiciones en verso contra Gálvez y el Marqués de Croix, de hacia 1771*, Biblioteca Nacional de España (BNE), MSS/20258–31.

11. Croix was despised by the end of his mandate, seen as a toady of Gálvez. One verse bid farewell to the viceroy this way: "Adios, Marqués de Croix / que ocupaste tu tiempo / en estar en tu cuarto / firmando, siempre, como en un barbecho." To "firmar en barbecho" means to sign something without first reading it. *Varias composiciones en verso contra Gálvez y el Marqués de Croix, de hacia 1771*, BNE, MSS/20258–31.

12. On Bucareli see Priestley, *José de Gálvez*, 287–88; Bobb, *The Viceregency of Antonio Maria Bucareli in New Spain*.

13. Bucareli to Arriaga, February 22, 1772, Real Academia de la Historia, Bucareli 4308.

14. Croix to Urrutia, December 20, 1771, AGI, Mexico 2778.

15. Opinion of fiscals, April 7, 1778, AGI, Mexico 2778.

16. Permission to depart, AGI, Contratación, 5516, n. 186. Perón may have been with Gamboa since 1764, when as a teenager he traveled to New Spain with Gamboa.

17. Cámara de Indias, October 6, 1769, AGI, Mexico 1641.

18. In 1776 the crown increased the size of the audiencia from eight oidores and four alcaldes del crimen to ten and five, respectively. In 1788, however, the numbers were reduced, through attrition, back to eight and four. On the role of oidores in

government see also Sanciñena Asurmendi, *La Audiencia en México en el reinado de Carlos III*, 44–47. Cañeque, *The King's Living Image*, 65.

19. Gamboa's representation, March 14, 1781, AGI, Mexico 1876. Romero de Terreros, "Epigrafía de la Hacienda de Xalpa," 418–21.

20. Tutino, *Making a New World*, 281–87.

21. Representation by Encarnación, December 15, 1777, AGI, Mexico 1862.

22. Gamboa's representation, March 14, 1781, AGI, Mexico 1876; Brading, *The First America*, 178.

23. BNE, Papeles referentes a Hacienda, MSS/3535, no. 187.

24. Gamboa's representation, March 14, 1781, AGI, Mexico 1876.

25. BNE, Papeles referentes a Hacienda, MSS/3535, no. 294; Luque Alcaide, "Francisco Javier Gamboa y la educación del indígena en México (siglo XVIII)," 47–61.

26. Gamboa's representation to the crown, March 14, 1781, AGI, Mexico 1876.

27. Sarría to Gálvez, May 25, 1781, AGI, Mexico 1867.

28. Sarria, *Ensayo de metalurgia*.

29. Instructions, March 16, 1765, quoted by Priestley, *José de Gálvez*, 416–17.

30. Fabry, *Compendios a demostracion de los crecidos adelantamientos*.

31. Gálvez, *Discurso y reflexiones de un vasallo sobre la decadencia de Nuestras Indias*, RB, MS Ayala II/2816.

32. Gamboa, *Comentarios*, 379. Borda was focused at the time on his own proposal for the rehabilitation of the Quebradilla mine in Zacatecas, which the crown approved with a package of concessions in 1768. Cédula on Quebradilla project, March 12, 1768, AGI, Mexico 2235.

33. Representation on mercury prices, March 28, 1767, AGI, Mexico 1266.

34. Relación de méritos, 1759, AGI, Ind. Gen. 158, no. 20. Landázuri proposed the construction of a second mint in Guadalajara, as had Gamboa, and lobbied for a university there, a project finally accomplished in 1792. López-Hidalgo Preciado, "Fundación de la Real Universidad de Guadalajara," 62–67. On Landázuri, see also Bernard, *Le Secrétariat d'État et le Conseil espagnol des Indes*, 126–32; Burkholder, *Biographical Dictionary of Councillors of the Indies*, 88–89.

35. Stein and Stein, *Apogee of Empire*, 69–79.

36. Llombart Rosa, *Campomanes*, 130–34.

37. See Burkholder, "The Council of the Indies in the Late Eighteenth Century," 404–23.

38. Gamboa, "Breve Noticia del origen y formación de las Perlas," RB, MS Ayala, 2834.

39. Landázuri, "Noticia de los Minerales de Oro y Plata que contienen las Provincias de el Reyno de la Nueva España, con expresión de los nombres de las Minas principales, y de el estado, en que actualmente se hallan," RB, MS Ayala, 2824.

40. See Stein and Stein, *Apogee of Empire*, 151–53. The Steins's view of Landázuri is not entirely consistent. On the one hand, they describe him as colonialist to the core, opposed to both manufacturing and mercury mining in New Spain. On the

other hand, they admit his close ties to the merchants of Mexico City, who invested in domestic manufacturing and mining.

41. Opinion of Landázuri on unminted silver, July 20, 1767, AGI, Mexico 1266.

42. Tau Anzoátegui, *Casuismo y sistema*, 115.

43. On dissimulation as a legal mechanism see Tau Anzoátegui, "La disimulaión en el Derecho Indiano," 223–43.

44. Landázuri opinion on mercury prices, July 13, 1767, AGI, Mexico 1266.

45. In the 1750s, the crown invited foreign scientists to Almadén, including the Irishman William Bowles and the German Heinrich Storr, to overhaul operations. Lowering the cost of production at Almadén and thus expanding output gave the crown the confidence to lower mercury prices in New Spain. See Motten, *Mexican Silver and the Enlightenment*, 7.

46. Dobado and Marrero accept that the improved mercury supply was the main factor in the growth of mining and with it the entire novohispano economy. See Dobado and Marrero, "The role of the Spanish imperial state in the mining-led growth of Bourbon Mexico's economy," 866–70. The crown also stimulated production by making blasting powder, another state monopoly, more available. Stein and Stein, *Apogee of Empire*, 234–36.

47. Gálvez to the crown, February 17, 1771, AGI, Mexico 1129; Council of the Indies opinion on Real del Monte, June 12, 1773, AGI, Mexico 1129.

48. Representation by Regla, Sepember 2, 1771, AGI, Mexico 1129.

49. Quoted in *La administración de D. Frey Antonio María de Bucareli y Ursua*, 366.

50. *La administración de D. Frey Antonio María de Bucareli y Ursua*, 374.

51. Opinion of Landázuri on Regla, July 19, 1772, AGI, Mexico 1129.

52. Royal cédula, July 20, 1773, AGI, Mexico 2235. At the same time, Bucareli requested that treasury officials across New Spain send to Mexico City detailed information about the mines in their districts, including ownership, production levels, mercury consumption, and fiscal revenue. For a compilation of the original reports see López Miramontes and Urrutia de Stebelski, *Las minas de Nueva España en 1774*.

53. Alzate y Ramírez, *Asuntos varios sobre ciencias y artes*, November 30, 1772.

54. Motten, *Mexican Silver and the Enlightenment*, 33. On Velázquez de León see Moreno, *Joaquín Velázquez de León y sus trabajos científicos sobre el valle de México*, 21–44.

55. Lassaga and Velázquez de León, *Representación que a nombre de la Minería de esta Nueva España, hacen al Rey Nuestro Señor*.

56. Lassaga and Velázquez de León, *Representación que a nombre de la Minería de esta Nueva España, hacen al Rey Nuestro Señor*.

57. Lassaga and Velázquez de León, *Representación que a nombre de la Minería de esta Nueva España, hacen al Rey Nuestro Señor*.

58. On the consulado's role in the drainage project, see Candiani, *Dreaming of Dry Land*, esp. chapter six.

59. Acuerdo opinion, August 14, 1774, AGI, Mexico 2240

60. Opinion of Valcárcel, August 29, 1774, AGI, Mexico 2240

61. Lassaga to Gálvez, June 27, 1778, AGI, Mexico 2240.

62. Howe, *Mining Guild of New Spain*, 49.

63. Resolution of Council of the Indies, April 23, 1776, AGI, Mexico 2240.

64. Landázuri opinion, February 9, 1776, AGI, Mexico 2240.

65. Quoted in MacKay, *"Lazy, Improvident People" Myth and Reality in the Writing of Spanish History*, 147.

66. Llombart Rosa, "Campomanes, el economista de Carlos III," 236–37.

67. Campomanes, "Del beneficio de las minas," 443.

68. Smith, *An Inquiry into the Nature and Causes of the Wealth of Nations*, 606.

69. TePaske and Brown, *A New World of Gold and Silver*, 77; Tutino, *Making a New World*, 160–64.

70. Garner and Stefanou, *Economic Growth and Change in Bourbon Mexico*, 36.

71. Gálvez, *Informe del marqués de Sonora al virrey don Antonio Bucarely y Ursúa*, 70.

72. Ordinance thirty-seven, analyzed by Gamboa, *Comentarios*, 323–40.

73. Audiencia representation to the crown, April 26, 1778, AGI, Mexico 2240.

74. Lassaga to Gálvez, June 27, 1778, AGI, Mexico 2240.

75. In September 1778 Antonio de Ulloa, in New Spain as commander of the last organized fleet, warned his close friend Bucareli that Gálvez was planning to elevate his brother Matías, who in his opinion was "limitadísimo, sin talentos ni instrucción." Quoted in Solano, *Antonio de Ulloa y la Nueva España*, 378.

76. On Cossío see Brading, *Miners and Merchants*, 61–63.

77. Cossío to Gálvez, November 20, 1780, AGI, Mexico 1511.

78. Quoted in Sanciñena Asurmendi, *La Audiencia en México en el reinado de Carlos III*, 202.

79. See Tutino, *Mexico City, 1808*, 128–32. For the financing of Spain's contribution to the United States' independence see Valle Pavón, *Donativos, préstamos y privilegios*.

80. The royal order of Gamboa's appointment was dated December 19, 1780.

81. Gamboa to the king, March 14, 1781, AGI, Mexico 1876. This submission, with eleven supporting documents, reviewed his entire career as an audiencia minister.

82. Bartolache certificate included in Gamboa's March 1781 submission, AGI, Mexico 1876.

83. Mayorga to Gálvez, March 16, 1781, AGI, Mexico 1876.

84. Cossío to Gálvez, March 14, 1781, AGI, Mexico 1511.

85. Gamboa to Flores, April 16, 1788, AGI, Mexico 1879. Berrio died during construction of his family's mansion in the center of Mexico City, today known as the Palacio de Iturbide and maintained as a cultural center by Citibanamex.

86. Mariana Berrio to Gálvez, January 11, 1782 AGI, Mexico 1876

87. Gamboa and Condesa de San Mateo to Gálvez, January 12, 1781, AGI, Mexico 1876.
88. Gamboa to Mayoraga, December 31, 1782, AGI, Mexico 1876. The Berrio estate case was hardly settled. The crown refused to accept the mayorazgo and the Moncadas divorced, amid mutual accusations of adultery. It was a huge scandal in the early 1790s. Revillagigedo to the king, August 31, 1792, Archivo Histórico Nacional (AHN), Consejos, 21807.
89. Membership in the cathedral chapter was the most prestigious position open to priests in New Spain. These officers assisted and advised the bishop, handled diocesan protocol and conducted religious services in the cathedral itself. See Taylor, *Magistrates of the Sacred*, 121–24.
90. Juan José de Gamboa to Gálvez, May 30, 1783, AGI, Mexico 1876.
91. Cossío to Gálvez, November 17, 1781, AGI, Mexico 1511.
92. Letter regarding tribunal's accounts, August 12, 1786, AGI, Mexico, 2240.
93. Valdés, *Gazetas de Mexico*, August 11, 1784; Pérez Melero, *Minerometalurgia de la plata en México*, 44–52.
94. Posada to Valdés, December 30, 1788, AGI, Mexico, 2238.
95. Miners' representation to the viceroy, August 7, 1782, AGI, Mexico, 2241.
96. Posada to Gálvez, September 2, 1786, AGI, Mexico, 2241.
97. Gamboa opinion on the Mining Tribunal, January 1, 1790, AGI, Mexico, 2238. See also Méndez Pérez, "El licenciado don Francisco Xavier de Gamboa en las Juntas de Arreglo de Minería de la Nueva España, 1789–1790," 161–96.
98. Gamboa opinion on the Mining Tribunal, January 1, 1790, AGI, Mexico, 2242.
99. Elhuyar opinion on the Mining Tribunal, January 27, 1790, AGI, Mexico, 2242.
100. Ladrón de Guevara's opinion, June 21, 1777, AGI, Mexico 2240.
101. Joaquín Velázquez de León to crown, May 26, 1778, *Nuebas ordenanzas de minas*, Hispanic Society of America, HC 336/645.
102. Howe, *Mining Guild of New Spain*, 62.
103. He could have been thinking about Juan Ordóñez Montalvo, a priest who headed the mining operations of the Valle Ameno family and who in 1758 had published a book about mercury refining.
104. Frederick Sonneschmidt, *Descripción de los diferentes methodos que hay en este reyno de N. E. de beneficiar metales por amalgmación*, manuscript, prologue, unpaginated, John Carter Brown Library.
105. This derision of local practical knowledge and the inflated expectations for the implementation of abstract scientific principles resembles modern statecraft as described by James C. Scott. See Scott, *Seeing Like a State*, 309–41.
106. Observations on Physics, July 30, 1787, AGI, Mexico 1878.
107. Alamán, *Historia de México desde los primeros movimientos que prepararon su independencia en el año de 1808, hasta la época presente*, vol. 1, 28.
108. Quoted in Howe, *Mining Guild of New Spain*, 383.
109. Grafe and Irigoin, "A stakeholder empire: the political economy of Spanish imperial rule in America," 626.

110. Revillagigedo to Pedro Lorena, July 29, 1790, AGI, Mexico 2242.

111. In 1790, as part of the review of mining in New Spain, Viceroy Revillagigedo remitted to Madrid files on the concessions. The criteria used to structure concessions can be glimpsed in the opinion of José Antonio de la Cerda, a mercury official, to Pedro Lorena, October 5, 1790, AGI Mexico 2243.

112. Gamboa, *Comentarios*, 477–82.

Chapter Seven

Note to Epigraph: Revillagigedo to Floridablanca, August 29, 1790, AGI, Estado 20, no. 52.

1. See Garriga, "Los límites del reformismo borbónico."

2. This argument is made by Michael Scardaville in the context of the criminal justice system of Mexico City. See Scardaville, "(Habsburg) Law and (Bourbon) Order," 501–25.

3. Dubois, *Avengers of the New World*, 39.

4. Dubois, *Avengers of the New World*, 16.

5. Burkholder, *Biographical Dictionary of Councillors of the Indies*, 62.

6. Iriarte to Gamboa, December 24, 1784, British Library (BL), Egerton Manuscripts 517.

7. Gamboa to Iriarte, March 25, 1785, BL, Egerton Manuscripts 517.

8. Gamboa to Iriarte, March 25, 1785, BL, Egerton Manuscripts 517.

9. Gamboa report, March 25, 1785, BL, Egerton Manuscripts 517.

10. The slave code has been erroneously attributed to Gamboa by several authors. On Emparán's role see Malagon Barceló, ed., *Código Negro Carolino*, xlv–li.

11. On the reform in Mexico City see Scardaville, "(Habsburg) Law and (Bourbon) Order."

12. Audiencia to crown on new urban ordinances, February 25, 1786, Archivo General de Indias (AGI), Santo Domingo 989.

13. Iriarte's report, June 8, 1785, BL, Egerton Manuscripts 517.

14. Real Cédula, April 12, 1786, BL, Egerton Manuscripts 517.

15. Gamboa to Iriarte, April 25, 1787, BL, Egerton Manuscripts 517.

16. On the Haitian revolution see Dubois, *Avengers of the New World*.

17. In 1785 the audiencia reported to Madrid that it heard 422 cases. Ventura de Taranco to the Audiencia, June 24, 1786, AGI, Santo Domingo 991.

18. Ventura de Taranco to the Audiencia, June 24, 1786, AGI, Santo Domingo 991; Audiencia to Council, December 25, 1787, AGI, Santo Domingo 991.

19. Response of crown attorney of Council of the Indies, March 1, 1788, AGI, Santo Domingo 991.

20. Garcia to Gálvez, March 23, 1786, AGI, Santo Domingo, 989

21. Audiencia to the crown, April 25, 1786, AGI, Santo Domingo 989.

22. Gamboa to the crown, May 6, 1767, AGI, Mexico 1707.

23. Fiscal's opinion endorsed by the Council, September 4, 1786, AGI, Santo Domingo 989.

24. Maria Manuela de Urrutia to Gálvez, December 2, 1785, AGI, Mexico 1876.

25. Burkholder and Chandler, *Biographical Dictionary of Audiencia Ministers*, 312–13.

26. Gamboa to the king, August 25, 1787, and Opinion of the fiscal, March 31, 1788, AGI, Santo Domingo 1006.

27. Gálvez also approved the establishment of the Archivo General de Indias in Seville, for which he deserves the everlasting gratitude of historians. See Solano, "José de Gálvez: Fundador del Archivo de Indias," 7–52.

28. See Salvucci, "Costumbres viejas, 'hombres nuevos.'"

29. Tau Anzoátegui, "La formación y promulgación de las Leyes Indianas: En torno a una consulta del Consejo de Indias en 1794," 148–49.

30. For the most recent accounts of the rebellion see Walker, *The Tupac Amaru Rebellion*; Serulnikov, *Revolution in the Andes*. See also Serulnikov, *Subverting Colonial Authority*.

31. Matías de Gálvez served from April 1783 to October 1784 and Bernardo de Gálvez from June 1785 to November 1786.

32. Eusebio Sánchez Pareja to Gálvez, January 27, 1787, AGI, Mexico 1743.

33. Gamboa to Porlier, January 25, 1788, AGI, Mexico 1879.

34. Gamboa to Porlier, March 25, 1788, AGI, Mexico 1879.

35. Gamboa to the Audiencia, April 30, 1789, Archivo General de La Nación (AGN), Civil 23.

36. Moncada to the crown, August 16, 1794, AGI, Estado 40, no. 7. Gamboa recused himself from any ongoing legal actions relating to the estate. Revillagigedo to king, August 31, 1792, Archivo Histórico Nacional (AHN), Consejos, 21807.

37. Gamboa to Porlier, May 27, 1788, AGI, Mexico 1879.

38. Garriga, "Los límites del reformismo borbónico," 801–04.

39. Brading, "Nuevo plan para la mejor administración de justicia en América," 127–38.

40. Solórzano Pereyra, *Política Indiana*, book 5, chapter 3, paragraph 7; Brading, "Nuevo plan," 377.

41. Brading, "Nuevo plan," 379.

42. Quoted in Cañeque, *The King's Living Image*, 166.

43. For a revisionist interpretation of this practice, see Baskes, *Indians, Merchants and Markets*. See also Taylor, *Magistrates of the Sacred*, 399–405.

44. Gaspar de Zuñiga, viceroy from 1595 to 1603, said that the only solution was to raise the salaries of local officials significantly so they would not have to engage in business on the side. See Borah, *Justice by Insurance*, 112.

45. Gálvez, *Informe del marqués de Sonora al virrey don Antonio Bucarely y Ursúa*, 10.

46. Herrera returned to Spain in 1787 with his young wife and served as a *consejero togado* on the Council of the Indies until his death in 1794. See Burkholder and Chandler, *Biographical Dictionary of Audiencia Ministers*, 161–62; Tutino, *Mexico City, 1808*, 55–56.

47. Campillo y Cossío, *Nuevo sistema de gobierno ecónomico para América*.

48. Intendancy Plan, January 15, 1768, AGI, Ind. Gen. 1713.

49. San Juan de Piedras Alvas to Arriaga, May 24, 1768, AGI, Ind. Gen. 1713.

50. Tau Anzoátegui, "La variedad indiana, una clave de la concepción jurídica de Juan de Solórzano," 209.

51. Yuste, "El Conde de Tepa ante la Visita de José de Gálvez," 131.

52. Viana was likely the richest member of the audiencia, thanks to his 1771 marriage to sixteen-year-old María Josefa Rodríguez de Pedroso García y Arellano, the heiress of New Spain's largest pulque fortune. He later served on the Council of the Indies. On Viana see Burkholder and Chandler, *Biographical Dictionary of Audiencia Ministers*, 353–54; Tutino, *Mexico City, 1808*, 51–52. See also Viana Pérez, "La actividad comercial de un oidor de la Audiencia de México: Francisco Leandro de Viana," 117–38.

53. Owensby, "Between Justice and Economics: "Indians" and Reformism in Eighteenth-Century Spanish Imperial Thought," 152.

54. On Ulloa see Solano, *La pasión de reformar*.

55. Solano, *Antonio de Ulloa y la Nueva España*, 151–52.

56. Solano, *Antonio de Ulloa y la Nueva España*, 158.

57. See Stein, "Bureaucracy and Business in the Spanish Empire, 1759–1804," 2–28.

58. Gálvez's intervention in customs collection in Mexico City in 1767 was also undermined by the crown's failure to pay officials decent salaries. The new men felt just as obliged to collect "gratifications" as the men whom they replaced, whom Gálvez had charged with fraud. See Salvucci, "Costumbres viejas, 'hombres nuevos,'" 249–53.

59. Porlier's opinion on intendancies, December 2, 1801, AGI, Ind. Gen. 886. See also Tau Anzoátegui, *Casuismo y sistema*, 222–23.

60. Brading, *Miners and Merchants*, 67, 74, 83–87.

61. Flon to Porlier, July 28, 1789, AGI, Mexico 1976.

62. Audiencia to Porlier, January 10, 1790, AGI, Mexico 1881.

63. Gamboa representation to the king, December 22, 1791, Biblioteca Nacional de España (BNE), Papeles referentes a Hacienda, MSS/3535.

64. Flon to Gardoqui, June 27, 1792, AGI, Mexico 1876.

65. Güemes-Pacheco y Padilla, "Carta al excelentísimo señor don Antonio Valdés, 1789," 274.

66. Güemes-Pacheco y Padilla, "Carta al excelentísimo señor don Antonio Valdés, 1789," 274.

67. BNE, Papeles referentes a Hacienda, MSS/3534, no. 241.

68. Revillagigedo to Porlier, November 6, 1789, AGI, Mexico, 1782.

69. Audiencia to the king, November 26, 1789, AGI, Estado 20, no. 47.

70. Revillagigedo to crown, November 26, 1789, AGI, Estado 20, no. 47.

71. Núñez de Haro to Porlier, November 26, 1789, AGI, Mexico 1879. On the importance of public display of political authority, see Cañeque, *The King's Living Image*, 120–49.

72. Güemes-Pacheco y Padilla, "Relación Reservada (1794)," 1123–24.

73. Revillagigedo to Gamboa, December 14, 1789, BNE, Papeles referentes a Hacienda, MSS/3524, no. 280.

74. Revillagigedo to Gamboa, July 14, 1790, BNE, Papeles referentes a Hacienda, MSS/3534, no. 311.

75. Gamboa to Revillagigedo, August 30, 1791, BNE, Papeles referentes a Hacienda, MSS/3524, no. 392.

76. Sedano and García Icazbalceta, *Noticias de México*, vol. 2, 86–88.

77. Sedano and García Icazbalceta, *Noticias de México*, vol. 2, 86–88.

78. Residencia of Revillagigedo II, AHN, Consejos, 20723.

79. Both carvings were described in an early work of Mexican archaeology by the novohispano polymath Antonio de León y Gama in *Descripción histórica y cronológica de las dos piedras*, written in 1792. See also Brading, *The First America*, 461–63. Both carvings occupy prominent places today in Mexico City's Museo Nacional de Antropología. On the most recent theory on the Aztec calendar stone, see Stuart, "El emperador y el cosmos," 20–25.

80. Güemes-Pacheco y Padilla, "Relación Reservada," 1084–85.

81. Gamboa to Revillagigedo, September 21, 1790, BNE, Papeles referentes a Hacienda, MSS/3534, no. 337.

82. Antonio Bassoco served as the treasurer of Nuestra Señora de Aránzazu at the same time Gamboa served as the brotherhood's rector in the mid-1770s. Ruiz de Azúa y Martínez de Ezquerecocha, *Vascongadas y América*, 224.

83. Revillagigedo to Gamboa, September 19, 1790, BNE, Papeles referentes a Hacienda, MSS/3534, no. 335.

84. Revillagigedo to Floridablanca, August 29, 1790, AGI, Estado 20, no. 52.

85. Revillagigedo to Floridablanca, September 30, 1790, AGI, Estado 20, no. 53.

86. Güemes-Pacheco y Padilla, "Relación Reservada," 1041.

87. On the theater in late-eighteenth-century Mexico City, focusing on enlightenment reforms of productions, see chapter two of Viqueira Albán, *Propriety and Permissiveness in Bourbon Mexico*.

88. Revillagigedo to Porlier, January 10, 1792, AGI, Mexico 1131.

89. Güemes-Pacheco y Padilla, "Relación Reservada," 1041.

90. Güemes-Pacheco y Padilla, "Relación Reservada," 1047.

91. Güemes-Pacheco y Padilla, "Relación Reservada," 1050.

92. Güemes-Pacheco y Padilla, "Relación Reservada," 1054.

93. Güemes-Pacheco y Padilla, "Relación Reservada," 1176.

94. Brading, *Miners and Merchants*, 128.

95. Geneological information drawn from familysearch.org, accessed on July 2, 2019.

96. Branciforte, July 25, 1794, AGN, Correspondencia de virreyes, 179, no. 16. On the institution of the Montepío see Sanciñena Asurmendi, *La Audiencia en México en el reinado de Carlos III*, 73.

97. Alzate y Ramírez, "Elogio de Gamboa."

98. Alzate y Ramírez, "Advertencia del Autor de esta Gazeta en orden al siguiente Elogio, dispuesto por el Licenciado D. Mariano Castillejos, Abogado de esta Real Audiencia e Individuo de su Ilustre y Real Colegio (1794)," 279.

99. Alzate y Ramírez, "Elogio de Gamboa," 445.

100. Alzate y Ramírez, "Elogio de Gamboa,"445.

101. Alzate y Ramírez, "Elogio de Gamboa," 447.

102. Alzate y Ramírez, "Elogio de Gamboa," 451.

103. Alzate y Ramírez, "Elogio de Gamboa," 452.

<#>

Conclusion

1. Borah, *Justice by Insurance*, 40.

2. In the words of Brian Owensby, "By then [1700], law had become a chief means by which individuals and communities defended and contested liberty, land and local autonomy. It served as the fulcrum for balancing community and individual tensions in criminal and civil matters. It was the weapon of choice, sword as well as shield, in disputes between Indian communities. It bridged distances between Spaniards and Indians, but it also established boundaries. It offered ordinary Indians a means of approaching a distant king whose decrees were all that stood between them and innumerable opportunists." Owensby, *Empire of Law*, 296.

3. Carlos Garriga argues that the decline in the number of creoles serving on the audiencias of America was the most important change that the Bourbon reforms effected in the administration of justice. See Garriga, "Los límites del reformismo borbónico."

4. Observations on Physics, July 30, 1787, AGI, Mexico 1878.

5. See North, *Institutions, Institutional Change, and Economic Performance*; Acemoglu and Robinson, *Why Nations Fail*. For a convincing rebuttal of this claim, see Dobado and Marrero, "The role of the Spanish imperial state in the mining-led growth of Bourbon Mexico's economy."

Bibliography

Abbreviations

AGI   Archivo General de Indias, Seville
AGN   Archivo General de la Nación, Mexico City
AGS   Archivo General de Simancas
AHCV   Archivo Histórico del Colegio de las Vizcaínas, Mexico City
AHN   Archivo Histórico Nacional, Madrid
BL   British Library, London
BNE   Biblioteca Nacional de España, Madrid
RB   Real Biblioteca, Madrid

Books and Articles

Certamen Poetico, con que la humilde lealtad y reconocida gratitud del Real, y mas antiguo Colegio de S. Ildefonso de México, Seminario de la Compañia de Jesus, celebró el dia 23 de Enero del año de 1748 la exaltacion al Solio de su Augustissimo Protector. Salamanca: Imprenta de la Santa Cruz, 1748.

Extractos de las juntas generales celebradas por la Real Sociedad Bascongada de los Amigos del País (1771–1773). San Sebastian: Sociedad Guipuzcoana de Ediciones y Publicaciones (Real Sociedad Bascongada de Amigos del País), 1985.

Extractos de las juntas generales celebradas por la Real Sociedad Bascongada de los Amigos del País (1774–1776). San Sebastian: Sociedad Guipuzcoana de Ediciones y Publicaciones (Real Sociedad Bascongada de Amigos del País), 1985.

La administración de D. Frey Antonio María de Bucareli y Ursua, cuadragesimo sexto Virrey de México. Vol. 2, edited by Rómulo Velasco Ceballos. Mexico City: Talleres Gráficos de la Nación, 1936.

Noticia del origen, fundación, objeto y constituciones de la Real Congregación de naturales y originarios de las tres provincias vascongadas establecida bajo la advocación del glorioso San Ignacio de Loyola. Madrid: Tipografía de los hijos de M. G. Hernández, 1896.

"Representación vindicatoria que en el año de 1771 hizo a Su Majestad la ciudad de México." In *El criollo como voluntad y representación*, edited by Salvador Albert Bernabéu, 77–159. Madrid: Fundación MAPFRE, 2006.

Acemoglu, Daron, and James A. Robinson. *Why Nations Fail: The Origins of Power, Prosperity, and Poverty.* New York: Crown, 2012.

Acevedo, Diego de. *El discreto estudiante: Reglas de buena crianza, para la educacion de los colegiales del Colegio real de S. Ildefonso, a cuyas expensas se reimprime.* Mexico City: Con licencia en Mexico, F. Rodriguez Lupercio hrs., 1722.

Agüero, Alejandro. "Las categorías básicas de la cultura jurisdiccional." In *De Justicia de Jueces a Justicia de Leyes: Hacia la España de 1870*, edited by Marta Lorente Sariñena, 19–58. Madrid: Consejo General del Poder Judicial, 2006.

Aguirre Salvador, Rodolfo. *El mérito y la estratégia: Clérigos, juristas y médicos en Nueva España.* Mexico City: Universidad Nacional Autónoma de México, 2003.

Alamán, Lucas. *Historia de México desde los primeros movimientos que prepararon su independencia en el año de 1808, hasta la época presente.* 5 vols. Mexico City: Fondo de Cultura Económica, 1985.

Alencastre Noraña y Silva, Fernando de. "Relación dada por el Excmo Señor Duque de Linares Fernando de Alencastre Noraña y Silva a D. Baltasar de Zúñiga y Guzman." In *Instrucciones y memorias de los virreyes novohispanos*, edited by Ernesto de la Torre. Mexico City: Editorial Porrua, 1991.

Alzate y Ramírez, José Antonio de. "Advertencia del Autor de esta Gazeta en orden al siguiente Elogio, dispuesto por el Licenciado D. Mariano Castillejos, Abogado de esta Real Audiencia e Individuo de su Ilustre y Real Colegio (1794)." In *Gacetas de literatura de México.* Puebla: Reimpresos en la Oficina del Hospital de S. Pedro, a cargo del ciudadano M. Buen Abad, 1831.

———. *Asuntos varios sobre ciencias y artes.* Mexico City: Imprenta de la Bibliotheca Mexicana, 1772–1773.

———. "Elogio Histórico del Señor D. Francisco Xavier de Gamboa, Regente que fue de esta Real Audiencia de México (1794)." In *Ilustrados en la Nueva España: Los socios de la Real Sociedad Bascongada de los Amigos del País*, edited by Josefina María Cristina Torales Pacheco, 444–52. Mexico City: Universidad Iberoamericana, 2001.

Angulo Morales, Alberto. "La Real Congregación de San Ignacio de Loyola de los naturales y originarios de las tres provincias vascas en la corte de Madrid (1713–1896)." In *Los vascos en las regiones de México, siglos XVI–XX.* Vol. 5, edited by Amaya Garritz, 15–34. Mexico City: Universidad Nacional Autónoma de México, 1999.

Azcona Pastor, José Manuel. *Possible Paradises: Basque Emigration to Latin America.* Reno: University of Nevada Press, 2004.

Barrientos Grandón, Javier. *La cultura jurídica en la Nueva España*. Mexico City: Universidad Nacional Autónoma de México, 1993.

Baskes, Jeremy. *Indians, Merchants and Markets: A Reinterpretation of the Repartimiento and Spanish-Indian Economic Relations in Oaxaca, 1750–1821*. Stanford: Stanford University Press, 2000.

———. *Staying Afloat: Risk and Uncertainty in Spanish Atlantic World Trade, 1760–1820*. Stanford: Stanford University Press, 2013.

Bellomo, Manlio. *The Common Legal Past of Europe, 1000–1800*. Translated by Lydia G. Cochrane. Washington, DC: Catholic University of America Press, 1995.

Benton, Lauren. *Law and Colonial Cultures: Legal Regimes in World History, 1400–1900*. Cambridge, UK: Cambridge University Press, 2002.

Bergamo, Ilarione da. *Daily Life in Colonial Mexico: The Journey of Friar Ilarione da Bergamo, 1761–1768*. Translated by William J. Orr. Edited by Robert Ryal and Orr Miller, William J. Norman, OK: University of Oklahoma Press, 2000.

Bernard, Gildas. *Le Secrétariat d'État et le Conseil espagnol des Indes, 1700–1808*. Geneva: Droz, 1972.

Berní Catalá, José. *El abogado instruído en la práctica civil de España (1738)*. Valladolid: Editorial Lex Nova, 2006.

Bobb, Bernard E. *The Viceregency of Antonio Maria Bucareli in New Spain, 1771–1779*. Austin: University of Texas Press, 1962.

Borah, Woodrow. *Justice by Insurance: The General Indian Court of Colonial Mexico and the Legal Aides of the Half-Real*. Berkeley: University of California Press, 1983.

Brading, David A. *The First America: The Spanish Monarchy, Creole Patriots, and the Liberal State, 1492–1867*. Cambridge: Cambridge University Press, 1991.

———. "Government and Elite in Late Colonial Mexico." *Hispanic American Historical Review* 53, no. 3 (August 1973): 389–414.

———. *Mexican Phoenix, Our Lady of Guadalupe: Image and Tradition Across Five Centuries*. Cambridge: Cambridge University Press, 2001.

———. *Miners and Merchants in Bourbon Mexico, 1763–1810*. Cambridge: Cambridge University Press, 1971.

———. "Nuevo plan para la mejor administración de justicia en América." *Boletin del Archivo General de la Nación* 9, nos. 3–4 (1968): 368–400.

———. "Tridentine Catholicism and Enlightened Despotism in Bourbon Mexico." *Journal of Latin American Studies* 15 (1983): 1–22.

Bravo Lira, Bernardino. "La literatura jurídica indiana en el Barroco." *Revista de Estudios Histórico-Jurídicos* 10 (1985): 227–68.

Burkholder, Mark A. *Biographical Dictionary of Councillors of the Indies, 1717–1808*. Westport, CT: Greenwood Press, 1986.

———. "The Council of the Indies in the Late Eighteenth Century: A New Perspective." *The Hispanic American Historical Review* 56, no. 3 (August 1976): 404–23.

Burkholder, Mark A., and D. S. Chandler. *Biographical Dictionary of Audiencia Ministers in the Americas, 1687–1821*. Westport, CT: Greenwood Press, 1982.

———. *From Impotence to Authority: The Spanish Crown and the American Audiencias, 1687–1808*. Columbia: University of Missouri Press, 1977.

Burns, Robert I., ed. *Las Siete Partidas*. Philadelphia: University of Pennsylania Press, 2001.

Cadalso, José. *Cartas marruecas*. 24th ed. Madrid: Espasa, 1999.

Callahan, William James. *Honor, Commerce, and Industry in Eighteenth-Century Spain*. Boston: Kress Library of Business and Economics, 1972.

Campillo y Cossío, José de. *Nuevo sistema de gobierno ecónomico para América*. Edited by Manuel Ballesteros Gaibrois. Oviedo: Grupo Editorial Asturiano, 1993.

Campomanes, Pedro Rodríguez de. "Del beneficio de las minas." In *Reflexiones sobre el comercio español a Indias (1762)*, edited by Vicente Llombart Rosa, 435–45. Madrid: Instituto de Estudios Fiscales, 1988.

———. *Reflexiones sobre el comercio español a Indias (1762)*. Edited by Vicente Llombart Rosa. Madrid: Instituto de Estudios Fiscales, 1988.

Candiani, Vera. *Dreaming of Dry Land: Environmental Transformation in Colonial Mexico City*. Stanford: Stanford University Press, 2014.

Cañeque, Alejandro. *The King's Living Image: The Culture and Politics of Viceregal Power in Colonial Mexico*. New York: Routledge, 2004.

Cañizares-Esguerra, Jorge. "Introduction." In *Science in the Spanish and Portuguese Empires, 1500–1800*, edited by Daniela Bleichmar, Paula De Vos, and Kristin Huffine, 1–6. Stanford: Stanford University Press, 2009.

Canterla, Francisco, and Martin de Tovar. *Vida y obra del primer Conde de Regla*. Sevilla: Escuela de Estudios Hispano-Americanos, 1975.

Caro Baroja, Julio. *La hora navarra del XVIII (personas, familias, negocios, e ideas)*. Pamplona: Institución Príncipe de Viana, 1969.

———. *Los vascos*. Madrid: Istmo, 1972.

Castañeda, Jorge G. *Manaña Forever? Mexico and the Mexicans*. New York: Vintage, 2012.

Castro Gutiérrez, Felipe. *Nueva ley y nuevo rey: Reformas borbónicas y rebelión popular en Nueva España*. Zamora Colegio de Michoacán, 1996.

Castro, Juan Francisco de. *Discursos críticos sobre las leyes y sus interpretes*. Madrid: Joaquín Ibarra, 1765.

Chavez Orozco, Luis, ed. *Conflicto de trabajo con los mineros de Real del Monte, año de 1766*. Mexico City: Instituto Nacional de Estudios Históricos de la Revolución Mexicana, 1960.

Chiaramonte, José Carlos. *Pensamiento de la Ilustración: Economía y sociedad iberoamericanas en el siglo XVIII*. Venezuela: Biblioteca Ayacucho, 1979.

Clavijero, Francisco Javier. "Breve descripción de la Provincia de México de la Compañía de Jesús, segun el estado en que se hallaba en año de 1767." In *Tesoros*

Documentales de México, siglo XVIII, edited by Mariano Cuevas, 295–309. Mexico City: Editorial Galatea, 1944.

Coatsworth, John H. "Inequality, Institutions and Economic Growth in Latin America." *Journal of Latin American Studies* 40, no. 3 (2008): 545–69.

Cope, R. Douglas. *The Limits of Racial Domination: Plebeian Society in Colonial Mexico City, 1660–1720.* Madison: University of Wisconsin Press, 1994.

Couturier, Edith Boorstein. *The Silver King: The Remarkable Life of the Count of Regla in Colonial Mexico.* Albuquerque: University of New Mexico, 2003.

Crawford, Matthew. *The Andean Wonder Drug: Cinchona Bark and Imperial Science in the Spanish Atlantic, 1630–1800.* Pittsburgh: University of Pittsburgh Press, 2016.

Cutter, Charles R. *The Legal Culture of Northern New Spain, 1700–1810.* Albuquerque: University of New Mexico Press, 1995.

Danks, Noblet Barry. "The Labor Revolt of 1766 in the Mining Community of Real del Monte." *The Americas* 44, no. 2 (1987): 143–65.

Decorme, Gerard. *La obra de los jesuitas mexicanos durante la epoca colonial, 1572–1767.* Vol. 1 of 2. Mexico City: Editorial Porrúa, 1941.

Dobado, Rafael, and Gustavo A. Marrero. "The Role of the Spanish Imperial State in the Mining-Led Growth of Bourbon Mexico's Economy." *The Economic History Review* 64, no. 3 (August 2011): 855–84.

Domínguez Ortiz, Antonio. *Carlos III y la España de la Ilustración.* Madrid: Alianza Editorial, 1988.

Dubois, Laurent. *Avengers of the New World: The Story of the Haitian Revolution.* Cambridge, MA: Harvard University Press, 2004.

Duve, Thomas, and Heikki Pihlajamaki, eds. *New Horizons in Spanish Colonial Law: Contributions to Transnational Early Modern Legal History.* Frankfurt am Main: Max Planck Institute for European Legal History, 2015.

Echave, Baltasar de. *Discursos de la antiguedad de la lengua cántabra bascongada.* Mexico City: La Imprenta de Henrico Martinez, 1607.

Espinosa de los Monteros, Ignacio. *Oración contua funebre, . . . al Theniente Coronel D. Joseph Velázquez Lorea; alguacil mayor del Santo Tribunal de la Inquisición, Alcalde de la Santa hermandad, y Juez por S. Mag. de la Acordada de este Reyno, y de el de la Nueva Galicia.* Mexico City: Por los Herederos de la Viuda de D. Joseph Bernardo de Hogal, 1756.

Esquivel Obregón, Toribio. *Biografía de Don Francisco Javier Gamboa: Ideario político y jurídico de Nueva España en el siglo XVIII.* Mexico City: La Sociedad Mexicana de Geografia y Estadistica, 1941.

Fabry, José Antonio. *Compendios a demostracion de los crecidos adelantamientos que pudiera lograr la Real Hacienda de Su Magestad mediante la rebaja en el precio de azogue.* Mexico City: Viuda de D. Joseph Bernardo de Hogal, 1743.

Feijóo, Benito Jerónimo. *Cartas eruditas y curiosas.* Oviedo: Instituto Feijóo de Estudios del Siglo XVIII, 2014.

Feingold, Mordechai. "Preface." In *Jesuit Science and the Republic of Letters*, edited by Mordechai Feingold. Cambridge, MA: MIT Press, 2003.

Fernández Pardo, Francisco. *La independencia vasca: La disputa sobre los fueros.* Madrid: Nerea, 1990.

Ferrone, Vincenzo. *The Enlightenment: History of an Idea.* Princeton: Princeton University Press, 2015.

Flores Clair, Eduardo. *El Banco de avío minero novohispano: Crédito, finanzas y deudores.* Mexico City: Instituto Nacional de Antropología e Historia, 2001.

Gálvez, José de. "Abril 20 de 1765, Inventorio de los bienes, créditos y alhajas pertenecientes al Señor Don Joseph de Gálvez Gallardo." In *Mexico en el Siglo XVIII*, edited by Francisco Rodas de Coss, 7–58. Mexico City: Secretaria de Relaciones Exteriores, 1983.

——. *Informe del marqués de Sonora al virrey don Antonio Bucarely y Ursúa.* Edited by Clara Elena Suárez Argüello. Mexico City: Editorial Porrúa, 2002.

——. *Informe sobre las rebeliones populares de 1767 y otros documentos inéditos.* Edited by Felipe Castro Gutiérrez. Mexico City: Universidad Nacional Autónoma de México, 1990.

Gamboa, Francisco Xavier de. *Comentarios a las Ordenanzas de Minas.* Madrid: Joachin Ibarra, 1761.

——. *Por el coronel D. Manuel de Rivas-Cacho, en el pleyto que sobre testamento de Da. Josepha Maria Franco Soto, su muger, le ha movido el Br. D. Juan Joseph de la Roca, presbytero de este arzobispado de México; para que los Señores de la Real audiencia se sirvan de confirmar la sentencia de visita de 1 de junio de este año: en que declaraon por ultima voluntad de Doña Josepha el testamento nuncupativo de 24 de febrero de 1751.* Mexico City: Nueva imprenta de la Biblioteca mexicana, 1753.

García, Clara. "Sociedad, crédito y cofradía en la Nueva España a fines de la época colonial: El caso de Nuestra Señora de Aránzazu." *Historias* 3 (1983): 53–68.

García Hernán, Enrique. *Consejero de ambos mundos: Vida y obra de Juan de Solórzano Pereira (1575-1655).* Madrid: Fundación MAPFRE, Instituto de Cultura, 2007.

Garcidueñas, José Rojas. *El antiguo Colegio de San Ildefonso.* 2nd ed. Mexico City: Universidad Nacional Autónoma de México 1985.

Garner, Richard L., and Spiro E. Stefanou. *Economic Growth and Change in Bourbon Mexico.* Gainesville: University Press of Florida, 1993.

Garriga, Carlos. "¿De qué hablamos los historiadores del derecho cuando hablamos de derecho?" *Revista Direito Mackenzie* 14, no. 1 (2020): 1–24.

——. "Los límites del reformismo borbónico: A propósito de la administración de la justicia de Indias." In *Derecho y administración oública en las Indias hispánicas*, edited by Feliciano Barrios Pintado, 781–821. Cuenca: Ediciones de la Universidad de Castilla-La Mancha, 2002.

———. "Orden jurídico y poder político en el Antiguo Régime." *Istor* 4, no. 16 (2004): 13–44.

Gayol, Víctor. *Laberintos de justicia: Procuradores, escribanos y oficiales de la Real Audiencia de México (1750–1812)*. 2 vols. Zamora: El Colegio de Michoacán, A.C., 2007.

Gómez Mendoza, Oriel. "Las nociones normativas de justicia y gobierno en la minería mexicana del siglo XVIII al XIX." *Cuadernos de Historia* 34 (June 2011): 109–26.

Gonzalbo, Pilar. *Historia de la educacion en la epoca colonial: La educacion de los criollos y la vida urbana*. Mexico City: El Colegio de México, 1990.

González Caizán, Cristina. "La Biblioteca de Agustín Pablo de Ordeñana." *Brocar* 21 (1998): 227–67.

Grafe, Regina, and Alejandra Irigoin. "A Stakeholder Empire: The Political Economy of Spanish Imperial Rule in America." *The Economic History Review* 65, no. 2 (2012): 609–51.

Greene, Jack P. "Negotiated Authorities: The Problem of Governance in the Extended Polities of the Early Modern Atlantic World." In *Negotiated Authorities: Essays in Colonial Political and Constitutional History*, 1–24. Charlottesville, VA, and London: University Press of Virginia, 1994.

Güemes y Horcasitas, Francisco de. "Relación de Don Francisco de Güemes y Horcasitas a Agustín de Ahumada y Villalón (1755)." In *Instrucciones y memorias de los virreyes novohispanos*, edited by Ernesto de la Torre, 795–843 Mexico City: Editorial Porrua, 1991.

Güemes-Pacheco y Padilla, Juan Vicente. "Carta al excelentísimo señor don Antonio Valdés, 1789." In *El ocaso novohispano*, edited by D. A. Brading. Mexico City: Instituto Nacional de Antropología e Historia, 1996.

———. "Relación Reservada (1794)." In *Instrucciones y Memorias de los Virreyes Novohispanos*, edited by Ernesto de la Torre, 1030–1273. Mexico City: Editorial Porrua, 1991.

Guerrero, Saúl. *Silver by Fire, Silver by Mercury: A Chemical History of Silver Refining in New Spain and Mexico, 16th to 19th Centuries*. Leiden, NL: Brill, 2017.

Guimerá, Agustín, ed. *El reformismo borbónico: Una visión interdisciplinar*. Madrid: Alianza Editorial, 1996.

Hamnett, Brian. *The Enlightenment in Iberia and Ibero-America*. Cardiff: University of Wales Press, 2017.

Hanke, Lewis. "A Modest Proposal for a Moratorium on Grand Generalizations: Some Thoughts on the Black Legend." *The Hispanic American Historical Review* 51, no. 1 (1971): 112–27.

Haslip-Viera, Gabriel. *Crime and Punishment in Late Colonial Mexico City, 1692–1810*. Albuquerque: University of New Mexico Press, 1999.

Hay, Douglas. "Property, Authority and the Common Law." In *Albion's Fatal Tree: Crime and Society in Eighteenth-Century England*, edited by Douglas Hay, Peter Linebaugh, and John G. Rule, 17–64. New York: Pantheon Books, 1975.

Heiberg, Marianne. *The Making of the Basque Nation*. Cambridge: Cambridge University Press, 1989.

Herzog, Tamar. *Upholding Justice: Society, State, and the Penal System in Quito (1650–1750)*. Ann Arbor: University of Michigan Press, 2004.

Hevía Bolaños, Juan de. *Curia Philipica*. Valladolid: Lex Nova, 1989. Facsimile of the 1797 edition.

Hidalgo Nuchera, Patricio. *Antes de la Acordada: La represión de la criminalidad rural en el México colonial (1550–1750)*. Seville: Secretariado de Publicaciones de la Universidad de Sevilla, 2013.

Hirschman, Albert O. *The Passions and the Interests: Political Arguments for Capitalism before its Triumph*. Princeton, NJ: Princeton University Press, 1996.

Howe, Walter. *The Mining Guild of New Spain and its Tribunal General, 1770–1821*. New York: Greenwood Press, 1949. Reprinted in 1968.

Jovellanos, Gaspar Melchor de. "Discurso académico en su recepción a la Real Academia de la Historia (1780)." In *Gaspar Melchor de Jovellanos: Obras en Prosa*, edited by José Caso González, 71–102. Madrid: Clásicos Castalia, 1987.

Juan, Jorge, and Antonio de Ulloa. *Discourse and Political Reflections on the Kingdoms of Peru: Their Government, Special Regimen of Their Inhabitants, and Abuses Which Have Been Introduced into One and Another, with Special Information on Why They Grew Up and Some Means to Avoid Them (1749)*. Edited by John J. TePaske. Norman: University of Oklahoma Press, 1978.

Kagan, Richard L. *Lawsuits and Litigants in Castile, 1500–1700*. Chapel Hill: University of North Carolina Press, 1981.

Keen, Benjamin. "The Black Legend Revisited: Assumpions and Realities." *The Hispanic American Historical Review* 49, no. 4 (1969): 703–19.

———. "The White Legend Revisited: A Reply to Professor Hanke's 'Modest Proposal.'" *The Hispanic American Historical Review* 51, no. 2 (1971): 336–55.

Kellogg, Susan. *Law and the Transformation of Aztec Culture, 1500–1700*. Norman: University of Oklahoma Press, 1995.

Kicza, John E. *Colonial Entrepreneurs, Families and Business in Bourbon Mexico City*. Albuquerque: University of New Mexico Press, 1983.

Knight, Alan. *Mexico: The Colonial Era*. New York: Cambridge University Press, 2002.

Kuethe, Allan J., and Kenneth J. Andrien. *The Spanish Atlantic World in the Eighteenth Century: War and the Bourbon Reforms, 1713–1796*. New York: Cambridge University Press, 2014.

Ladd, Doris. *The Making of a Strike: Mexican Silver Workers' Struggles in Real del Monte 1766–1775*. Lincoln: University of Nebraska Press, 1988.

Lamikiz, Xabier. *Trade and Trust in the Eighteenth-Century Atlantic World: Spanish Merchants and Their Overseas Networks*. Woodbridge, UK: Royal Historical Society, 2010.

Lassaga, Juan Lucas de, and Joaquín Velázquez de León. *Representación que a nombre de la Minería de esta Nueva España, hacen al Rey Nuestro Señor.* Mexico City: D. Felipe de Zúñiga y Ontiveros, 1774.

Lira, Andrés. "La actividad jurisdiccional del virrey y el carácter judicial del gobierno novohispano en su fase formativa." In *El gobierno de un mundo: Virreinatos y Audiencias en la América Hispánica,* edited by Feliciano Barrios, 299–318. Cuenca: Universidad de Castilla-La Mancha, 2004.

Llombart Rosa, Vicente. "Campomanes, el economista de Carlos III." In *Economía y economistas españoles.* Vol. 3, *La Ilustración,* edited by Enrique Fuentes Quintana, 201–55. Madrid: Galaxia Gutenberg, Círculos de Lectores, 2000.

———. *Campomanes: Economista y Político de Carlos III.* Madrid: Alianza Editorial, 1992.

———. "Introducción: El pensamiento económico de la Ilustración en España (1730–1812)." In *Economía y economistas españoles.* Vol. 3, *La Ilustración,* edited by Enrique Fuentes Quintana, 7–89. Madrid: Galaxia Gutenberg, Círculo de Lectores, 2000.

López de Priego, Antonio. "Carta de un religioso de los extintos Jesuitas, a una hermana suya, religiosa del convento de Santa Catarina de la Puebla de los Angeles (1785)." In *Tesoros documentales de México, siglo XVIII,* edited by Mariano Cuevas. Mexico City: Editorial Galatea, 1944.

López, François. "Aspectos específicos de la Ilustración española." In *II Simposio sobre el Padre Feijóo y su siglo,* 23–39. Oviedo: Centro de Estudios del S. XVIII, 1981.

———. "El libro y su mundo." In *La república de las letras en la España del siglo XVIII,* edited by Joaquín Álvarez Barrientos, 63–123. Madrid: Consejo Superior de Investigaciones Científicas, 1995.

López García, José Miguel. *El Motín contra Esquilache: Crisis y protesta popular en el Madrid del siglo XVIII.* Madrid: Alianza Editorial, 2006.

López Miramontes, Alvaro, and Cristina Urrutia de Stebelski. *Las minas de Nueva España en 1774.* Mexico City: Instituto Nacional de Antropología e Historia, 1980.

López-Hidalgo Preciado, Juan. "Fundación de la Real Universidad de Guadalajara." *Podium Notarial* 27 (June 2003): 62–67.

Luque Alcaide, Elisa. "Asociacionismo vasco en Nueva España." In *Los vascos en las regiones de México, siglos XVI–XX.* Vol. 2, edited by Amaya Garritz, 67–86. Mexico City: Universidad Nacional Autónoma de México, 1996.

———. "Francisco Javier Gamboa y la educación del indígena en México (siglo XVIII)." In *Los vascos en las regiones de México, siglos XVI–XX.* Vol. 5, edited by Amaya Garritz, 47–61. Mexico City: Universidad Nacional Autónoma de México, 1999.

———. *La cofradía de Aránzazu de México (1681–1799).* Pamplona: Ediciones Eunate, 1995.

————. *La educación en Nueva España en el siglo XVIII*. Seville: Escuela de Estudios Hispano-americanas, 1970.

Luque Talaván, Miguel. *Un universo de opiniones: La literatura jurídica indiana.* Madrid: Consejo Superior de Investigaciones Científicas, 2003.

Luzuriaga, Juan de. *Paranympho celeste: Historia de la mystica zarza, milagrosa imagen, y prodigioso santuario de Aránzazu, de religiosos observantes de nuestro seráfico padre San Francisco en la provincia de Guipúzcoa de la region de Cantabria.* Mexico City: Por los herederos de la viuda de Bernardo Calderón, 1686.

MacKay, Ruth. *"Lazy, Improvident People": Myth and Reality in the Writing of Spanish History.* Ithaca: Cornell University Press, 2006.

MacLachlan, Colin M. "Acordada." In *Los tribunales de la Nueva España: Antologia,* edited by José Luis Soberanes, 85–122. Mexico City: Universidad Nacional Autónoma de México, 1980.

————. *Criminal Justice in Eighteenth Century Mexico: A Study of the Tribunal of the Acordada.* Berkeley: University of California Press, 1974.

————. *Spain's Empire in the New World: The Role of Ideas in Institutional and Social Change.* Berkeley: University of California Press, 1988.

Malagon Barceló, Javier, ed. *Código Negro Carolino (1784).* Santo Domingo: Editora Taller, 1974.

Maneiro, Juan Luis, and Manuel Fabri. *Vidas de mexicanos ilustres del siglo XVIII.* Edited by Bernabé Navarro. Mexico City: Universidad Nacional Autónoma de México, 1989.

Mariluz Urquijo, José M. "El indiano en la Corte: La Real Congregación de Nuestra Señora de Guadalupe." In *Tres estudios novohispanos: Sociedad, letras, artes,* edited by Daisy Rípodas Ardanaz, 10–38. Buenos Aires: Libros de Hispanoamérica, 1983.

Martiré, Eduardo. *Las audiencias y la Administración de Justicia en las Indias.* Madrid: Universidad Autónoma de Madrid, 2005.

Masters, Adrian. "A Thousand Invisible Architects: Vassals, the Petition and Response System, and the Creation of Spanish Imperial Caste Legislation." *Hispanic American Historical Review* 98, no. 3 (2018): 377–406.

Mayagoitia, Alejandro. "Los rectores del Ilustre y Real Colegio de Abogados de México: La primera generación." In *Carrera, Linaje y Patronazgo: Clérigos y juristas en Nueva España, Chile y Perú, siglos XVI–XVIII,* edited by Rodolfo Aguirre Salvador, 267–315. Mexico City: Universidad Nacional Autónoma de México, 2004.

McKinley, Michelle A. *Fractional Freedoms: Slavery, Intimacy, and Legal Mobilization in Colonial Lima, 1600–1700.* New York: Cambridge University Press, 2016.

McNeill, John Robert. *Mosquito Empires: Ecology and War in the Greater Caribbean, 1620–1914.* New York: Cambridge University Press, 2010.

Mehl, Eva María. *Forced Migration in the Spanish Pacific World: From Mexico to the Philippines, 1765–1811*. Cambridge: Cambridge University Press, 2016.

Méndez Pérez, Juan. "El licenciado don Francisco Xavier de Gamboa en las Juntas de Arreglo de Minería de la Nueva España, 1789–1790." *Estudios de historia novohispana* 47 (July–December 2012): 161–96.

Mendoza Muñoz, Jesús, and Enrique D'abbadie Soto. *El capitán Miguel Velázquez Lorea y el Real Tribunal de la Acordada de la Nueva España: Antología documental*. Querétaro: Fomento Historico y Cultural de Cadereyta, 2006.

Merryman, John Henry. *The Civil Law Tradition*. 2nd ed. Stanford: Stanford University Press, 1985.

Molina del Villar, América. *Por voluntad divina: Escasez, epidemias y otras calamidades en la Ciudad de México, 1700–1762*. Mexico City: Centro de Investigaciones y Estudios Superiores en Antropología Social, 1996.

Morales Folguera, José Miguel, María Isabel Pérez de Colosía Rodríguez, Marion Reder Gadow, and Siro Villas Tinoco. *Los Gálvez de Marcharaviaya*. Málaga: Junta de Andalucía, Benedito Editores, 1991.

Moreno, Roberto. *Joaquín Velázquez de León y sus trabajos científicos sobre el valle de México, 1773–1775*. Mexico City: Universidad Nacional Autónoma de México, 1977.

Motten, Clement G. *Mexican Silver and the Enlightenment*. New York: Octagon Books, 1972.

Muriel, Josefina. "El Real Colegio de San Ignacio de Loyola (1734–1863)." In *Los vascos en México y su Colegio de las Vizcaínas*, edited by Josefina Muriel, 1–73. Mexico City: Universidad Nacional Autónoma de México 1987.

Navarro García, Luis. "Campillo y el Nuevo sistema: Una atribución dudosa." *Temas americanistas* 2 (1983): 22–29.

———. *La política americana de José de Gálvez según su "discurso y reflexiones de un vasallo."* Málaga: Editorial Algazara, 1998.

Navarro, Victor. "Tradition and Scientific Change in Early Modern Spain: The Role of the Jesuits." In *Jesuit Science and the Republic of Letters*, edited by Mordechai Feingold, 331–87. Cambridge, MA: MIT Press, 2003.

North, Douglass. *Institutions, Institutional Change, and Economic Performance*. Cambridge and New York: Cambridge University Press, 1990.

Novoa, Mauricio. *The Protectors of Indians in the Royal Audience of Lima: History, Careers and Legal Culture, 1575–1775*. Leiden, NL: Brill, 2016.

O'Hara, Matthew D. *A Flock Divided: Race, Religion, and Politics in Mexico, 1749–1857*. Durham, NC: Duke University Press, 2010.

Olavarría y Ferrari, Enrique de. *El Real colegio de San Ignacio de Loyola, vulgarmente, Colegio de las vizcaínas, en la actualidad, Colegio de la Paz: Reseña histórica escrita, por Enrique de Olavarria y Ferrari e impresa por acuerdo y con la aprobación de su Junta directiva*. Mexico City: F. Díaz de León, 1889.

Osores, Felix. *Historia de todos los colegios de la ciudad de México desde la conquista hasta 1780.* Mexico City: Tallers Graficos de la Nación, 1929.

———. *Noticias bio-bibliograficas de alumnos distinguidos del Colegio de San Pedro, San Pablo y San Ildefonso de Mexico.* 2 vols. Mexico City: Viuda de C. Bouret, 1908.

Otero, Mariano. "Apuntes para una biografía de don Francisco Javier Gamboa." In Otero, *Manuscritos.* Guadalajara: Gobierno de Jalisco, Secretaria General, Unidad Editorial, 1985.

Owensby, Brian. "Between Justice and Economics: "Indians" and Reformism in Eighteenth-Century Spanish Imperial Thought." In *Legal Pluralism and Empires, 1500–1850,* edited by Lauren Benton and Richard J. Ross, 143–69. New York and London: New York University Press, 2013.

———. *Empire of Law and Indian Justice in Colonial Mexico.* Stanford: Stanford University Press, 2008.

Pagden, Anthony. "Law, Colonization, Legitimation, and the European Background." In *The Cambridge History of Law in America: Early America (1580–1815),* edited by Michael Grossberg and Christopher Tomlins, 1–31. Cambridge: Cambridge University Press, 2008.

Paquette, Gabriel B. *Enlightenment, Governance, and Reform in Spain and its Empire, 1759–1808.* Basingstoke, UK: Palgrave Macmillan, 2008.

Parry, J. H. *The Audiencia of New Galicia in the Sixteenth Century: A Study in Spanish Colonial Government.* Cambridge, UK: Cambridge University Press, 1948.

Pérez Melero, Joaquín. *Minerometalurgia de la plata en México (1767–1849): Cambio tecnológico y organización productiva.* Valladolid: Universidad de Valladolid, 2006.

Pérez-Perdomo, Rogelio. *Latin American Lawyers: A Historical Introduction.* Stanford, California: Stanford University Press, 2006.

Pescador, Juan Javier. *The New World inside a Basque Village: The Oiartzun Valley and its Atlantic Emigrants, 1550–1800.* Reno: University of Nevada Press, 2004.

Porras Muñoz, Guillermo. "La situación jurídica del Colegio de las Vizcaínas." In *Los vascos en México y su colegio de las vizcaínas,* edited by Josefina Muriel, 109–37. Mexico City: Universidad Nacional Autonóma de México, 1987.

Premo, Bianca. *The Enlightenment on Trial: Ordinary Litigants and Colonialism in the Spanish Empire.* New York: Oxford University Press, 2017.

Priestley, Herbert Ingram. *José de Gálvez: Visitor-General of New Spain (1765–1771).* Philadelphia: Porcupine Press, 1980 (1916).

Ramos Lara, María de la Paz. *Difusión e institucionalización de la mecánica newtoniana en México en el siglo XVIII.* Mexico City: Sociedad Mexicana de Historia de la Ciencia y de la Tecnología, A. C. and Universidad Autónoma de Puebla, 1994.

Reyna, Maria del Carmen. "La biblioteca de José Miguel Calixto de Berrio y Zaldívar, segundo conde de San Mateo de Valparaíso y primer marqués del Jaral de

Berrio." In *Un recorrido por archivos y bibliotecas privados*.Vol. 2, 33–44. Mexico City: Asociación Mexicana de Archivos y Bibliotecas Privados, A.C., 1997.

Romero de Terreros, Manuel. "Epigrafia de la Hacienda de Xalpa." *Anales del Museo Nacional de México* 7 (1931): 418–21.

Ross, Richard J. "Legal Communications and Imperial Governance: British North America and Spanish America Compared." In *The Cambridge History of Law in America: Early America (1580–1815)*, edited by Michael Grossberg and Christopher Tomlins, 104–43. New York: Cambridge University Press, 2008.

Roura i Aulinas, Lluis. "Expectativas y frustración bajo el reformismo borbónico." In *Historia de España Siglo XVIII: La España de los Borbones*, edited by Ricardo Garcia Carcel, 167–221. Madrid: Cátedra, 2002.

Ruiz de Azúa y Martínez de Ezquerecocha, María Estibaliz. *Vascongadas y América*. Madrid: Editorial MAPFRE, 1992.

Sahagún de Arévalo Ladrón de Guevara, Juan Francisco, Juan Ignacio de Castorena y Ursúa, and Francisco González de Cossío. *Gacetas de Mexico: Castorena y Ursua (1722)—Sahagún de Arévalo (1728 a 1742)*. 3 vols. Mexico City: Secretaria de Educación Pública, 1949.

Sainz, Luis Ignacio. "Un retrato olvidado del salón General de Actos del Colegio de San Ildefonso: Don Cayetano Antonio Torres Tuñón en el pincel de Andrés López." *Revista Casa del Tiempo* 9, no. 98 (May 2002): 48–57.

Salvucci, Linda. "Costumbres viejas, 'hombres nuevos': José de Gálvez y la burocracia fiscal novohispana (1754–1800)." *Historia Mexicana* 33, no. 2 (1983): 224–64.

Salvucci, Richard J. *Textiles and Capitalism in Mexico: An Economic History of the Obrajes, 1539–1840*. Princeton, NJ: Princeton University Press, 1987.

Sánchez-Arcilla Bernal, José. *Manual de Historia del Derecho*. Madrid: Manuales Jurídicos Dykinson, 2004.

Sánchez-Blanco, Francisco. *El absolutismo y las luces en el reinado de Carlos III*. Madrid: Marcial Pons, 2002.

———. *Europa y el pensamiento español del siglo XVIII*. Madrid: Alianza Editorial, 1991.

Sanciñena Asurmendi, Teresa. *La Audiencia en México en el reinado de Carlos III*. Mexico City: Universidad Nacional Autónoma de México, 1999.

Sarria, Francisco Xavier de. *Ensayo de metalurgia*. Mexico City: Felipe Zuñiga y Ontiveros, 1784.

Scardaville, Michael C. "Alcohol Abuse and Tavern Reform in Late Colonial Mexico City." *Hispanic American Historical Review* 60, no. 4 (1980): 643–71.

———. "(Habsburg) Law and (Bourbon) Order: State Authority, Popular Unrest, and the Criminal Justice System in Bourbon Mexico City." *The Americas* 50, no. 4 (1994): 501–25.

Schell, William. "Silver Symbiosis: ReOrienting Mexican Economic History." *Hispanic American Historical Review* 81, no. 1 (February 2001): 89–133.

Scott, James C. *Seeing Like a State: How Certain Schemes to Improve the Human Condition Have Failed*. New Haven and London: Yale University Press, 1998.

Sedano, Francisco, and Joaquín García Icazbalceta. *Noticias de Mexico*. 2 vols. Mexico City: Imprenta de J. R. Barbedillo y Ca., 1880.

Sembolini Capitani, Lara. *La construcción de la autoridad virreinal en Nueva España, 1535–1595*. Mexico City: Colegio de México, 2014.

Sempat Assadourian, Carlos. "La bomba de fuego de Newcomen y otros artificios de desague: Un intento de transferencia de tecnología inglesa a la minería novohispana, 1726–1731." *Historia Mexicana* 50, no. 3 (2001): 385–457.

Sequeiros, Leandro. "*El Aparato para la Historia Natural Española* del franciscano granadino fray José Torrubia (1698–1761): Aportaciones postridentinas a la Teología de la Naturaleza." *Archivo Teológico Granadino* 64 (2001): 59–127.

Serulnikov, Sergio. *Revolution in the Andes: The Age of Túpac Amaru*. Durham, NC: Duke University Press, 2013.

———. *Subverting Colonial Authority: Challenges to Spanish Rule in Eighteenth-Century Southern Andes*. Durham and London: Duke University Press, 2003.

Simon-Díaz, José. *Historia del Colegio Imperial de Madrid*. Madrid: Consejo Superior de Investigaciones Científicas, 1952.

Smith, Adam. *An Inquiry into the Nature and Causes of the Wealth of Nations (1776)*. New York: Random House, 1994.

Smith, Robert Sidney. "The Wealth of Nations in Spain and Hispanic America, 1780–1830." *Journal of Political Economy* 65, no. 2 (1957): 104–25.

Solano, Francisco de. *Antonio de Ulloa y la Nueva España*. Mexico City: Universidad Nacional Autónoma de México, 1987.

———. "José de Gálvez: Fundador del Archivo de Indias." In *Ordenanzas del Archivo de Indias*, 7–52. Seville: Junta de Andalucia, 1986.

———. *La pasión de reformar: Antonio de Ulloa, marino y científico, 1716–1795*. Cádiz: Universidad de Cádiz; Escuela de Estudios Hispano-Americanos, 1999.

Solórzano Pereyra, Juan. *Política Indiana*. Edited by Francisco Tomás y Valiente and Ana María Barrero. Madrid: Biblioteca Castro, 1996.

Stein, Peter. *Roman Law in European History*. New York: Cambridge University Press, 1999.

Stein, Stanley J. "Bureaucracy and Business in the Spanish Empire, 1759–1804: Failure of a Bourbon Reform in Mexico and Peru." *Hispanic American Historical Review* 61, no. 1 (February 1981): 2–28.

Stein, Stanley J., and Barbara H. Stein. *Apogee of Empire: Spain and New Spain in the Age of Charles III, 1759–1789*. Baltimore: Johns Hopkins University Press, 2003.

———. *Silver, Trade, and War: Spain and America in the Making of Early Modern Europe*. Baltimore: Johns Hopkins University Press, 2000.

Stuart, David. "El emperador y el cosmos: Nueva mirada a la piedra del sol." *Arquelogía mexicana* 25, no. 149 (January–February 2018): 20–25.

Tandeter, Enrique, and Jorge Hidalgo Lehuedé, eds. *Procesos americanos hacia la redefinición colonial.* Paris: UNESCO, 2000.

Tau Anzoátegui, Víctor. *Casuismo y sistema: Indigación histórica sobre el espíritu del Derecho Indiano.* Buenos Aires: Instituto de Investigaciones de Historia del Derecho, 1992.

———. "El *Gobierno del Perú* de Juan de Matienzo: En la senda del humanismo jurídico." In *El Jurista en el Nuevo Mundo: Pensamiento. Doctrina. Mentalidad,* 45–69. Frankfurt am Main: Max Planck Institute for European Legal History, 2016.

———. *El Jurista en el Nuevo Mundo: Pensamiento. Doctrina. Mentalidad.* Frankfurt am Main: Max Planck Institute for European Legal History, 2016.

———. *El poder de la costumbre: Estudios sobre el derecho consuetudinario en América hispana hasta la emancipación.* Buenos Aires: Instituto de Investigaciones de Historia del Derecho, 2001.

———. "Entre leyes, glosas y comentos: El episodio de la Recopilación de Indias (1996)." In *El Jurista en el Nuevo Mundo: Pensamiento. Doctrina. Mentalidad,* 147–66. Frankfurt am Main: Max Planck Institute for European Legal History, 2016.

———. "La disimulación en el Derecho Indiano." In *El Jurista en el Nuevo Mundo. Pensamiento. Doctrina. Mentalidad,* 223–43. Frankfurt am Main: Max Planck Institute for European Legal History, 2016.

———. "La formación y promulgación de las Leyes Indianas: En torno a una consulta del Consejo de Indias en 1794 (1986)." In *La Ley en América Hispana del Descubrimiento a la Emancipación,* 145–72. Buenos Aires: Academia Nacional de la Historia, 1992.

———. *La ley en América hispana del descubrimiento a la emancipación.* Buenos Aires: Academia Nacional de la Historia, 1992.

———. "La variedad indiana, una clave de la concepción jurídica de Juan de Solórzano." In *El Jurista en el Nuevo Mundo: Pensamiento. Doctrina. Mentalidad,* 207–22. Frankfurt am Main: Max Planck Institute for European Legal History, 2016.

———. *Nuevos Horizontes en el Estudio del Derecho Indiano.* Buenos Aires: Instituto de Investigaciones de Historia del Derecho, 1997.

Taylor, William B. *Drinking, Homicide, and Rebellion in Colonial Mexican Villages.* Stanford: Stanford University Press, 1979.

———. *Magistrates of the Sacred: Priests and Parishioners in Eighteenth-Century Mexico.* Stanford: Stanford University Press, 1996.

TePaske, John Jay, and Kendall W. Brown. *A New World of Gold and Silver.* Leiden and Boston: Brill, 2010.

Tomás y Valiente, Francisco. *Manual de Historia del Derecho Español.* 4th ed. Madrid: Tecnos, 1983.

Torales Pacheco, Josefina María Cristina. *Ilustrados en la Nueva España: Los socios de la Real Sociedad Bascongada de los Amigos del País.* Mexico City: Universidad Iberoamericana, 2001.

———, ed. *La compañía de comercio de Francisco Ignacio de Yraeta (1767–1797)*. 2 vols. Mexico City: Instituto Mexicano de Comercio Exterior, 1985.

Torre Barrio y Lima, Lorenzo Felipe de la. *Arte del nuevo beneficio de la plata en todo genero de metales frios, y calientes*. Lima: La imprenta de Antonio Joseph Gutierrez de Zevallos, 1738.

Tortella, Jaime. "La España discreta." In *Historia de España Siglo XIII: La España de los Borbones*, edited by Ricardo García Cárcel, 121–55. Madrid: Cátedra, 2002.

Trabulse, Elías. "Francisco Xavier de Gamboa y sus Comentarios a las Ordenanzas de Minas de 1761." In *Comentarios a las Ordenanzas de Minas*, 17–52. Mexico City: Casa de Moneda de México, 1986. Facsimile edition.

———. *Francisco Xavier Gamboa:Un político criollo en la Ilustración Mexicana (1717–1794)*. Mexico City: Colegio de México, 1985.

Tutino, John. *Making a New World: Founding Capitalism in the Bajío and Spanish North America*. Durham, NC: Duke University Press, 2011.

———. *Mexico City, 1808: Power, Sovereignty, and Silver in an Age of War and Revolution*. Albuquerque: University of New Mexico, 2018.

Uribe-Uran, Victor. "Innocent Infants or Abusive Patriarchs? Spousal Homicides, the Punishment of Indians and the Law in Colonial Mexico, 1740s–1820s." *Journal of Latin American Studies* 38, no. 4 (November 2006): 793–828.

Valdés, Manuel Antonio. *Gazetas de Mexico: Compendio de noticias de Nueva-España desde principios del año de 1784*. Mexico City: Por D. Felipe Zúñiga y Ontiveros, 1784–85.

Valle Pavón, Guillermina del. *Donativos, préstamos y privilegios: Los mercaderes y mineros de la Ciudad de México durante la guerra anglo-española de 1779–1783*. Mexico City: Instituto Mora, 2016.

———. "Los excedentes del ramo Alcabalas: Habilitación de la minería y defense del monopolio de los mercaderes de México en el siglo XVIII." *Historia Mexicana* 56, no. 3 (2007): 969–1016.

Valle-Arizpe, Artemio de. *Historia de la Ciudad de México segun los relatos de sus cronistas*. Mexico City: Editorial Pedro Robredo, 1939.

Van Young, Eric. *Hacienda and Market in Eighteenth-Century Mexico: The Rural Economy of the Guadalajara Region, 1675–1820*. Berkeley and Los Angeles: University of California Press, 1981.

Viana Pérez, Francisco. "La actividad comercial de un oidor de la Audiencia de México: Francisco Leandro de Viana." In *Los vascos en las regiones de México, siglos XVI–XX*, edited by Amaya Garritz, 117–38. Mexico City: Universidad Nacional Autónoma de México, 1999.

Viqueira Albán, Juan Pedro. *Propriety and Permissiveness in Bourbon Mexico*. Translated by Sonya Lipsett-Rivera and Sergio Rivera Ayala. Wilmington, DE: Scholarly Resources, 1999.

Walker, Charles F. *The Tupac Amaru Rebellion*. Cambridge, MA: Harvard University Press, 2014.

Weisser, Michael. "Crime and Punishment in Early Modern Spain." In *Crime and the Law: The Social History of Crime in Western Europe since 1500*, edited by V. A. C. Gatrell, Bruce Lenman, and Geoffrey Parker, 76–96. London: Europa Publications, 1980.

Winchester, Simon. *The Map that Changed the World: William Smith and the Birth of Modern Geology*. New York: Harper Perennial, 2001.

Yannakakis, Yanna. *The Art of Being In-between: Native Intermediaries, Indian Identity, and Local Rule in Colonial Oaxaca*. Durham, NC: Duke University Press, 2008.

Yuste, Carmen. "El Conde de Tepa ante la Visita de José de Gálvez." *Estudios de Historia Novohispana* 11, no. 11 (1991): 119–34.

Zaballa Beascoechea, Ana de. "Cartas de vascos en México: Vida privada y relaciones de paisanaje." In *Los vascos en las regiones de México, siglos XVI–XX*. Vol 5, edited by Amaya Garritz, 83–100. Mexico City: Universidad Nacional Autónoma de México, 1999.

———. "Mentalidad e identidad de los vascos en México, siglo XVIII." In *Los vascos en las regiones de México, siglos XVI–XX*. Vol. 2, edited by Amaya Garritz, 157–70. Mexico City: Universidad Nacional Autonóma de México, 1996.

Index

～℘

Page numbers in italic text indicate illustrations.